Palm™

FOR

DUMMIES®

2ND EDITION

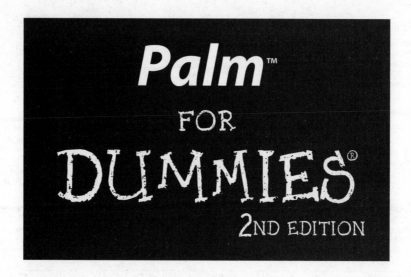

Palm™
FOR
DUMMIES®
2ND EDITION

by Bill Dyszel

Wiley Publishing, Inc.

Palm™ For Dummies®, 2nd Edition

Published by
Wiley Publishing, Inc.
909 Third Avenue
New York, NY 10022
www.wiley.com

Published by Wiley Publishing, Inc., Indianapolis, Indiana

Published simultaneously in Canada

No part of this publication may be reproduced, stored in a retrieval system or transmitted in any form or by any means, electronic, mechanical, photocopying, recording, scanning or otherwise, except as permitted under Sections 107 or 108 of the 1976 United States Copyright Act, without either the prior written permission of the Publisher, or authorization through payment of the appropriate per-copy fee to the Copyright Clearance Center, 222 Rosewood Drive, Danvers, MA 01923, (978) 750-8400, fax (978) 750-4744. Requests to the Publisher for permission should be addressed to the Legal Department, Wiley Publishing, Inc., 10475 Crosspoint Blvd., Indianapolis, IN 46256, (317) 572-3447, fax (317) 572-4447, e-mail: permcoordinator@wiley.com.

Trademarks: Wiley, the Wiley Publishing logo, For Dummies, the Dummies Man logo, A Reference for the Rest of Us!, The Dummies Way, Dummies Daily, The Fun and Easy Way, Dummies.com and related trade dress are trademarks or registered trademarks of Wiley Publishing, Inc., in the United States and other countries, and may not be used without written permission. Graffiti, HotSync, and Palm are trademarks or registered trademarks of Palm, Inc. All other trademarks are the property of their respective owners. Wiley Publishing, Inc., is not associated with any product or vendor mentioned in this book.

For general information on our other products and services or to obtain technical support, please contact our Customer Care Department within the U.S. at 800-762-2974, outside the U.S. at 317-572-3993, or fax 317-572-4002.

Wiley also publishes its books in a variety of electronic formats. Some content that appears in print may not be available in electronic books.

Library of Congress Control Number: 2002110286

ISBN: 0-7645-1674-4

Manufactured in the United States of America

10 9 8 7 6 5 4 3 2 1

2O/RQ/RQ/QS/IN

Ⓦ Wiley Publishing, Inc. is a trademark of Wiley Publishing, Inc.

About the Author

Bill Dyszel, author of 15 books including *Microsoft Outlook 2000 For Dummies* and *Treo & Handspring Visor For Dummies,* is also a nationally known expert on personal information management and sales automation technology. His dynamic, fun-filled seminars and keynote speeches reveal the secrets to making life simple by using technology well. He also consults with organizations that need to select, develop, and implement business solutions on the Palm platform and Microsoft Exchange.

The goal of Bill's work is to help people get beyond technology and make life better by intelligently using the best high-tech tools. He acts as a resource to people who want to sell more, work less, and be more effective with the help of their Palm organizer.

An accomplished entertainer as well, Bill sang with the New York City Opera for 14 years, appeared frequently on the New York stage as an actor and singer, and won critical praise for his off-Broadway opera spoof, *99% ARTFREE!* He still appears in concerts from time to time. Check out his Web site (www. palmpilotfordummies.com) to find out more about what Bill is doing.

Author's Acknowledgments

Thanks to the many people who have made this book possible — most of all, to Tiffany Franklin, my very capable acquisitions editor; Gayle Ehrenman my top-notch technical reviewer, as well as everyone on the staff of Wiley Publishing, Inc., who helped get this book to you.

Special thanks to the good folks at A & R Partners, Inc., for lending Palm devices during the development and production of this book, particularly Bob Angus and Rosie Pulido. Above all, thanks to the people at Palm Computing for keeping the Palm platform as powerful and vital as it is.

Publisher's Acknowledgments

We're proud of this book; please send us your comments through our online registration form located at www.dummies.com/register/.

Some of the people who helped bring this book to market include the following:

Acquisitions, Editorial, and Media Development

Project Editor: Kala Schrager *(Previous Edition: Paul Levesque)*

Acquisitions Editor: Tiffany Franklin

Copy Editors: Barry Childs-Helton, Diana Conover

Technical Editor: Gayle Ehrenman

Editorial Manager: Kevin Kirchner

Media Development Manager: Laura VanWinkle

Media Development Supervisor: Richard Graves

Editorial Assistant: Amanda Foxworth

Cartoons: Rich Tennant (www.the5thwave.com)

Production

Project Coordinator: Maridee Ennis

Layout and Graphics: David Bartholomew, Beth Brooks, Sean Decker, Carrie Foster, Joyce Haughey, Tiffany Muth, Barry Offringa, Julie Trippetti, Jeremey Unger

Proofreaders: Laura Albert, David Faust, John Greenough, Andy Hollandbeck, Carl Pierce, TECHBOOKS Production Services

Indexer: TECHBOOKS Production Services

Publishing and Editorial for Technology Dummies

Richard Swadley, Vice President and Executive Group Publisher

Mary C. Corder, Editorial Director

Andy Cummings, Vice President and Publisher

Publishing for Consumer Dummies

Diane Graves Steele, Vice President and Publisher

Joyce Pepple, Acquisitions Director

Composition Services

Gerry Fahey, Vice President of Production Services

Debbie Stailey, Director of Composition Services

Contents at a Glance

Table of Contents

Introduction

● ●

*1*f you use a Palm organizer, it's a good bet that you have things to do (probably lots of them). In fact, you probably have better things to do than waste time figuring out how to *use* a Palm organizer. That's why I wrote this book — to help busy people with Palm organizers get on with their busy lives and get the most from their Palm devices with a minimum of fuss. I promise I'll get right down to brass tacks to save you time.

If you're like me, using a Palm organizer may make you impatient with your regular desktop computer. The Palm device pops right on and does what you want without a lot of booting up and waiting around. Perhaps those bigger computers can take a hint from Palm's example and get down to business.

Sadly, I can't dispense with my regular computer just yet. A Palm organizer isn't meant to replace conventional computers; it's intended to give you a handy and portable window for accessing information, much of which you keep on your computer. But don't be fooled — your Palm device is a powerful little machine in itself.

About This Book

If you've never read a *For Dummies* book, welcome. Buying and reading this book proves that you're one smart cookie who doesn't want to deal with those overgrown paperweights that litter the shelves of your local bookstore's computer section. Instead, you want a clear, no-nonsense explanation of the things you really need to know, and nothing else. That's what you get here.

If you fit in any of the following categories, this book is meant for you:

- ✔ You're planning to buy a Palm organizer, and you want to know which model to buy, what you can do with it, and what it can do for you.

- ✔ You already own a Palm device, and you want to get the most from it quickly.

- ✔ You're looking for a gift to give someone who already has a Palm organizer. Palm devices are very popular gifts. (You can send me one anytime.)

- ✔ You own one of those Microsoft Pocket PC machines (say it isn't so!) and have realized the error of your ways.

Even if you're just curious about the Palm phenomenon, this book is aimed at showing you what all the excitement is about. Nearly anyone in any walk of life can receive some benefit from a Palm organizer — even if all that person wants is a little fun.

Foolish Assumptions

I figure that you know how to push a button. This skill will get you far with a Palm organizer; it's simple to use. And although you can use a Palm device without HotSyncing it with a desktop computer, I assume that you already know how to use your desktop computer — and that you'll probably use your Palm device with a desktop machine at some point. If you're still a little iffy on using your desktop computer, I suggest picking up a copy of the *For Dummies* book that covers the operating system your computer uses. The following titles, all published by Wiley, may be helpful:

- *Macs For Dummies,* 6th Edition, by David Pogue
- *PCs For Dummies,* 7th Edition, by Dan Gookin
- *Red Hat Linux 7 For Dummies,* by Jon "maddog" Hall, Paul G. Sery
- *Windows 95 For Dummies,* 2nd Edition, by Andy Rathbone
- *Windows 98 For Dummies,* by Andy Rathbone
- *Windows Me For Dummies,* by Andy Rathbone
- *Windows 2000 Professional For Dummies* by Andy Rathbone and Sharon Crawford
- *Mac OS 9 For Dummies,* by Bob LeVitus

In this book, I try to cover the whole range of the products based on the design from Palm Computing, Inc. When the first handheld units were produced, they were simply called Pilots. When the little Pilots became popular, the Palm people changed the name to PalmPilot to avoid confusion with the popular Pilot-brand pens. Then the Palm people decided to drop the Pilot thing altogether and call their product Palm III (presumably so they could name all future models after famous Roman numerals). Nowadays, the official name is the Palm Connected Organizer for the Palm Computing Platform. Technically, it's not a PalmPilot anymore.

Just to keep things clear, I try to stay generic sounding when I'm talking about features that appear on all Palm whatchamacallits. When I discuss a feature that appears on only a particular model of Palm device, such as the Palm i705, I say so. (For general information about what each model does, see Appendix B.)

You may also be using another product that's based on Palm Computing technology but has a different name. The Handspring Visor was the first popular Palm clone, but you'll also find products by IBM, Sony, Kyocera, and a whole slew of other manufacturers in the near future. The general principles in this book should work for those products as well.

Conventions Used in This Book

You may be a diehard reader of *For Dummies* books, living in a beautiful black-and-yellow home filled with black-and-yellow books. You may be familiar with the approach — this book works much like all the other books in the series.

To lessen confusion as you read this book, keep the following in mind:

- When I refer to a *desktop computer,* I mean a conventional computer running either Microsoft Windows or the Mac OS. If your main computer is a laptop, that's fine. Please forgive me if I always say "desktop" — they all look so big next to a Palm device.

- Because the Palm organizer is made to work as an extension of more than one type of computer system, the terms I use to describe what you should do on your desktop machine usually cover both the Windows and Macintosh platforms. The book also has a chapter about using the Windows version of the Palm Desktop.

Here are a few tidbits and terms you need to understand:

- *Tapping* means touching your Palm stylus to a named area on the Palm display.

- *Clicking* means pressing the left mouse button on an item if you're using a Windows computer or pressing the only mouse button if you're using a Mac.

- *Choosing* means to either tap a menu choice on your Palm screen or click a specific menu choice with your desktop computer's mouse.

- *Right-clicking* means to press the right mouse button if you're using a computer running Windows (and a mouse with two or more buttons). The Mac has no right mouse button to click. Seems suspicious to me, but that's how it is.

- *Double-clicking* means quickly clicking the left mouse button (or the only mouse button) twice.

- *Dragging* (on the Palm screen) means touching an item with your stylus and sliding the point of the stylus from one spot on the display to another.

> ✔ *Dragging* (on a Windows PC or a Mac) means holding down the mouse button while moving the mouse.

> ✔ *Selecting* or *highlighting* means either tapping a choice on a list or sliding your stylus across a specific area of text, which prepares the Palm device for you to do something to that piece of text.

All the tasks I describe in the preceding list are much easier to do than they sound. You'll catch on in almost no time. In the meantime, here are a few items I mention from time to time:

> ✔ *Dialog boxes* are rectangles that pop up on the screen and can include messages for you to read, buttons for you to tap or click, lists for you to choose from, blanks for you to fill in, and check boxes for you to tap. Don't worry: I tell you what to do with each dialog box as you encounter it.

> ✔ *Buttons* are (normally) real, physical buttons on the case of your Palm device. I normally call each button by the name of the application it runs. Your Palm organizer comes with two types of buttons: hard and soft. *Hard buttons* are those at the bottom of your Palm device, mounted below the screen. *Soft buttons* are "virtual" — they appear just above the hard buttons but are part of the screen. You can find more about all this button stuff in Chapter 1.

I normally simplify menu commands by saying something like "Choose Go⇨Cubs," which means *Choose Go from the menu bar and then choose Cubs*. Also, whenever I describe text that's shown on the screen, it appears in a special typeface, `like this`.

How This Book 1s Organized

To help you more easily find out how to do what you want to do, I've divided this book into seven parts. Each part covers a different aspect of using your Palm organizer. The first couple of parts focus on the Palm device itself — what you can do if you just have that thing. In later parts, I discuss add-ons for your Palm thingy, as well as the desktop computer program that comes with your Palm device. (Yes, your Palm organizer can talk to your desktop computer. If this possibility really floats your boat, jump right into Part IV.)

Here's a quick-and-dirty outline of this book — just enough to whet your appetite and make you want to buy it!

Part I: Getting to Know Your Palm Organizer

Nothing about using a Palm organizer is difficult, although many features and options aren't exactly obvious. The first part of this book describes what you have to work with on your Palm device and how you work with what you have. I explain what all those funny-looking buttons and other doodads on the outside of your Palm organizer do, and I give you a lesson in Graffiti — and no, not so you can join a gang and practice spray-can art. Graffiti is the special alphabet you can use for entering information into your Palm device. If you're in the secret-agent biz (or if you're just security-minded), you can find out how to keep confidential information on your Palm organizer safe from prying eyes.

Part II: Getting Down to Business

Yes, Virginia, a Palm device is a computer. It doesn't act grouchy and forbidding like other computers, but it can do many of the jobs typically performed by enormous desktop units (once called *microcomputers,* back in the days of dinosaurs and enormous mainframes). The Palm organizer comes with a set of preinstalled programs when you buy it. Those programs act as a personal information manager (PIM) to help you keep track of your schedule, and include the Address Book and To Do List.

If you've ever used a computer for personal organizing, the methods of the Palm organizer may seem familiar. It also has a program called Memo Pad for jotting down random notes to yourself or others, and you can even copy your e-mail to your Palm organizer and read it while you're sitting by the pool. (Sorry, the pool isn't included.) Palm devices also feature infrared beaming, a method for sending information through the air between two Palm devices, using an invisible beam of infrared light. How cool is that?

Part III: Palm Organizers and the Outside World

Many of the coolest things you can do with your Palm device come from outside your Palm device. You can beam items from one Palm to another, connect your Palm device to a phone, or automatically synchronize copies of documents from your desktop computer to your Palm device. This part shows you how to make the Palm connection to all sorts of exciting and useful resources and also tells you what to do with those connections after you've made them. And when you're out and about and you want to use the PalmModem to HotSync to your computer . . . well, I show you how to do that, too. How's that for a bargain?

Part IV: Making the Palm Connection to Bigger Things

No computer is an island, especially the tiny Palm device. If it were, you'd be in trouble at high tide. The Palm people always figured that folks would use their Palm devices in conjunction with some other computer. This is simply because there's no denying the physical limitations of a tiny computer when you're entering data and connecting to other resources like the Internet or a CD-ROM. This part of the book tells you all you need to know about HotSyncing, which is the process through which your Palm device and your desktop computer talk to each other. I also walk you through the steps for installing and operating the desktop programs that come with your Palm device.

Part V: Going Outside the Box with Your Palm Organizer

As with any appliance, the day may come when you need more from your Palm organizer and the equivalent of a Maytag repairman is nowhere in sight. Or perhaps you need to make your Palm device do something new. In this part, I show you some options for making your little Palm thingy do big things. I cover software add-ons and hardware accessories that may impress your peers in your particular profession as well as e-mail and wireless capabilities. Whether you're a doctor or a bartender, add-on software is out there for you.

Part VI: The Part of Tens

Why ten? Beats me! All the other *For Dummies* books get a Part of Tens, so I'll be darned if mine doesn't get one too! In this part, you find out what your Palm device *can't* do (sorry, teleporting is out), and how to stylishly accessorize your organizer without having to call Calvin Klein for wardrobe advice. I also include a few troubleshooting tips and a list of places to look on the Internet for help with your Palm device.

Part VII: Appendixes

Just in case you were wondering what kinds of things other people are doing with their Palm devices or what kind of Palm devices they're using to do those things, I've added a pair of appendixes (appendices for you Latin purists). One discusses Palm programs designed for big business, and the other lists the Palm models that are available as I write this.

What You Don't Have to Read

I discovered that busy people like using a Palm device, but those people are often too busy to learn how to use it effectively. That's understandable; it's part of the territory. It takes only a few minutes to learn each feature of your Palm organizer, so I put this book together in independent chunks for busy people who want to read only a few pages at a time while they jet from place to place.

Icons Used in This Book

Sometimes the fastest way to find information in a book is to look at the pictures. In this case, icons draw your attention to specific types of information that are useful to know. Here are the icons I use in this book:

I use this icon for really important info you shouldn't forget.

The Tip icon notes a hint or trick for saving time and effort — or highlights text that makes the Palm organizer easier to understand.

The Warning icon alerts you to something you should be careful about in order to prevent problems.

Where to Go from Here

If this were the Land of Oz, I could tell you to follow the Yellow Brick Road. But I'll have to settle for saying, "Turn the page." And ignore that man behind the curtain; he's just another Wizard, fussing with his Palm organizer.

Part I

Getting to Know Your Palm Organizer

The 5th Wave   By Rich Tennant

"Yes, it's wireless; and yes, it weighs less than a pound; and yes, it has multiuser functionality... but it's a stapler."

In this part . . .

You can do lots with the Palm organizer's few tiny buttons and little plastic stylus. Although you may figure out a great deal by just fiddling around with your Palm device, this part's quick tour gives you a head start. I also show you how to customize your Palm device to your specific needs.

Chapter 1

What Can a Palm Device Do?

Asking, "What can I do with a Palm device?" is like asking, "Where can I go on a bicycle?" You can go nearly anywhere you want on a bicycle — you can take a ride in the park or cross the Rocky Mountains. Most normal people are better off crossing the Rockies by car or bus, but they can handle the ride in the park quite nicely on a bike. Likewise, your Palm device is just the right tool for jotting down a quick note, although you probably wouldn't use it to write the sequel to *Moby Dick*.

Your Palm device can do many of the things that a desktop or laptop computer can do, although some tasks are easier to handle on a larger computer (say, surfing the Web) and others are perfect for the Palm device (such as looking up a phone number). If you ask people what they do most with their Palm devices, you get a wide variety of answers: Some need to find addresses or check schedules; others play games, entertain themselves with an electronic book, or read their e-mail.

Although the Palm device comes in a small, friendly package, it has plenty of power inside. Even though the unit is barely larger than a couple of candy bars, it has enough computing power inside to do more than some of the early 1980s Macintosh machines that took up most of your desktop (and may still be taking up your desktop today). Every day, people are finding clever new things to do with their Palm devices, and you'll probably figure out a few unique things on your own.

Does my Palm device do Windows?

On the whole, your Palm device is just as compatible with your desktop machine as those other handhelds that run Microsoft's Pocket PC program. You can't run your desktop Windows programs (such as Excel) on your Pocket PC, although the Pocket PC includes brain-damaged replicas of the desktop programs you may already know. Also, more software is being written for Palm devices than is being written for Pocket PCs. When I wrote this chapter, I found nearly 15,000 programs available for Palm devices, compared to barely a tenth of that number for Pocket PC machines.

(Is somebody winning this competition? Hmmm . . . could be. . . .)

Both Palm devices and Pocket PCs can connect to your desktop computer and match up your lists of names and appointments, which is called *synchronizing*. One way or another, you probably want to synchronize your palm-size computer to a desktop or laptop computer — and a Palm device synchronizes every bit as well as a Pocket PC. My recommendation: Stick with Palm devices. You've got more options.

You can add an endless variety of functions to your Palm device by installing programs that don't come in the package with it. Throughout most of this book, I focus on things that you can do with the stuff that comes in the box with your Palm device, and that's plenty. In addition, I provide a selection of useful applications on a Web site called `www.palmpilotfordummies.com`, as well as links to Web sites that offer literally thousands of Palm programs. (See Chapter 12 for more info about installing Palm applications.)

What Is This Thing, Anyway?

A Palm device is a simple little contraption with almost no moving parts. Sometimes it's hard to believe that it's a computer at all. After all, computers are supposed to have zillions of buttons and lights and make scary sounds when they start up, right? Well, you don't have to think of your Palm device as a computer — instead, think of it as your little electronic friend that helps you keep track of your real friends. Unlike some of your real friends, your Palm device never asks to borrow 50 bucks 'til payday. On the other hand, it never offers to pick up the check in a restaurant, either, so don't lose track of those real friends.

A Palm device really has only three elements: the buttons, the screen, and the stylus. No mouse, no cables, no disks — none of it. You probably want to use your Palm device along with a normal computer that has all those annoying gizmos, but as long as you're just using your Palm device, you can keep things simple. Figure 1-1 shows you what a typical Palm device looks like, and the following sections tell you what all those funny little doodads do.

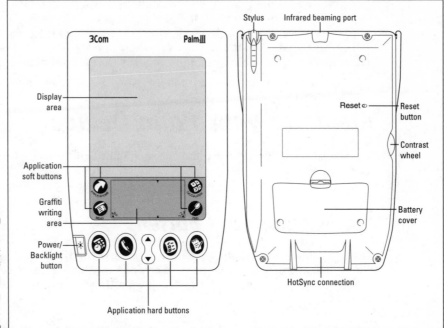

Figure 1-1: The front and back of a typical Palm organizer.

Choosing a Palm Device

This book covers the most recent models of the Palm devices, but you may be using an earlier version. Users of earlier versions can find plenty of value here, too, because the Palm people tend to not make wholesale changes to basic applications, incorporating only slight changes and improvements with each new release. So newer versions should look familiar to you.

New developments occur so often in the Palm world that you may find it difficult to keep up. As I write this, a whole new kind of Palm device called Palm OS 5 is on the way — a faster, smarter Palm device with the same friendly face and features that everybody loved in earlier Palms. The new version offers better security, slicker multimedia functions, and sharper, brighter screens. Rest assured, however, that all the basic functions I describe in this book also work on a Palm OS 5 device — so if you buy one, you'll be totally comfortable from the get-go.

Because so many different versions of the Palm organizer exist, I've included a quick-and-dirty guide to all the currently available Palm devices in Appendix B.

So far, no single model offers every feature that you may want — the one disappointment common to all the new types of Palm devices. Some have color screens, others come in sleek, shiny cases, others connect to the Internet wirelessly — but none do everything at once. Pick the features that matter most to you — and wait a few months to see what comes next.

The Outside of Your Palm Device

The case of your Palm device offers a bunch of little buttons that do all sorts of cool stuff. This section explains what those buttons do.

Application hard buttons

The *application hard buttons* are easy to use. I use the word *hard* to mean real, actual, physical buttons that you can push with your finger to make something happen. Figure 1-2 shows you what those buttons look like.

Figure 1-2:
The buttons
at the
bottom of
the case are
hard
buttons.

The *application buttons* are the four round buttons at the bottom of the case on a Palm device. Push any of these buttons at any time, and the Palm device shows you the application (or program) assigned to that button. (Think of *applications* as jobs that the Palm device is ready to do for you.)

You can even push an application button when the Palm device is turned off. When you do so, your Palm device automatically turns on and opens the application assigned to that button. A Palm device is a little like a microwave oven in that way: You don't have to turn on your microwave and then tell it to start cooking — you just push the button and you're cooking. Unlike your microwave oven, however, your Palm device needs very little cleaning, and it doesn't make your breakfast eggs explode.

Here's what those buttons do:

- **Date Book:** The leftmost application button — easy to identify by the little icon that looks like a clock on top of a bent-out-of-shape calendar. You don't need to get bent out of shape when you use the Date Book, which shows you dates and appointments. (See Chapter 8 for more info about the Date Book.)

- **Address Book:** The second button from the left — the one with the little telephone icon — is where you go to find names, addresses, and (naturally) phone numbers. (See Chapter 5 for more info about the Address Book.) The two applications at the right of the Palm device are separated from the ones on the left by the scroll buttons (which I describe later in this chapter, in the "Scroll buttons" section).

- **To Do List:** The third application button, second from the right side of the case and decorated with a little checklist. The To Do List button opens the application that tracks your tasks. (See Chapter 6 for more info about the To Do List.)

- **Memo Pad:** The rightmost button, the one with the picture of the tiny pen writing on an itty-bitty notebook. The Memo Pad is the place where you enter and store text. (See Chapter 7 for more info about the Memo Pad.)

Now that several different companies offer dozens of different Palm-powered devices, you may run across a Palm device that assigns the four buttons to programs other than those described here. For example, wireless devices often assign one of the four buttons to an e-mail program; Palm-powered cell phones sometimes devote a button to telephone-related features such as a speed-dial list.

Palm devices: Real computers

Don't be fooled — a Palm device is a real computer. Although it may look like those little electronic organizers that have been around for years, it contains the same Motorola computer chip that powered the first Macintosh. Yes, you can manage addresses and appointments on a Palm device, just as you can on those old organizers — *and* you can also run and load software, in much the same way you can on a conventional computer.

The biggest difference between a Palm device and a regular computer is what computer geeks call the *user interface*. The typical Palm device has no keyboard. Instead of using a keyboard, you write and tap on its touch-sensitive screen. Many types of programs that people commonly use on conventional computers are being developed for Palm devices — including spreadsheets, database managers, and Web browsers.

You can assign different programs to the four application buttons; you don't have to stick to the ones that come installed on your Palm device. If you don't use the To Do List or the Memo Pad much (for example), and you want to reassign those buttons to other programs, then see Chapter 3 to find out how it's done.

Scroll buttons

At the bottom-center of the case on a Palm device is the *scroll button.* This button works like the power-window button in a car. If you want to move down through a screen to see what doesn't fit on one screen, use the bottom part of the button. If you want to go back to the top of the screen, use the top part of the button. The scroll button may change the way that it acts in different applications. Sometimes pressing the scroll button makes the information in the display area leap, rather than crawl, to the next screen. Sometimes the scroll button does nothing, especially when there's nothing more to see.

Power button

The button somewhere on the edge of the case is the *power* button. Different Palm device manufacturers put the power button in different places, but wherever the button is located, it does the same job; it turns your Palm device on and off, just like you'd expect.

The power button also controls the *backlight,* a little light that brightens the screen. To turn the backlight on, hold the power button down for at least two seconds. (You can also customize your Palm device so the backlight goes on with a certain stroke of your stylus. I discuss that subject in Chapter 3.) The backlight makes text on the screen much easier to read in complete darkness, although it helps only a little in dim light.

Although the backlight makes it possible to read the text on your Palm device in complete darkness, it also drains the batteries like crazy. If you want your batteries to last, use the backlight sparingly.

A nice thing about the way that Palm devices work is a quality called a *persistent state.* No, that's not the feeling you get after you meet all the salesmen in Utah; it means that whatever is happening on the screen when you turn the power off is still happening when you turn the Palm device on again. It's like sleep mode on your desktop computer. Persistent state is a handy feature when you get interrupted in the middle of doing something and want to get right back to it, even if you get a call from a long-winded salesman in Utah.

Reset button

If you suddenly have to tell your Palm device to stop what it's doing and start all over again, you *reset* the device with a handy button. Rarely (well, we can *hope* rarely), an installed program misbehaves, making your Palm device hang up or act crazy. Resetting the Palm device usually fixes the problem.

You can reset your Palm device the hard-bitten way or the kinder, gentler, soft way:

✔ **Soft reset:** A *soft* reset just makes everything stop and start again. You can perform a soft reset on your Palm device by pushing the end of a bent paper clip into the little hole labeled Reset located on the back. The stylus that comes with many Palm devices includes a secret, built-in reset pin. Just unscrew the end of the stylus to find the reset pin.

✔ **Hard reset:** A *hard* reset erases all your data and your username. Needless to say, you don't want to do a hard reset without a good reason. If you're selling your Palm device to someone else, you can do a hard reset to make the unit act like it did when it was brand-new. (I wish I could do that to myself now and then.) To perform a hard reset, hold down the power button and then press the end of a paper clip into the hole marked Reset located on the back of your Palm device. When you do, a prompt appears on the screen, asking whether you really want to erase all your data. Think hard again about whether you want to do that — and then press the scroll-up hard button (if you do) or the scroll-down hard button (if you don't).

The Screen

You can't miss the most important part of a Palm device — the *screen,* which you can see in Figure 1-3. It shows you the information that you've stored in your applications and lets you know what the applications are ready to do for you next.

An equally important function of the Palm organizer screen is to take information from you. Two parts of the screen accomplish this purpose — the display area and the Graffiti area (about which more in a moment) —, and the soft buttons (not to be confused with the hard buttons described earlier in this chapter) put lots of other neat capabilities at your fingertips.

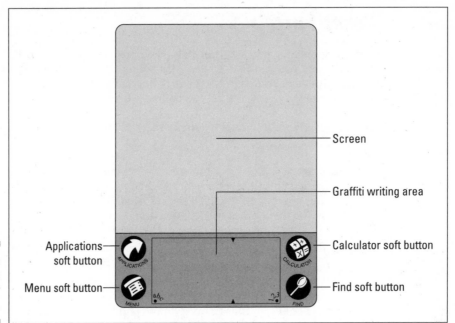

Screen

Graffiti writing area

Calculator soft button

Find soft button

Applications soft button

Menu soft button

Figure 1-3:
The Palm
organizer
screen.

The display area

The largest part of the Palm organizer screen is the main *display area,* as shown in Figure 1-4. The display area shows the text that you're working with, and it also contains some active areas that you can tap with your stylus to do things like display the contents of a memo or mark a task as complete. You can also slide your stylus across the surface of the screen to select (or highlight) text that's displayed in some applications.

Most standard Palm Computing applications organize the display with consistent areas that do much the same job from one application to the next:

- ✔ The upper-left corner of the screen displays a tab showing the name of the application you're currently using (such as Address List, To Do List, or Memo Pad).

- ✔ The upper-right corner usually tells you what kind of item you're viewing.

- ✔ The bottom of the display area usually contains buttons that you can tap to create, find, or edit items in the application you're using.

- ✔ The main, central part of the display area shows the bulk of your information.

✔ Some applications offer a scroll bar at the right edge of the screen. You can scroll through the display area to show information that's higher or lower on the list of items that you're currently viewing. This scroll bar does the same thing as the scroll buttons at the bottom of your Palm device. (For more information, refer to the "Scroll buttons" section earlier in this chapter.)

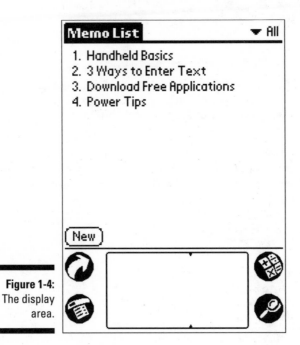

Figure 1-4:
The display
area.

I use the words *sometimes* and *usually* when I describe the display area because every program works a little differently. Although not every element works the same way all the time, the preceding description is how most well-designed Palm Computing programs tend to work.

Soft buttons

Soft buttons aren't really soft, like a pillow — they're virtual. Unlike hard buttons, soft buttons aren't physical buttons, have no moving parts, and don't do anything until your Palm device is powered on. Then they appear on the screen of the Palm device, as shown in Figure 1-5.

Figure 1-5:
The soft
buttons are
really just
four spots
alongside
the Graffiti
box.

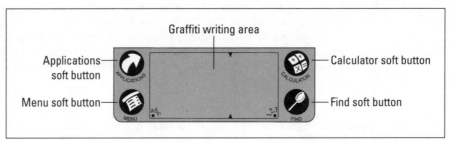

The four jobs assigned to the four soft buttons are Applications, Menu, Calculator, and Find. To use one of the soft buttons, just tap it with your stylus. The following sections outline what each soft button does.

Applications

The *Applications* soft button calls up a list of all the applications on your Palm device, showing their icons. Figure 1-6 shows the icons that you see.

Figure 1-6:
Every
program on
your Palm
device has
an icon on
the list of
applica-
tions.

Several applications come already installed on your Palm device, including the following:

- ✔ **Graffiti:** This little teaching program helps you figure out the special Palm alphabet.

- ✔ **HotSync:** Makes your Palm device communicate with your desktop computer.

- ✔ **Preferences:** Use this application to configure your Palm device to suit your needs.

- ✔ **Security:** Sets up passwords; hides or shows private items.

The next two applications show up on most Palm devices, but they've been excluded from certain models to keep the price down. You probably won't miss them, but just in case you wanted to know, they are

- ✔ **Mail:** Exchanges messages with the e-mail program on your desktop.

- ✔ **Expense:** Helps you keep track of what you spend.

Any applications you install on your Palm device also show up on this list. I tell you more about the applications that come with your Palm device later in this chapter (in the "The Standard Palm Applications" section); in Chapter 12, I show you how to install other applications. You can start any application you see on the applications list by tapping the icon for that program once. A little battery icon at the top of the applications list tells you how much power is left in your batteries (in case you get too tap-happy).

Menu

The *Menu* button activates the menus in any application that you're running. Most Palm Computing programs have a set of menus that enable you to cut, copy, or paste text, as well as create new items or delete old ones. (These menus are similar to those you find in the applications for your desktop computer — except these menus are not as complex.) To use the menus in any application, start the application, tap the Menu button, and then tap the menu that you want to use. Figure 1-7 shows a sample menu.

Calculator

The *Calculator* button contains no mysteries; it simply starts up the on-screen calculator, as shown in Figure 1-8. Tap the numbers just like you do on a handheld calculator. You can even press the on-screen calculator buttons with your finger. Naturally, it's not a good idea to put your fingers on the screen if you have gooey stuff like chocolate on your hands, because it leaves a mess on your screen, which makes your calculations hard to read. I don't know what happens if you try to lick chocolate off your Palm organizer screen (or worse, somebody else's Palm organizer screen). I wouldn't try it.

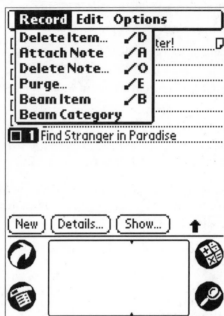

Figure 1-7:
If you don't
like the
specials,
just order
from the
menu.

Figure 1-8:
You can
perform
simple
calculations
on your
Palm
calculator.

Find

The *Find* button starts up a little program that searches your entire Palm device for a certain string of text. Follow these steps to find every item on your Palm device that contains the word *chocolate:*

1. **Tap the Find button.**

2. **Enter the word** chocolate, **as shown in Figure 1-9.**

   You can enter the text by using either a Palm keyboard, the on-screen keyboard, or Graffiti. (See Chapter 2 for more info about entering text.)

3. **Tap OK with your stylus.**

   The Find program finds all the *chocolate* on your Palm device, which is faster and healthier than finding all the chocolate in your grocery store.

Figure 1-9:
Use Find to
find a word
that occurs
in any Palm
application.

I have to tell you one odd thing about the Find tool: If you enter only the first part of a word, it finds the word you're looking for; if you enter only the *last* part of the word, however, your word doesn't turn up. If you enter *choco,* you still find *chocolate,* but if you enter *late,* you come up with *late, later,* and *latest,* but not *chocolate.*

Contrast adjustment

Most Palm devices offer a method of adjusting the contrast on the screen, just like your TV. In certain kinds of light, you can see the text on the screen better if you adjust the contrast a little. Usually you'll find a contrast soft button somewhere on the Palm screen; it's normally a tiny circle, colored half black, half white. If your Palm device doesn't have a contrast circle, then it has a contrast button on the edge of the case. Pressing the contrast button makes the Adjust Contrast box appear on the screen. You can use your stylus to adjust the contrast by sliding the little button to the left or right.

The Graffiti area

Most of the bottom part of the screen is occupied by a large box, located between the soft buttons, called the *Graffiti area,* as shown in Figure 1-10. A pair of tiny triangles at the top and bottom of the Graffiti area separates the left section where you enter letters from the right section where you enter numbers. You can use the Palm organizer's stylus to write letters on the left side in the Palm Computing special alphabet, called Graffiti. You can enter Graffiti-style numbers on the right side. Graffiti is much like the plain block printing that you were taught to use in kindergarten, although a few letters are written a little differently. (For more info about using Graffiti to enter text, see Chapter 2.)

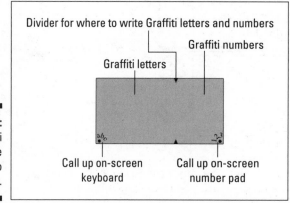

Figure 1-10: The Graffiti area is the place to enter text.

The letters *abc* appear in the lower-left corner of the Graffiti area, and the numbers *123* appear in the lower-right corner. As you may have guessed, tapping *abc* calls up an on-screen keyboard, and tapping *123* calls up a number pad. (For more information about entering text via the on-screen keyboard and number pad, see Chapter 2.)

The Standard Palm Applications

Palm devices aren't designed to be just cool little computers (although they *are* cool little computers). They are designed to do useful things for you as soon as you take them out of the box. I like nothing better than instant gratification, and that's what you get with a Palm device. (I do, anyway.)

The standard Palm Computing applications don't have to be installed, configured, or fussed with in any way — they're ready to use with one press of a button. You can configure the preferences for the applications, of course, to get them exactly the way that you want them (for more info about preferences, see Chapter 3). To get started, just press the button assigned to that application or tap the Applications soft button for a list of your Palm Computing programs, and then pick the one that you want to use.

The programs that you can use as soon as you take your Palm device out of the box include the following:

- ✔ **Address Book:** This is your "little black book" of names, addresses, and phone numbers. You can keep a detailed description of everything that you need to know about the people in your list by attaching a note to each record. You can also keep track of everyone's e-mail address, and you can use the Address Book as your personal address book for e-mail that you compose on your Palm device. (For more info about e-mail on a Palm device, see Chapter 10, and for more info about the Address Book, see Chapter 5.)

- ✔ **Calculator:** The calculator is a simple tool for punching in numbers and performing arithmetic. The Palm calculator does one trick that a hand-held calculator can't handle, however: It shows a list of recent calculations. After doing a series of calculations, tap Menu and then choose Options⇨Recent Calculations to recap your last few calculations, as shown in Figure 1-11.

- ✔ **Date Book:** Think of this program as your calendar of appointments and events. The Date Book (shown in Figure 1-12) lets you set appointments and alarms to remind yourself of those appointments. You can also add notes to any appointment so you can keep some details about it handy. (For more info about the Date Book, see Chapter 8.)

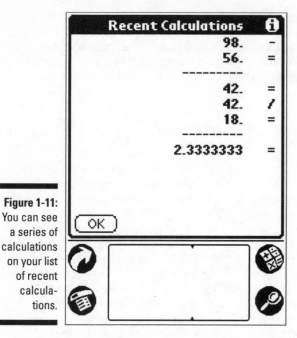

Figure 1-11:
You can see
a series of
calculations
on your list
of recent
calcula-
tions.

Figure 1-12:
Stay on
schedule by
using your
Date Book.

✓ **Expense:** This is a program for keeping track of what you spend. The Expense program, as shown in Figure 1-13, synchronizes, or matches up the information you enter to special Microsoft Excel spreadsheets on your desktop computer, enabling you to collect expense figures on the road and then pull them together when you get home. Unfortunately, the Expense program is not really useful because you can only enter a few types of expenses in the program, and you can't customize the program to include types of expenses that you may need to record. The Palm people put many great features in the Palm operating system, but the Expense program isn't one of them. In fact, they dropped the Expense program completely from the Palm m100, figuring that most people wouldn't miss it. I don't use it at all. (See Chapter 12 for more info about Expense.)

Figure 1-13:
You can
keep tabs
on your
spending
with the
Expense
application.

✓ **HotSync:** This program *is* a great feature; it links your Palm device to your desktop computer. The HotSync program has two parts: one part on the Palm device and one on the desktop. Either a PC or a Mac can synchronize data with the same Palm device, although the PC and the Mac need different desktop software. (See Chapter 11 for more information about using HotSync.)

✓ **Mail:** This simple e-mail program enables you to HotSync your e-mail with your desktop computer so you can read e-mail, compose replies, and create messages to be sent through your desktop e-mail system — without having to stay at your desk. (For more info about the Mail program, see Chapter 10.)

✔ **Memo Pad:** The Memo Pad is your collection of plain old text notes that you can keep around for future reference. Figure 1-14 shows the memos that exist in your Palm device when you buy it, plus a few that I've added. You can either create notes on your desktop computer and transfer them to your Palm device (so critical information is handy) or create memos on your Palm device for later transfer to desktop computer programs, such as your word processor. (For more info about the Memo Pad, see Chapter 7.)

✔ **Preferences:** This program lets you customize your Palm device by changing application button assignments, time and number formats, modem setup, and shortcuts. Figure 1-15 shows the General Preferences screen. For other preferences screens, choose from the pull-down menu in the upper-right corner. (For more info about setting preferences, see Chapter 3.)

✔ **Security:** This program lets you hide or show all the items that you've marked Private on your Palm device. You can also set, remove, or change a password to protect your information. Figure 1-16 shows what to expect from the Security screen. (For more info about using the security features, see Chapter 3.)

✔ **To Do List:** Here's a list of tasks that you need to remember, sorted by order of priority, due date, or by the name of the task. You can also keep track of tasks that you've completed on the To Do List for reference. (For more info about the To Do List, see Chapter 6.)

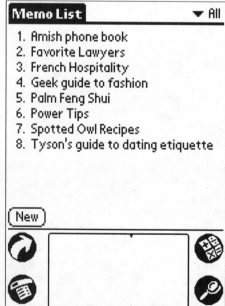

Figure 1-14:
The Memo list stores any kind of text that you want to keep handy.

Figure 1-15:
Make your
Palm device
your own by
setting your
Prefer-
ences.

Figure 1-16:
Protect your
sensitive
information
by setting a
password in
the Security
application.

HotSyncing Is Hot Stuff

HotSyncing is making your desktop computer and Palm device talk to each other like friends at lunch. They compare days, talk about what they did, and maybe exchange notes — only more efficiently than people trying to talk around a mouthful of salad.

During a HotSync, the two machines compare data and then match up that data exactly, keeping each other current on who you know, what you've done, when you did it, and what you gotta do tomorrow. HotSyncing also gives you a handy way to install additional applications on your Palm device, as well as back up (or *archive*) all your Palm data to your big, safe desktop computer just in case. (Your Palm device does this automatically; you don't even have to think about it.)

HotSyncing is easy — just put your Palm device in its cradle and push the button on the cradle. Of course, you have to connect the cradle to your desktop computer before you can HotSync. For more info about HotSyncing and using your Palm device with your desktop computer, see Chapters 12 through 14.

Powering Up Your Palm

Your Palm organizer is so thrifty with electricity that some models operate on standard AAA batteries that you can buy at any drugstore or newsstand. However, if your Palm device has fancy features like a color screen, a built-in phone, or comes in a sleek, super-slim case, you may end up with a rechargeable Palm device with a permanent battery hidden inside. You need to deal with the two different kinds of Palm devices differently.

Charge it — your Palm device, that is

Most Palm devices feature a built-in, rechargeable battery. Because you can't change the battery in those models, you have to be sure that you keep the unit charged up at all times.

When you take your brand-new rechargeable Palm out of the box, the battery has no charge in it. You have to plug the cradle into the AC adapter that comes in the box and then plug the adapter into a wall socket. When the cradle is plugged in and you set the Palm in the cradle, a light on the cradle comes on to show you that the Palm device is charging. Leave the Palm device in the cradle for a few hours before you use it for the first time.

You can plug the cradle into the back of your computer and set up your Palm device to work with the Palm desktop software while the battery is charging. Is that cool, or what?

I like to leave a rechargeable Palm in its cradle to charge whenever I'm not out and about. I also make it a point to HotSync my Palm at least once a day by putting the Palm in the cradle and pushing the button on the cradle. I often HotSync two or three times a day, just to keep my data safe. Although a rechargeable Palm can run for several weeks on a charge, I still prefer to keep mine topped off.

When batteries are included

If you don't have a rechargeable Palm, your Palm device doesn't plug into the wall. Although the cradle may look like it can recharge your Palm device, it doesn't do that for the Palm devices that use regular batteries. Instead, your Palm device runs on a pair of plain old AAA batteries, which should last nearly a month with normal use.

If you use the backlight frequently, you drain the batteries faster.

When you change batteries, it's a good idea to HotSync first by putting the Palm in the cradle and pressing the button on the cradle just in case something goes wrong. When you take out a set of batteries, you have 30 seconds to insert a new set before the Palm device starts forgetting things.

If you tap the Applications soft button to the left of the Graffiti area, you can see on the Applications screen how much power remains in your batteries. A Palm device's battery power is indicated by a silhouette of a battery at the top of the Applications screen. When your batteries are at maximum power, the battery is completely black. As the batteries drain, the black part of the battery indicator gets smaller and smaller. Earlier Palm devices show just a bar graph labeled Battery at the bottom of the screen.

You can't change the batteries on a rechargeable Palm device, of course. You can only recharge the built-in battery by leaving the Palm device in its cradle for a few hours. You can also buy a travel charger for your Palm device to keep the charge fresh when you're on the road.

Getting Started

Palm computer users are busy people. They're often too busy to learn to use their Palm devices well. Whether or not you're a Type-A, in-a-hurry personality, these tips get you off to a quick start with your Palm device.

- ✔ **Connect your Palm device to your computer.** To keep your information safe, you should connect your Palm device to a desktop or laptop computer. Just plug the wire on your Palm cradle into the only place on your computer where it fits, which is either something called a *serial port* or something different called a *USB port*. The two things are quite different; you won't be able to confuse one for the other, so don't worry about it. Insert the Palm software CD into your CD-ROM drive and follow the instructions. For more details on installing your Palm device, see Chapter 14.

- ✔ **Set the date and time.** You need to set the time and date on your Palm device so that it can keep track of your appointments. Follow these steps to set the date and time:

    1. **Tap the Applications soft button.**

    2. **Choose Preferences.**

    3. **Select the General tab.**

    4. **Tap the hour and date boxes to set the time.**

    For more about setting the time and customizing your Palm device, see Chapter 3.

- ✔ **Fill your Address Book with names from your desktop computer.** If you're already using a desktop address program like Microsoft Outlook or Act!, you can just "pour" your list of addresses into your Palm organizer by pressing the button on the Palm cradle to start a HotSync. The Palm desktop installation program automatically connects your Palm to Microsoft Outlook when you insert the Palm CD in your CD-ROM drive.

- ✔ **Check out the keyboard.** You have no reason to wait to start using your Palm organizer. Take out the stylus from the side of the Palm case, press any of the buttons on the Palm case to start a program, tap the spot labeled *abc* on the Palm screen to open the on-screen keyboard, and start entering information. Of course, entering information on your desktop computer and then shooting the info over to your Palm by doing a HotSync can be far more efficient, but something can also be said for instant gratification.

✔ **Learn Graffiti.** If you really want get things done with your Palm device, you need to learn Graffiti. Your Palm device includes an excellent ten minute tutorial program for learning Graffiti. To start it up, tap the Applications button to the right of the Graffiti area, and then tap the Graffiti icon. You can be even more efficient when you know the tricks for drawing certain finicky letters. To become a Graffiti whiz in no time flat, see Chapter 2.

✔ **Create your business card.** Your Palm device can "beam" your business card to another PalmPilot or Visor user. But you need to enter and set up your business card first. Enter your own name and address in your Palm Address Book, and then tap the Menu button and choose Record/Select Business Card. Then when you want to beam your business card to your new acquaintance, just hold the Address Book button for two seconds while pointing the red "beaming" spot on your Palm device toward the other Visor or PalmPilot. See Chapter 9 for more about beaming.

✔ **Enter an appointment.** The Date Book is the most popular Palm feature. To enter an appointment, press the Date Book button on the Palm case (the leftmost button), tap the line corresponding to the time of your appointment, and enter the name of your appointment with either Graffiti or the on-screen keyboard. For more about entering, changing, or deleting appointments see Chapter 8.

✔ **Install a program.** Your Palm device can run any of the 15,000 programs that have been created for the Palm platform. You can download thousands of these programs for free and install them to your Palm device. If you use Windows, just double-click the name of a downloaded Palm program and then HotSync your Palm computer to install your new program. Nothing could be simpler. If you want to make your Palm computer an incredible, all-in-one information resource by installing extra programs, see Chapter 13.

Chapter 2

Going in Stylus

*T*o enter information into your Palm device, just write on the screen. Isn't that easy? Well, there's a small catch; you have to write using a special alphabet called *Graffiti*. Fortunately, writing Graffiti is very, very simple (no, you don't use a spray can). In fact, many people are unaware of how simple Graffiti is so they don't use it at all. With about half an hour of practice, you can learn to write anything you want in Graffiti. Current Palm devices even have a game to help you learn to write Graffiti. In this chapter, I show you the basics of Graffiti, plus I reveal some tricks on how to make the Graffiti system work better.

The people who make Palm devices recommend that you enter most of your data via the Palm Desktop program (described in Chapters 12, 13, and 14). Although this is the clearest way to deal with data entry, I think that being able to jot down a memo while riding on a train or sitting by a pool is half the fun of having a Palm device, so I like to use either Graffiti or the on-screen keyboard that's built into a Palm device. Programmers are creating products that offer interesting new ways to enter text into your Palm device, but those products have to be bought separately. (I discuss these products at the end of this chapter, in the section "Other Text-Entry Tricks.")

Graffiti

Using words to explain Graffiti is like trying to describe a spiral staircase without using your hands. Even though a spiral staircase is tricky to describe, it's easy to use; the same goes for Graffiti. After you've used Graffiti for even a little while, you find it comes naturally.

To write in Graffiti, you have to use a *stylus* — a special pen with no ink. You can use the stylus that comes with your Palm device, which is stored in a holder on the back or side of your Palm device (depending on which model you're using). Although you can also go out and buy a fancy, expensive stylus from people who also sell fancy, expensive writing pens, the cheap, plastic stylus that comes with your Palm device does the job just as well.

Although your Palm device will probably work perfectly for a long time with little or no trouble, if you accidentally scratch the screen, you'll start having problems. Don't use a sharp object as a stylus. To be safe, use a stylus that was designed to work with a Palm device.

You can use the stylus to tap on-screen buttons and select text. To write text in Graffiti, though, you have to write in the box at the bottom of the screen (cleverly named the Graffiti area), as shown in Figure 2-1.

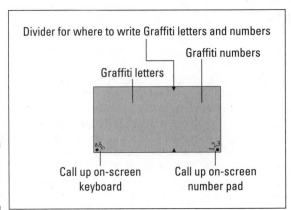

Figure 2-1:
The Graffiti
writing area.

Divider for where to write Graffiti letters and numbers

Graffiti numbers

Graffiti letters

Call up on-screen keyboard

Call up on-screen number pad

The Graffiti tutorial

More recent versions of the Palm organizer — such as the Palm m515, and Palm i705— include a Graffiti tutorial so that you have a chance to figure out the Palm Computing writing system. I think that you'll get the hang of Graffiti after about 20 minutes of practice, and the tutorial helps by giving you step-by-step exercises for the characters that you use most often. It also displays a trace of the actual characters you write — as you write them — so you understand why your Palm device sometimes misunderstands the letters you enter. (I'm often shocked at how well it interprets my hieroglyphics — half the time, I can't read the stuff myself.)

Graffiti letters and numbers

The letters abc hang around in the lower-left corner of the Graffiti area to remind you that you have to write letters on the left side of the box. The numbers 123 (in the lower-right corner) remind you that — you guessed it — you can write only numbers on the right side of the screen. Two tiny triangles separate the letter-writing area from the number-writing area.

Graffiti is a special alphabet that you have to learn; it's not handwriting-recognition software that learns your handwriting style. Most of the letters and numbers in the Graffiti alphabet are the same as the plain block letters that you were taught to use in the first grade, with one important adjustment: *Graffiti letters must be written with a single stroke of the stylus*. If you remember this one rule, Graffiti is simple. Figure 2-2 shows the letter *A* in Graffiti.

Figure 2-2:
The letter A.

The Graffiti letter *A* looks just like a normal capital letter *A* without the cross-bar. (That dot on the lower-left end of the *A* shows where you begin the stroke — it's the same place most people begin writing a capital *A*.) You don't write a crossbar because writing it requires a second stroke of the stylus, and picking up the stylus is the way you tell Graffiti that you've moved on to the next letter. For the letter *A*, just draw the upper, triangular part of the *A* and then move on to the next letter. (It takes much less time to do this than to read about doing it.)

Your Palm device comes with a little sticker that shows you the whole Graffiti alphabet. You can put the sticker on the back of your unit so that you always have it as a reference. In case you've lost the little sticker, Figure 2-3 shows the whole Graffiti alphabet.

Nearly all Graffiti charts display the alphabet as little squiggles or shapes with a dot at one end. The dot tells you where to begin drawing the Graffiti stroke.

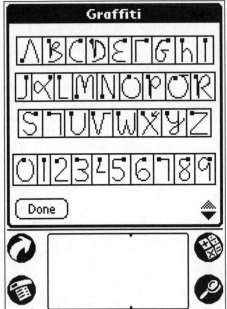

Figure 2-3:
The whole
Graffiti
alphabet.

As you can see, the Graffiti alphabet is easy to understand. The trick is to remember the tiny differences between regular printing and printing Graffiti.

Your Graffiti guru

Spiritual guides tell us that it's good to ask for help. If you need help with Graffiti, just call on your little Graffiti guru. You can display the Graffiti Help screen from most Palm programs as follows:

1. Tap the Menu soft button.

The menu bar appears.

2. Choose Edit⇨Graffiti Help.

The Graffiti Help screen appears.

After you find the Graffiti letter that you want to use, tap the Done button to return to your program and write the letter.

The Graffiti Help screen appears only in situations when it is possible to enter text. For example, if you're looking at your To Do List, you cannot enter text, so you can't access the Graffiti Help screen. You need to select a To Do item or create a new To Do (or some other function that allows you to enter text) before you can access the Help screen.

You may find that getting used to writing Graffiti takes a little time. Don't despair — that's normal. Like most computers, your Palm device can be finicky about what it accepts when it comes to individual things like human handwriting. Because my handwriting is pretty awful, I often have to write more slowly and carefully when I'm writing Graffiti characters than when I'm writing normal text on paper.

If you're a touch typist, you probably won't achieve the kind of speed when you're entering text in Graffiti that you do when typing. The point of Graffiti is not so much speed as convenience; you use Graffiti when dragging a keyboard around just isn't practical.

Moving the Graffiti cursor

When you're creating text in Graffiti, you always see a little blinking line in the display area, called the *insertion point* or the *cursor,* which shows you where the next letter that you enter will appear. Sometimes, you want to make the cursor move without entering a letter, you want to enter a space between words, or you want to produce a line between paragraphs.

To create a space, draw the Graffiti space character in the Graffiti area, as shown in Figure 2-4. (The space character is just a horizontal line drawn from left to right.)

Figure 2-4:
The space character.

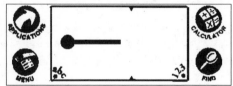

If you make a mistake, you may want to backspace to erase the last letter that you wrote. The backspace character works just like the Backspace key on a regular desktop computer. To backspace, draw the Graffiti backspace character in the Graffiti area, as shown in Figure 2-5. (The backspace character is just a horizontal line drawn from right to left — the opposite of the space character.) Although some characters have to be entered either in the letters or numbers area of the Graffiti box, you can enter spaces and backspaces in either area.

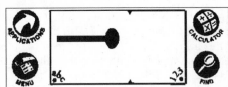

Figure 2-5:
The
backspace
character.

When you want to delete an entire word or a large block of text, it's quicker to select the text before drawing the backspace character to delete everything that you've selected. To select text, draw an imaginary line through the text that you want to select in the display area (not in the Graffiti area). You can identify the selected text because it's highlighted. Backspacing after highlighting text erases that text. You can also just begin writing after selecting text — the new text replaces the old.

If you're finished with the line you're writing and you want to begin entering text on a new line, use the Graffiti Return character, as shown in Figure 2-6. The return character is a slanted line drawn from the upper-right to the lower-left part of the Graffiti area. It works a little like the Enter key on a regular desktop computer, although you use the Return character much less on a Palm device than you would use Enter on a regular computer.

Figure 2-6:
The Return
character.

Capitalizing without a Shift key

When you type a capital letter on a regular keyboard, you hold the Shift key while typing the letter. But because you can't hold a key while entering a Graffiti letter, you have to enter the shift character before entering a letter that you want capitalized.

The Shift character is simply an upward, vertical stroke in the Graffiti text area, as shown in Figure 2-7. To enter a capital *A,* draw a vertical line upward in the Graffiti text area, then enter the letter *A.* After you draw the shift character, an upward-pointing arrow appears in the lower-right corner of the screen to show you that your next letter will be capitalized.

Figure 2-7: The Shift character.

On a regular keyboard, if you want to capitalize a whole string of letters, you press the Caps Lock key and type away. After you finish typing the capital letters, you press the Shift key to return to regular, lowercase text.

Entering two shift characters in a row in Graffiti, as shown in Figure 2-8, is the same as pressing the Caps Lock key on a regular keyboard. After you enter the shift character twice, you see an arrow with a dotted tail in the lower-right corner of the display area, which tells you that all the text that you enter will be capitalized. You can cancel the Caps Lock action by entering the shift command again.

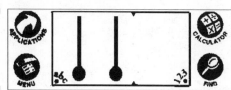

Figure 2-8: The Caps Lock command.

TIP

In certain situations, because Palm Computing applications assume that the first letter of a sentence or proper name should be capitalized, the shift arrow automatically shows up in the lower-right corner of the screen to indicate that your next letter is capitalized. If you don't want to capitalize the beginning of a sentence, enter the shift character twice to return to lowercase text.

Graffiti has another type of shift character — the Extended Shift, which is entered as a downward, diagonal line starting from the top-left, as shown in Figure 2-9. The Extended Shift character offers a way to enter special characters, such as the copyright symbol (©) and the trademark symbol ((tm)). You can also use Extended Shift to create certain punctuation characters, such as the upside-down question marks and exclamation points that you need for entering text in Spanish, in addition to some mathematical symbols like plus signs. When you enter the Extended Shift stroke, a little diagonal line appears in the lower-right corner of the screen. If you explore the Graffiti help screen, you'll see a list of the extended shift characters.

Figure 2-9:
The
Extended
Shift stroke.

Another special shift character that you may use is the Command Shift stroke — an upward diagonal line that starts in the lower-left part of the Graffiti screen, as shown in Figure 2-10. You can perform quite a few common tasks in many of the Palm computing programs by entering the Command Shift stroke followed by a letter. To delete a To Do item, for example, tap the item and then enter the Command Shift stroke followed by the letter *D*. This step opens the Delete dialog box, just as if you had chosen Record⇨Delete Item from the menu. You can see what the Command Shift stroke can do in any program by tapping the Menu soft button and looking at the list of commands on the right side of each menu.

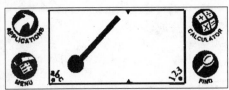

Figure 2-10:
The
Command
Shift stroke.

Punctuating your text

Although Graffiti letters and numbers look somewhat normal, Graffiti punctuation is strange. To enter punctuation characters, such as periods, dashes, and commas, you have to tap your stylus once in the Graffiti area before entering the character. Many punctuation characters have different meanings if you don't tap first before drawing them. When you tap once, a little dot appears in the lower-right corner of the display area to show that you've tapped.

You may want to avoid punctuation altogether when you're entering Graffiti text, except for the occasional period or dash:

- **Period:** The simplest punctuation character is the period. Tap twice in the Graffiti area to create a period. Figure 2-11 shows a dot that I drew to make a period.

- **Dash:** The second simplest punctuation character is the dash. Tap once in the Graffiti area, and then draw a horizontal line from left to right. After you've used Graffiti for a while, you think of this as tapping and then drawing the space character.

TIP

If you need to enter e-mail addresses into your Address Book, you almost certainly need to be able to enter the @ sign, for e-mail addresses that look like somebody@something.com. The @ sign is simply a tap in the Graffiti area followed by the letter *O*.

Figure 2-11:
The Graffiti
period.

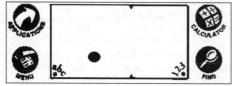

I have lots of Graffiti practice under my belt, but I still forget most of the punctuation characters. With the exception of commas, dashes, and apostrophes, I go to my on-screen keyboard for punctuation. Most of the punctuation that I tend to forget can be found on the number keyboard, so I just tap the spot labeled 123 in the lower-right corner of the Graffiti area to bring up the number keypad. I'll tell you more about the on-screen keyboard later in the chapter.

TIP

You can see how to write Graffiti punctuation characters in the Graffiti help screen; just tap the Memo hard button (the first physical button on the right at the bottom of your Palm device), then choose Edit⇨Graffiti help and press the scroll-down button until the characters you want to enter appear.

Graffiti whiz secrets

I think that most people can get a good handle on Graffiti within a few hours, except for people under 15 years of age, who usually pick it up in about five minutes. I've heard stories of kids in junior high school who write notes to each other in Graffiti, which I think is very clever. I hope that they don't write naughty words on walls in Graffiti, which would be redundant.

REMEMBER

Even with some experience, certain Graffiti letters stay finicky and can be hard to enter accurately. Make your Graffiti characters as large, square, and vertical as possible.

Another trick is to figure out which letters can be entered by writing a number on the letter side of the Graffiti area and a letter on the number side of the Graffiti area. If you write the number 3 on the letter side of the Graffiti area, for example, the letter B turns up more reliably than it does if you actually draw the Graffiti letter B. Table 2-1 shows a list of letters that are often a problem and how to get your Palm device to recognize them more reliably.

Table 2-1	Tricks of the Graffiti Trade
Character	**Keystroke**
B	Draw the number *3* on the letter side of the Graffiti area.
G	Draw the number *6* on the letter side of the Graffiti area.
K	This one is the trickiest Graffiti character. Just draw the "legs" on the side of the *K*, joined by a little loop. Leave out the vertical bar. To me, it looks a little like a fish swimming from right to left. I describe this subject in greater detail later in this chapter.
P	Begin at the bottom of the *P* and make the loop at the top pretty small.
Q	Draw an *O* with a long tail at the top.
R	Do this just like the *P*, but make the tail of the *R* extra long.
V	Draw the *V* backward (start from the top right).
Y	Just draw the lower loop of a cursive capital *Y*. It's just a loop, like the letter *K*, except that the fish is swimming down.
2	Draw the letter *Z* on the number side of the Graffiti writing area.
4	Draw the letter *L* on the number side of the Graffiti area.
5	Draw the letter *S* on the number side of the Graffiti area.
7	Draw a backward letter *C* on the number side of the Graffiti area.

Getting your numbers

Graffiti numbers are written pretty much like normal numbers (except that the number *4* is best written like a capital *L*). But the speediest way to enter numbers on a Palm device is to tap the number spot in the lower-right corner of the Graffiti box and tap out the numbers on the on-screen keypad. I stick with Graffiti for letters, but the keypad is faster when you want to enter numbers.

The amazing Graffiti fish loop

One Graffiti character has no counterpart in the normal alphabet, although knowing how to draw this character can help you enormously when you use Graffiti. Because the character doesn't have an official name, I just call it the *fish loop*.

I know that my fish story is a dopey explanation, but I bring it up for two reasons. First, because Graffiti seems to recognize this loop symbol more reliably than most other letters or numbers, finding out how to use it certainly makes you a quicker and slicker Graffiti-ist. The second reason for my fish story is because I find stupid explanations are the easiest to remember. By that measure, you'll *never* forget this explanation.

There are four fish strokes:

✔ **Left-facing:** If you draw a little loop that looks like a fish swimming from right to left, as shown in Figure 2-12, Graffiti translates that loop as the letter K.

Figure 2-12: This little fish goes by the name K.

✔ **Down-facing:** If you make the fish look like it's swimming downward, as shown in Figure 2-13, Graffiti translates that loop as the letter *Y*.

Figure 2-13: Why is this fish swimming down? It's forming the letter *Y*.

✔ **Right-facing:** If you make the fish look like it's swimming from left to right, as shown in Figure 2-14, Graffiti translates that loop as the letter *X*.

Figure 2-14: This fish signs its name with an X.

> ✔ **Up-facing:** If you make the fish look like it's swimming upward and you begin drawing from the left, as shown in Figure 2-15, Graffiti translates that loop as the shortcut symbol, a useful tool that I discuss in the next section, "The Graffiti ShortCut Symbol."

Figure 2-15: This fish knows the shortcut — straight up.

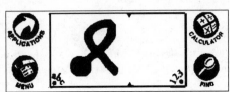

By the way, I did say that each Graffiti letter must be written in a single stroke, but the regular *X* is the exception that proves the rule. You can do a two-stroke *X* if you prefer, but I think the fish loop is a bit slicker.

The Graffiti ShortCut symbol

Another compelling reason to use Graffiti is that you can create and use ShortCuts. *ShortCuts* are abbreviations that automatically expand themselves into longer blocks of text or automated entries, such as the current date and time.

When you buy your Palm device, a few ShortCuts are already built in. Some of the preprogrammed ShortCuts are for useful words: *meeting, breakfast, lunch,* and *dinner.* You also get some useful time-stamp ShortCuts for entering the current date and time.

To add a time stamp to a memo or note, write the Graffiti ShortCut symbol, followed by the letters *TS,* as shown in Figure 2-16.

As soon as you finish writing the letter *S,* the three characters that you entered disappear, and the current time appears.

The following are three preprogrammed time-stamp ShortCuts:

> ✔ **TS (Time stamp):** Enters the current time
>
> ✔ **DS (Date stamp):** Enters the current date
>
> ✔ **DTS (Date-time stamp):** Enters the current date and time

Figure 2-16:
No, this is not the name of a fraternity — it's the Graffiti Time Stamp shortcut.

Other preprogrammed ShortCuts include the following:

- **ME:** For the word *meeting*
- **BR:** For the word *breakfast*
- **LU:** For the word *lunch*
- **DI:** For the word *dinner*

In Chapter 3, I show you how to create ShortCuts of your own.

The On-Screen Keyboard

Perhaps you don't want to spend time finding out about Graffiti. You may just want to get down to business, which is fine. You can call up the on-screen keyboard to enter letters by tapping on a tiny picture of a keyboard, as shown in Figure 2-17.

To make the on-screen keyboard appear, tap the dot in one of the two lower corners of the Graffiti area. When you tap the dot on the letter side of the Graffiti area, the alphabet keyboard appears. When you tap the dot on the number side, a numeric keypad appears, as shown in Figure 2-18. After you've entered the text that you want, tap Done to make the on-screen keyboard go away.

Figure 2-17:
The on-
screen
keyboard is
an easy way
to enter text,
too.

The on-screen keyboard is too small for touch-typing. You definitely need the stylus to pick out those tiny little keys. I use the on-screen keyboard as little as possible because I think that I type more slowly when I'm trying to find those tiny little keys. I know plenty of people who stick exclusively with the on-screen keyboard; they do just fine.

The on-screen keyboard appears only when it's possible for you to enter text. If you're looking at your list of memos, for example, the on-screen keyboard doesn't appear because you have to open a memo or create a new memo before you can enter text.

On the on-screen keyboard, you also see a button labeled Int'l, which unlocks a special set of keys for entering those festive international characters that English sadly lacks.

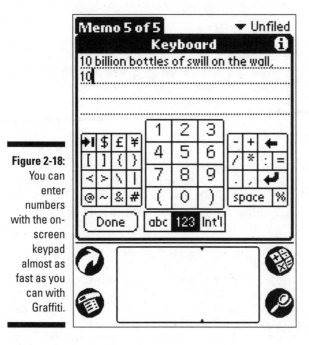

Figure 2-18:
You can enter numbers with the on-screen keypad almost as fast as you can with Graffiti.

Other Text-Entry Tricks

You can find dozens of programs and gizmos that almost totally eliminate the need to learn Graffiti. You'll pay a little extra and might need to carry another gadget, but most of these solutions can get you up and running in a jiffy.

However, you don't need any of these if you use a Palm device with a built-in keypad (such as certain Sony Clie models or the Handspring Treo). You can just let your fingers do the walking.

Writing systems

Graffiti is kindergarten-simple, but it can be fussy about understanding what you enter. Many people want a faster, better, or more flexible writing system for their Palm device. Here are a few of the top names.

Jot

Graffiti isn't the only way to enter written information into your Palm device. You can also buy Jot, a piece of software that uses a different but equally simple set of letters for entering text. Some people prefer Jot to Graffiti the way others might prefer Pepsi to Coke. Personally, I stick with Graffiti because it's free; if you're not satisfied, check out Jot by visiting `www.palm pilotfordummies.com/jot`.

Silkyboard

If you'd rather not look at the Graffiti writing area at all, you can buy Silkyboard, a tiny picture of a typewriter keyboard that sticks to the bottom part of your screen like a piece of adhesive tape. When you tap on the tiny keyboard, you get the same result as using Graffiti. You can get Silkyboard at `www.palmpilotfordummies.com/silkyboard`.

The Fitaly Keyboard

Did you even wonder why the letters on a typewriter keyboard spell QWERTY? The people who designed the Fitaly keyboard for your Palm device wondered the same thing, so they developed a tiny keypad (like Silkyboard) with the keys arranged in a pattern to help you type faster. However, if you don't have time to learn Graffiti, you probably don't have time to learn Fitaly either. You can find out more at `www.palmpilotfordummies.com/fitaly`.

Keyboards

You'll find more keyboard add-ons for your Palm device than eggs in a hen-house. Of course, hens don't need a keyboard because they can't touch type — they just hunt and peck. (Sorry!) I've seen at least ten Palm keyboards and used at least three. The following sections discuss the most popular keyboards.

Stowaway

My very favorite keyboard at the moment is the folding Palm keyboard, also known as the Stowaway keyboard, distributed by Targus for non-Palm-brand organizers. It's an amazing James-Bond-style gadget that folds out from a pocket-sized case to form a full-sized keyboard. People literally gasp when they see you unfold the Stowaway, so even if you don't type much, it's a great conversation starter. Because the Stowaway fits in a coat pocket (or even in a shirt pocket), you can carry it everywhere you take your Palm organizer. Pick up a Stowaway at `www.palmpilotfordummies.com/stowaway`.

GoType!

Before the Stowaway appeared, my favorite keyboard for handheld computers was the GoType! keyboard from LandWare. It doesn't fold up into your pocket, but it opens like a clam to reveal a slightly miniaturized keyboard. Because the GoType! doesn't fold the way the Stowaway does, you can rest it on your lap while typing, which makes it handy for taking notes in lectures and other situations when you're not sitting at a table. If you're sitting at your computer, you can find out more at www.palmpilotfordummies.com/gotype.

FX100

The oddest keyboard I've seen is the flexible rubber keyboard called the FX100. This contraption actually rolls up like a tiny rubber bathmat into a fist-sized case. I find that the keys are a bit too small to touch-type, but people with smaller hands say that the size is just right. You can find out more about the FX100 at www.palmpilotfordummies.com/flextype.

Wireless Link

The Wireless Link from Micro Innovations is an intriguing new product at the time of this writing. I find Wireless Link interesting but tricky to use. It's a tiny folding keyboard that connects to your Palm device through the Infrared link that you use for beaming business cards. That means that you can use it with just about any Palm device (or Pocket PC device, for that matter). Other keyboards only connect to certain Palm models, so if you upgrade to a new model, you need a new keyboard. My only gripe is that the keys are a bit too small for touch typing (for me, at least). Find out more at www.palmpilotfordummies.com/wirelesslink.

Chapter 3

Making Your Palm Device Your Own

● ●

In This Chapter

▶ Setting preferences

▶ Using the Security program

▶ Setting passwords

▶ Hiding and showing private items

▶ Saving time with ShortCuts

▶ Using Palm Computing hacks

● ●

*O*ver 20 million people use Palm computers, and there are probably 20 million different ways to use one. Most people use a Palm device exactly the way it comes out of the box; they don't change a thing. But if you get an itch to customize your Palm and give your unit some special zip, you can have it your way with very little fuss.

Later in the book, I suggest some extra programs and accessories you can get to make your Palm your own, but in this chapter, I stick to the simple ways you can customize your Palm to suit your fancy.

Setting General Preferences

When you start up your Palm device for the first time, the General Preferences screen appears automatically. Consider it an invitation to set the time and date accurately. You may also want to reset the time if you travel frequently to different time zones.

Follow these steps to access the General Preferences screen:

1. **Tap the Applications soft button, the upper spot on the left side of the Graffiti box.**

   The list of applications appears on the screen.

2. **Tap the Prefs icon.**

   The Preferences application launches, as shown in Figure 3-1.

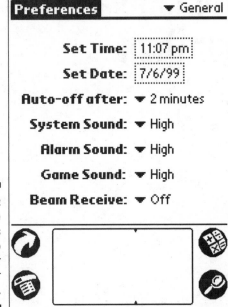

Figure 3-1:
Go to the
Prefs
program to
make your
Palm your
own.

3. **Tap the word in the upper-right corner of the screen.**

   The Preferences program has eight options for setting up different types of preferences: Buttons, Digitizer, Formats, General, Modem, Network, Owner, and ShortCuts. The name of the section you're looking at appears in the upper-right corner of the screen. The triangle next to the name of the section means you can tap the name of the section to see a pull-down menu of the other available sections.

4. **Choose General.**

   The General Preferences screen appears.

To change the individual settings of the General Preferences screen, continue with the following sections of the chapter.

Setting the time

I like having my Palm device remind me of my appointments shortly before they occur, just to avoid missing anything that I've scheduled. The Palm device is like an alarm clock, though: My alarm can't go off at the right time if I don't set it to the right time in the first place.

Follow these steps to set the time on your Palm device:

1. With the General Preferences screen visible, tap the time shown in the Set Time box.

The Set Time dialog box opens, showing the time for which the Palm device is now set, along with a pair of triangles for changing the time. The top triangle sets the time later, and the bottom triangle sets the time earlier, as shown in Figure 3-2.

Figure 3-2:
In the Set Time dialog box, tap the triangles to set the time.

2. Tap the hour in the Set Time dialog box.

The hour is highlighted to show you've selected it.

3. Tap the triangles until the hour you want appears.

The hour changes as you tap the triangles.

4. Set the minutes by following Steps 2 and 3 for each of the two minute boxes.

The minutes change as you tap the triangles.

5. Tap the AM or PM box to choose the appropriate setting.

The box you tap is highlighted to show that you've picked it.

6. Tap OK.

The Set Time dialog box closes.

If you want the time on your Palm device to appear in a format different from the standard 1:35 PM format, then see the section "Setting Format Preferences" later in this chapter, where I show you how to change the time format.

Setting the date

If you use the calendar frequently or if you enter lots of tasks with assigned due dates, then you may want your Palm device to know what day it is.

Follow these steps to set the date on your Palm device:

1. **With the General Preferences screen visible, tap the date shown in the Set Date box.**

   The Set Date dialog box opens, as shown in Figure 3-3.

Figure 3-3:
Set the date
on your
Palm device
by tapping
the current
date on the
calendar.

2. **Tap one of the triangles on either side of the year to set the current year.**

   After you tap the triangle on the left, the year shown moves to one year earlier. Tapping the triangle on the right moves the year shown to the next year. Keep tapping until the current year appears.

3. **Tap the month you want.**

   The name of the month you tap is highlighted to show you've selected it, and a calendar for the month you tap appears.

4. **Tap the day of the month that you want to set.**

   The Set Date dialog box closes; the date you chose appears on the Preferences screen.

After you've set the date, your Palm device remembers it and keeps track of the date automatically unless you let the batteries go dead. If you go around the world for 80 days and come home to a dead Palm device, just change the batteries (or recharge your Palm), HotSync, and reset the date and time. (For more info about batteries, see Chapter 1.)

Setting the Auto-off interval

Your Palm device goes a long way on a pair of AAA batteries or a single charge; mine usually runs for the better part of a month before I have to replace them. One method that the Palm device uses to stretch battery life is to turn off automatically if you haven't pressed a button for a few minutes.

Although you don't have many choices about how long your Palm device waits before shutting off, here's how you can choose from what's available:

1. **With the General Preferences screen visible, tap the triangle next to the words *Auto-off after*.**

   The pull-down list of Auto-off intervals appears. You can choose a 1-, 2-, or 3-minute Auto-off interval, as shown in Figure 3-4.

Figure 3-4:
The Auto-off feature can lengthen your Palm's battery life.

2. **Choose the Auto-off interval you want.**

   The interval you tap appears in the Auto-off after box.

You don't need to worry much about your Palm device turning off too fast; you only have to press the green power button to switch right back to the program you were working on when the Palm device turned off.

Setting the sound volume

A tiny little speaker inside your Palm device makes little chirping sounds when you tap the screen, and it plays a squeaky little fanfare when you run the HotSync program. If you think that a Palm device should be seen and not heard, then you can turn the sound off. If you have particularly sharp hearing, then you can also change the volume.

You can adjust three volume settings:

- ✔ **System:** System sounds are those sounds that the Palm OS is pro-grammed to make in certain events. For example, when you want to do something specific that your Palm device can't do at that particular moment, then you may get an error beep, just like when your desktop PC protests one of your actions.

- ✔ **Alarm:** An alarm sounds when you set a reminder for an appointment. You can also get some third-party Palm Computing programs that use the alarm sound.

- ✔ **Game:** Game sounds work only with games that are programmed to use them. Although most games are more fun with sounds, those gamelike boinks and bleeps are a dead giveaway that you're not using your Palm device for serious work. If you plan to secretly play a shoot-'em-up game at the weekly staff meeting (not that I'd suggest such a thing, of course), then a good career move may be to turn off your game sounds.

If your Palm device goes off when you're at the movies, you may get some dirty looks, so be a good sport and turn off the sounds when you go to the Mega-Multiplex. Follow these steps to adjust the volume on all three types of sounds:

1. **With the General Preferences screen visible, tap the triangle next to the type of sound you want to change.**

   A pull-down menu of volume choices appears. On a Palm III or later model you can choose between Off, Low, Medium, or High, as shown in Figure 3-5. Earlier Palm devices offer a check box in which you can only turn the sound on or off.

Figure 3-5:
You can turn
the volume
up or down
to suit your
taste.

2. **Choose the volume level you want.**

   The volume level that you tap appears in the System Sound box.

The term *Palm device volume* is an oxymoron like *military intelligence, postal service,* and *athletic scholarship.* The minuscule speaker inside the case can only make sounds that I'd describe as soft, softer, and softest. You may want to adjust the volume anyway, so at least you have a way to do so.

Turning off beaming

A Palm device can send or receive all sorts of things by *beaming,* which is the rather neat process of sending data between Palm devices via an invisible light beam that travels through the air. (Sounds kind of magical, doesn't it? To demystify beaming, see Chapter 9.) The Palm doesn't distinguish between truly useful information and useless junk when it sends stuff out over the air — kind of like television.

If you want to avoid having unwanted junk beamed to your Palm device, you can elect to not receive beamed items by following these steps:

1. **With the General Preferences screen visible, tap the triangle next to Beam Receive.**

   The pull-down list of choices appears.

2. **Choose either On or Off.**

   The choice that you tap appears in the Beam Receive box.

 Turning off Beam Receive doesn't stop you from beaming items to others. If you've turned off Beam Receive and you try to beam something, though, a dialog box opens, asking whether you want to turn Beam Receive back on. If you're exchanging business cards with another Palm device user, switching on Beam Receive makes sense. You don't want to be unsociable, do you?

Setting Button Preferences

You may use some programs more than others. As a result, you may want to assign a different program to one of the hard buttons at the bottom of your Palm organizer case.

You should be aware that some Palm devices have a different set of programs assigned to the buttons than the ones I describe here. For example, the Palm i705 has Web-browsing and e-mail buttons, and some Palm-powered phones assign buttons to telephone functions. So don't be alarmed if your settings look a little different than the ones I describe here. You can use the same process for changing the button assignments for any Palm device.

Here's how to switch the programs assigned to the Applications buttons:

1. **Tap the Applications soft button, the upper spot on the left side of the Graffiti box.**

   The list of applications appears, showing icons for all the programs installed in your Palm device.

2. **Tap the Prefs icon.**

   The Preferences screen appears.

3. **Tap the word in the upper-right corner of the screen.**

   A pull-down list of preferences options appears.

4. **Choose Buttons.**

   The Buttons Preferences screen appears and displays five icons, one for each of the buttons at the bottom of your Palm device and one for the Calculator soft button. (The other soft buttons aren't up for grabs.) The name of the assigned program shows up next to each icon.

5. **Tap the triangle next to the button of the program you want to change.**

   A pull-down list of all the applications installed in your Palm device appears; the program names are in alphabetical order, as shown in Figure 3-6. If your applications list gets too long to fit on the Palm organizer screen, little arrows appear at the top and bottom of the list, indicating that more programs are available. You can scroll up and down the list, either by tapping the arrows at the top and bottom of the list or by pressing the scroll-up and scroll-down buttons at the bottom center of the case.

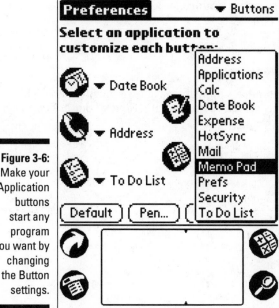

Figure 3-6:
Make your
Application
buttons
start any
program
you want by
changing
the Button
settings.

6. **Choose the name of the application you want to assign to that button.**

   The application name you tap appears on the Buttons Preferences screen next to the button to which it's assigned.

   Now, when you press that particular button, your Palm device runs the newly assigned program. All your programs still appear after you tap the Applications soft button, although only the assigned programs run from the hard buttons.

Setting Format Preferences

Because people express time and numbers differently in different places, your Palm device has settings to accommodate these differences.

Here's how to change the way that dates and numbers appear:

1. **Tap the Applications soft button.**

   The list of applications appears, showing icons for all the programs installed in your Palm device.

2. **Tap the Prefs icon.**

   The Preferences screen appears.

3. **Tap the word in the upper-right corner of the screen.**

   A pull-down list of Preferences options appears.

4. **Tap Formats.**

   The Format Preferences screen appears.

5. **Tap the triangle next to Preset To.**

   A pull-down menu of countries appears, as shown in Figure 3-7. When you choose a certain country, the preset date, time, and number formats for that country appear.

Figure 3-7:
Use your favorite country's number format by choosing it from the Preset To list.

6. **Choose the country whose presets you want to use.**

   The name of the country that you tap appears in the Preset To box, and all the number formats on the Format Preferences screen change to the formats common to the country you chose.

7. **If you want to change an individual type of formatting, then tap the triangle next to the example of that type.**

A pull-down list of formatting choices appears. If you choose the United States, for example, the entry in the Time box says HH:MM a.m./p.m., which means that all time entries on your Palm device appear the way that people write them in the United States, such as 11:13 a.m. If you want the time to appear the way that it's displayed in Italy — 11.13, for example — choose the HH.MM entry.

The format that you tap appears on the Format Preferences screen, as shown in Figure 3-8.

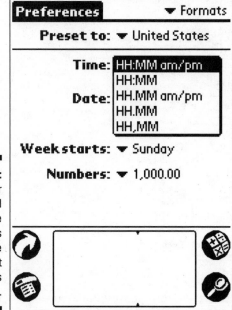

Figure 3-8:
Choose your
Time and
Date
formats
from the
Format
Preferences
screen.

Changing your format preferences also changes the way that numbers appear in all Palm Computing applications. If you want to use one format in one application and another format in a different application, then you're out of luck. One format per customer, please.

Using the Security Application

If you keep lots of sensitive business data on your Palm device, then you'd be wise to take advantage of the built-in security features. You can hide items that you want to protect from unauthorized eyes, and you can even assign a password to lock your Palm device from any unauthorized use.

Follow these steps to access the Security screen:

1. **Tap the Applications soft button.**

   The list of applications appears on your screen.

2. **Tap Security.**

   The Security screen appears, as shown in Figure 3-9.

Figure 3-9:
Keep your
secrets
secret with
the Security
Application.

To change the individual settings on the Security Preferences screen, read the following sections.

Setting your password

Although you can keep confidential information on either a desktop computer or a Palm device, few people misplace their desktop computers in airports or restaurants the way that they misplace their Palm devices. That makes password-protecting your Palm data all the more important.

Follow these steps to set a password:

1. **With the Security Preferences screen visible, tap Unassigned in the Password box.**

   The Password dialog box opens.

   If the word *Assigned* appears, you already have a password. If you want to delete your password, see the following section, "Deleting a forgotten password."

2. **Enter the password that you want to set by using Graffiti (refer to Chapter 2 for more information about entering text).**

   The password that you enter appears in the Password dialog box, as shown in Figure 3-10. Don't forget to remember your password.

Figure 3-10: Enter your password in the Password dialog box.

3. **Tap OK.**

   The Password dialog box opens again, asking you to verify your password.

4. **Re-enter the password that you entered in Step 2.**

   The password that you enter appears again in the Password dialog box. By the way, did I mention that you should remember your password?

5. **Tap OK.**

   The Password dialog box closes, and the word *Assigned* appears in the Password box.

Other Palm security options

Even if you set a password on your Palm device, the security still isn't exactly Fort Knox–level. If you're extremely concerned about keeping the information on your Palm device confidential, you might consider one of the many third-party security programs for the Palm platform. Some popular choices include the following:

✔ **Sign-On from CIC:** This program uses your signature in lieu of a password. Not only is your signature easier to remember than a password, but Sign-On measures the speed and pattern of your signature so carefully that it's nearly impossible for an intruder to forge. Find out more at www.palmpilot fordummies.com/signon.

✔ **One Touch Pass:** This program cleverly disguises itself as a picture-viewing program so that the bad guys will never know your Palm is locked up. When you start up your Palm device, One Touch Pass displays a photo or drawing of your choice. You enter your "password" by touching different parts of the picture in a sequence you've designated in advance. Find out more at www.palmpilotfordummies.com/one touchpass.

✔ **Handango Security Suite:** This package includes two different programs, one for password protection and the other for encrypting some or all of the information stored on your Palm device. It's available at www.palmpilotfordummies.com/ handangosecurity.

As time goes on, you can expect to see better security features built right into your Palm device, especially on newer models that use Palm OS 5. That'll certainly bring joy to the hearts of secret agents everywhere. It'll also make corporate IT managers happy.

Deleting a forgotten password

It happens. You've been asked to supply 1,001 passwords for various systems and situations, from your ATM pin number to your e-mail account. Then you get a Palm device and you also get your 1,002nd password, which you forget. To solve this problem, you can just delete the old password, as long as you can turn on the power and get to the Security application:

1. **With the Security screen visible, tap the Forgotten Password button.**

   The Delete Password dialog box opens, as shown in Figure 3-11, bearing a stern warning that all the items you've marked as private are removed until the next HotSync.

2. **If you want to proceed, tap Yes.**

   After a short pause, the word Unassigned appears in the Password box. You can then reassign a new password — and make it something easy to remember. Why make things hard on yourself?

If you lock down your Palm device by tapping Turn Off & Lock Device in the Security application and then forget your password — you're cooked. You can get back into your Palm device only by performing a hard reset, which wipes out all your data. (Refer to Chapter 1 for more information about resetting your Palm device.) You can recover all the items you entered before your last HotSync by doing another HotSync. Whatever you entered after the last HotSync, but before you have reset your Palm device, is gone for good.

Unless you're unusually security-conscious, I'd pass on the password. I don't use one myself because I'm sure I'd forget it. If I lose my Palm organizer and you find it, then you'll know whom I had dinner with last week. Big deal. (If you must know, it was my friends Bill and Alice. We had pizza. Aren't you thrilled to know that? I didn't think so.)

If I was worried about keeping my top-secret data secure, then I might consider adding some security software like CIC Sign-On, a program that uses your signature as your password. You wouldn't forget your signature, would you? The program costs about twenty bucks — a small price to pay for peace of mind. You can find out more about the program at www.palmpilot fordummies.com/signon.

Hiding private items

It may not be *Saving Private Ryan,* but *Hiding Private Items* can be heroic stuff, too. The main reason to mark items as private is so you can hide them from the prying eyes of supervisors, paparazzi, and secret agents, or if you want to hide all the phone numbers of the Bond girls from Miss Moneypenny — but I digress.

Follow these steps to hide private items:

1. **With the Security screen visible, tap the Hide button next to the words** *Private Records.*

   The Hide Records dialog box opens, as shown in Figure 3-12, telling you what happens when you hide records.

Figure 3-12: You can hide your private records by tapping Hide in the Hide Records dialog box.

2. **Tap Hide.**

   The Hide Records dialog box closes, and the Security screen reappears. The word *Hide* is highlighted, and your private items are hidden, as they should be!

After you've hidden your private items, you may want to make them appear again later. Just follow the preceding steps, and tap Show rather than Hide. If you've assigned a password, the Palm device makes you enter your password before revealing your private items. Of course, before you can hide Private items, you need to mark them so that the Palm device knows that they are private items. You can mark any item as private by tapping the item to open it, tapping the button labeled `Details`, and then tapping the Private check box.

Setting Up ShortCuts

One cute feature in the Palm Computing world is the *ShortCut* — an automatic abbreviation. If you write the words *New York* frequently, for example, you can make a ShortCut named *NY*. Then, whenever you want to write "New York," just enter the Graffiti ShortCut symbol (which looks like a cursive, lowercase letter *L*) and enter the letters **NY**. The words *New York* appear automatically. (For more info about entering Graffiti ShortCuts, see the section about the Graffiti ShortCut symbol in Chapter 2.)

ShortCuts can save you lots of tapping and scribbling when you want to enter information. I like to use the date-time stamp ShortCut to measure how long I've worked on projects, especially when I'm billing for those projects by the hour. You can create or edit your own collection of ShortCuts in a jiffy.

To access the ShortCuts screen, follow these steps:

1. **Tap the Applications soft button.**

   The list of applications appears, showing icons for all the programs installed in your Palm device.

2. **Tap the Prefs icon.**

   The Preferences screen appears.

3. **Tap the word in the upper-right corner of the screen.**

   A pull-down menu of Preferences options appears.

4. **Choose ShortCuts.**

   The ShortCuts screen appears, listing all your current ShortCuts.

Read the following sections to figure out how to add, change, or delete your ShortCuts.

Adding a new ShortCut

A collection of ShortCuts is already set up for your use when you buy a Palm device. To get your money's worth from ShortCuts, create some of your own.

Adding a new ShortCut is this simple:

1. **With the ShortCuts screen visible, tap New.**

2. **Use Graffiti to enter the ShortCut name you want (refer to Chapter 2 for more information about entering text).**

   The text that you enter appears on the ShortCut Name line. (See Figure 3-13)

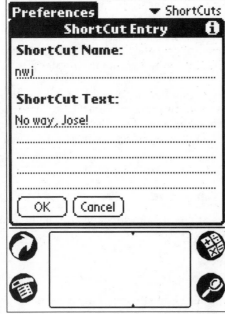

Figure 3-13: Enter the name of your ShortCut on the top line and enter the full text of the ShortCut in the lower area.

You can also use the on-screen keyboard to enter your ShortCut name, but make sure you can enter the characters you want in Graffiti; you can't use ShortCuts from the on-screen keyboard — only from Graffiti. For more about Graffiti and the on-screen keyboard, see Chapter 2.

3. **Tap the first line of the ShortCut Text section.**

   An insertion point appears at the point where you tap.

4. **Enter the text of your ShortCut by using either the on-screen keyboard or Graffiti.**

The text that you enter appears in the ShortCut Text section.

5. Tap OK.

Your new ShortCut appears on the list of ShortCuts.

Don't use a period as the first character of your ShortCut name. For some reason, the names of ShortCuts beginning with a period ("dot ShortCuts," to Palm Computing programmers) do nothing useful for you and me, although they can do nasty things to your Palm device, such as erase all your data or drain your batteries. Try to stick to names made up of letters and numbers when you're creating ShortCuts. Also, the names of ShortCuts can't contain spaces.

Editing a ShortCut

At some point, you may want to change either the name or the contents of a ShortCut.

Follow these steps to edit a ShortCut:

1. Tap the name of the ShortCut that you want to edit.

The ShortCut name you tap is highlighted to show you've selected it, as shown in Figure 3-14.

Figure 3-14:
Choose the
ShortCut
that you
want to edit.

2. **Tap Edit.**

   The ShortCut Entry dialog box opens.

3. **Select the part of the ShortCut that you want to replace.**

   The text you select is highlighted to show you've selected it.

4. **Enter the new text by using either the on-screen keyboard or Graffiti (refer to Chapter 2 for more info about entering text).**

   The text you enter replaces the text you selected.

5. **Tap OK.**

   The ShortCut Entry dialog box closes.

Your revised ShortCut is ready to use at the drop of a stylus.

Deleting a ShortCut

If you know how to edit a ShortCut, then you know how to delete a ShortCut. Just follow the same steps I describe in the preceding section, "Editing a ShortCut," and then tap the word Delete rather than the word Edit. Zap! Your ShortCut is long gone.

Hacking Up Your Palm Device

No, the heading for this section isn't the latest sequel to *Halloween.* In the Palm Computing universe, *hacks* are applications you can install on your Palm device to add features or to make it behave differently from a normal one. I'm not getting into hacks in any great degree here, although I do want you to know that they exist. Palm devices are catching on in the corporate world in a big way, and some big outfits customize their Palm devices to suit the work that they expect people to do by adding programs some call *Enterprise Applications.* That means you may have a company-issue Palm device with hacks installed that make it behave in a totally different way from the way I describe in this book. See Appendix A for more information about Enterprise Applications.

You can install hacks that change the functions of your buttons, that change the way your screen looks, or that change the things you can do with cut and paste, and lots more. Programmers are coming up with new Palm Computing hacks all the time. Most hacks are useful, such as AppHack, a program that enables you to assign as many as six different programs to each of the four hard buttons. Other hacks are less useful, such as BackHack, which reverses the spelling of all text on your Palm device, such that the word *Record* (for example) comes out as *droceR*. I can't begin to explain why someone would want a program to do that, but rest assured, someone does.

One of the most important hacks is HackMaster, the hack that manages other hacks. (Geesh, can this stuff get any more complicated?) Many hacks require you to install HackMaster before installing other hacks. If you're adventurous, check out the Palm Computing–related Web sites listed in Chapter 20, and download some hacks to install to your Palm device. When I say "adventurous," I mean you should be ready to deal with some problems, because some hacks are very experimental. The guy who developed HackMaster, a very smart and personable fellow named Edward Keyes, told me that Palm added a reset pin to the Palm stylus just because people using hacks tended to have problems with them. In my experience, hacks tend to be fussy and problematic, so I avoid them. Fortunately, they're easy to uninstall.

Chapter 4

Tips for Saving Time with Your Palm Computer

*U*sing your Palm computer isn't difficult. You can discover most of what you need to know by fiddling around for a few days. But most Palm owners don't want to waste precious time fiddling around with their Palm devices; they want to get right down to business. Here are the best tricks I know to become a speedy Palm user without much fuss.

For the moment, I stick to showing you tricks that don't require buying extra software or add-on thingamajigs. Your Palm computer does so many helpful things for you right out of the box that you may not need to fuss with adding anything to it. However, if you're interested, I show you how to find scads of Palm accessories and software in Chapters 19 and 20. I've organized all these time-savers into categories so you can easily find what you need. Enjoy!

General Time-Savers

General time-savers isn't the official name of anything. I use this term refer to time savers you can you can take advantage of at any time or in any application.

Using ShortCuts

The best time-savers are cleverly named *ShortCuts*. You can expand short abbreviations into words and phrases of as many as 45 letters (including spaces). You do this by entering the Graffiti ShortCut symbol (which looks like a cursive letter *L*) and then the abbreviation assigned to the ShortCut that you want to use to make the whole word or phrase appear. (For more info about the Graffiti ShortCut symbol, see Chapter 2.)

When you first buy a Palm device, several ShortCuts are already installed, including the words *Breakfast, Lunch,* and *Dinner,* just in case you're hungry. (To see the whole list or to find out how to create your own ShortCuts, see Chapter 3.)

Beaming from one device to another

If you've set up your business card for beaming, just hold down the Address Book button for about two seconds. The Beam dialog box opens, and your Palm device searches for any nearby Palm device that's ready to receive your card. (For more info about beaming, see Chapter 9.)

If you know lots of other Palm owners with whom you want to share information, then you can beam nearly anything on your Palm organizer with a single stroke of your stylus. Dragging your stylus from the bottom of the screen to the top opens the Graffiti Help screen, but you can assign the Beam feature to this action if you'd prefer. Doing so means dragging your stylus in this way automatically beams whatever is displayed on your Palm screen. To change what happens when you drag your stylus up the screen, go to the Preferences application and look under Button Preferences. (See Chapter 3 for more about setting button preferences.)

Using your finger rather than the stylus

You can't do anything with a stylus that you can't do with your finger. Because the Palm screen is touch-sensitive, your finger can serve as a perfectly good stylus at times. The only reason for a stylus is that many Palm organizer programs contain buttons too small to tap with a finger (unless you have very small fingers). A gentle tap with a fingernail can sometimes do just as well as a stylus tap. You're still better off using the stylus when you can because your fingertips can smudge up the screen after a while. However, you can always wash your screen with a dab of window cleaner. Be gentle, though; you don't want to scratch the screen.

Enter the current time

If you want to enter the current time in a memo, note, or other program, you can call on the time stamp ShortCut. Just enter the Graffiti ShortCut symbol, which looks like a cursive, lowercase letter *L,* and then enter *TS*. I like to use the time stamp as a primitive way to "punch in" when I'm trying to measure time spent on a job. I create a memo, enter a time stamp when I begin, and then enter another time stamp in the memo when I'm finished.

Reassigning a hard button to your favorite program

If you use a particular program more often than one of the standard Palm organizer applications, you can reassign one of the four application hard buttons to start that particular program. Many people don't use the Memo Pad or the To Do List nearly as much as the Date Book or the Address Book, so they reassign the Memo Pad button to make it run another program. I sometimes reassign my Memo Pad button to run a different memo program called Info Select.

You can also get a variety of programs that enable you to launch a variety of different programs from the hard buttons by pressing two buttons at one time. Some of those programs belong to a category of programs called *hacks,* which can be finicky at times, so I personally avoid them. (For more info about hacks, see Chapter 3.) I still just tap the Applications icon just to the left of the Graffiti area to go to the Applications screen and start my programs most of the time. You can take your pick.

Application Time-Savers

These time-savers apply directly to the four main applications that come with your Palm device. Every program you add to your Palm device has it's own set of shortcuts and time savers, but these tricks are available to every Palm owner, and they can save you loads of time.

Pressing hard buttons to change categories

When you first press the Memo hard button you see all your memos. If you press the Memo button a second time, then the memos in the Business category appear. Each time when you press the Memo button again, you see a different category until you've cycled around to the All category. All four standard application hard buttons behave in the same way: You push the button several times to run through several different categories. The Date Book button is slightly different; it shows you different views of the Date Book — the day and then the week and then the month — each time you press the hard button. If you don't have any items filed in a particular category, then your Palm device conveniently skips that category.

Viewing different dates by pressing buttons

Whenever you want to check your schedule in a jiffy, remember that you don't have to dig for your stylus, instead you can get to any date by pressing buttons:

- ✔ Press the Date Book button once to see Day view.
- ✔ Press the Date Book button twice to see Week view.
- ✔ Press the Date Book button three times to see Month view.

After you see the view you want, press the up or down scroll buttons at the bottom center of the case to move to the next day, week, or month. By cleverly combining button clicks, you can see your schedule for any day on the calendar. Granted, whipping out the stylus and picking the date you want to see is sometimes easier, but when your hands are full, the stylus can be one too many things to hold.

Uncluttering the Date Book

The Date Book shows a blank line for every hour of your workday. That can make your schedule look cluttered and hard to read. If you set up your Date Book preferences to have your day begin and end at the same time, then the display area shows only the entries for the times at which you've scheduled appointments; the rest of the screen is blank, as shown in Figure 4-1.

Figure 4-1:
To make your screen easier to read, set your workday to both begin and end at the same time.

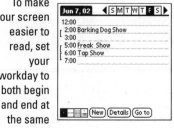

If you press the Date Book hard button twice, then you see the Week view of the Address Book. Week view shows a collection of bars representing appointments for the week. If you want to change the scheduled time of an appointment, just drag the bar representing that appointment to the time you prefer, as shown in Figure 4-2. Sad to say, you can't drag an appointment from one week to another.

Figure 4-2:
Just drag and drop to change appointment times.

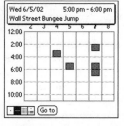

Cut, copy, and paste

Most people who use computers have been cutting, copying, and pasting text for years. You can do the same trick with your Palm device. Just select some text by drawing an imaginary line through the text with your stylus, and then tap the Menu soft button at the bottom left corner of the Palm screen and choose Edit⇨Cut or choose Edit⇨Copy. To make the text reappear in another place, just tap where you want to place the text and choose Edit⇨Paste.

Although cutting makes the text you selected disappear, don't worry — it's not gone forever. The text goes to a place called the *clipboard*. The same thing happens when you choose Edit⇨Copy, except the original text stays put, and a copy of that text goes to the clipboard. Even if you turn off your Palm device, the last text you put on the clipboard stays on the clipboard, so you may find you can paste text that you copied weeks or even months ago. Be aware, however, that every time you cut or copy text, whatever you cut or copy replaces any text previously on the clipboard.

Adding multiple items to a category

It's a bit laborious to add a bunch of items to your Palm device then go back and assign a category to each individual item. If you want to add a series of new items to a single category, simply display that category and begin creating items. Whatever category you display before creating new items becomes the category assigned to the new items. For example, if I want to make a list of things I need to do at Internet World, I press the To Do List hard button several times until my Internet World category appears (assuming I created an Internet World category). Then, I just start adding items. Because every new item I create while in a certain category turns up in that category, I can see everything in the category as I add items.

Graffiti Time-Savers

If you've really taken to Graffiti, you may appreciate the quick time-savers in this section. While about half of the Palm owners I know never learn Graffiti, I still think Graffiti is the quickest way to get lots of power out of your Palm device.

Start writing to create new items

If you want to add a new item to any standard Palm organizer application (except the Address Book), press the hard button for that application and begin entering text in the Graffiti area. This trick works only if you use Graffiti. Whenever the Palm device senses that you're entering Graffiti, it naturally does the right thing — it opens a new item in which to store the new text.

Open Graffiti Help with a single stroke

You can open Graffiti Help by drawing a line with your stylus from the Graffiti writing area to the top of the display area. If you've already earned your black belt in Graffiti, then you can assign that stroke to perform one of four other tasks:

  ✔ Turn on the backlight

  ✔ Display the on-screen keyboard

  ✔ Beam the current item to another Palm device

  ✔ Turn off and lock your Palm device

For some reason the Palm programmers didn't allow you to do really useful things with the Graffiti upstroke command, such as cook dinner or drive you home. I'm waiting for those features to appear in Palm OS99.

Follow these steps to reassign the upstroke command:

1. **Tap the Applications soft button.**

2. **Tap Prefs.**

3. **Choose Buttons from the pull-down menu in the upper-right corner.**

4. **Tap Pen.**

   The Pen dialog box appears, as shown in Figure 4-3. If the feature you want to activate with the Graffiti upstroke is shown, tap OK. Otherwise move on to Step 5.

Figure 4-3:
Customize
what
happens
when you
use the
Graffiti
upstroke.

    5. **Tap the downward-pointing triangle in the Pen dialog box.**

       A list of features to choose from appears.

    6. **Tap the feature you want the Graffiti upstroke to activate.**

       The item you tapped appears on the screen.

    7. **Tap OK**

       Now a swift upstroke of your stylus will activate the feature you chose.

For more info about customizing the functions of your Palm device, see Chapter 3.

Part II
Getting Down to Business

The 5th Wave   By Rich Tennant

"You can sure do a lot with a Palm Handheld, but I never thought dressing one up in GI.Joe clothes and calling it your little desk commander would be one of them."

In this part . . .

The programs that come with your Palm device can perform quite a range of helpful functions if you know all the options. You can create and manage appointments, addresses, tasks, and memos by following the steps in this part.

Chapter 5

Names and Addresses in a Zip

*A*fter carrying a Palm organizer for a while, you won't be able to imagine needing to get back to your office computer to look up an address or phone number. Your Palm device keeps everything that you need to know, right at your fingertips, everywhere that you go.

You can also make your Palm Address Book do tricks that you can't even dream of doing with a paper organizer. For example, if I need to know the names of everyone that I know in Indianapolis, I can look them all up in a snap with my Palm organizer. If I'm using a wireless e-mail program on my Palm device, I can also send an e-mail message right out to anyone that I have in my list at any time.

Accessing the Address Book

To call up the Address Book on your Palm device, just press the Address Book hard button (the second button from the left at the bottom, as shown in Figure 5-1), which calls up the Address List. My sample Address List is shown in Figure 5-2.

Address Book
hard button

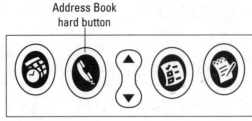

Figure 5-1:
The
Address
Book hard
button.

Figure 5-2:
Your
Address List
shows all
the names
that you've
collected.

Putting Names in Your Palm Device

I know more than a few people who enter and make changes to their Address
List on a desktop computer and then transfer the whole shebang to their
Palm device just to look up names while they're traveling. That's okay.
Actually, most of those folks have employees who enter the information for
them, which is the easiest method. However, most of us don't have that
luxury. (See Chapter 12 for more info about keeping up the Address List in
the Palm Desktop program.) The fact is that you can enter all the information
that you need right on your Palm device, no matter where you are.

Adding a new name

Many people have relied on a Little Black Book since even before Casanova. The paper kind served well until the computer came along and enabled you to find one name from a list of thousands faster than you can say, "What's-his-name." Speed isn't the only advantage of electronic Address Lists. For example, the Palm device can look up a name from your list and then plug that name into an item on the To Do List, the Memo Pad, or the Date Book to save you the trouble of retyping. Before you can look up a name, however, you have to add the name to the Address Book.

Use these steps to store a name in the Address Book:

1. **With the Address List visible, tap the New button at the bottom of the Address List.**

   The Address Edit screen appears.

2. **Tap anywhere on the Last Name line.**

   The words *Last Name* become highlighted to show that you've selected the Last Name line, as shown in Figure 5-3.

Figure 5-3:
The name of the line that you tap is highlighted to show where you're working.

3. **Enter the last name of the person that you're adding by using Graffiti or the on-screen keyboard (see Chapter 2 for more info about entering text).**

The letters that you enter appear on the Last Name line.

4. **Follow Steps 2 and 3 to enter information on the First Name, Title, and Company lines.**

   The text that you enter appears on the lines that you choose.

5. **Tap anywhere on the Work line.**

   The word becomes highlighted to show that you've selected it.

6. **Enter the person's work telephone number.**

7. **Follow Steps 5 and 6 to enter the person's home phone number.**

8. **If you want to enter a type of phone number that isn't shown, tap Other.**

   A list appears, showing the different types of phone numbers that you can enter, including pager and mobile numbers.

9. **Tap the name of the type of phone number that you want to enter, such as Mobile.**

   The type of phone number that you choose replaces the word *Other*, as you see in Figure 5-4.

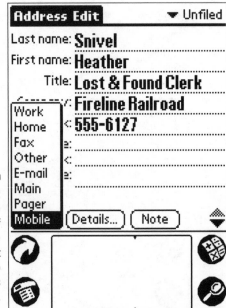

Figure 5-4:
Choose the type of phone number that you want to enter if it's not shown.

10. **Enter the phone number in the Graffiti number area.**

    The text that you enter appears on the new line.

11. **If you want to enter your contact's mailing address, press the scroll-down hard button at the bottom-center of the Palm device.**

   The lower half of the contact form appears, enabling you to enter mailing address information, as shown in Figure 5-5.

12. **Enter mailing address information on the appropriate lines, just as you did in the preceding steps.**

   The information that you enter appears on the appropriate lines.

13. **When you finish entering the information, click Done at the bottom of the Address Edit screen.**

   The Address Edit screen disappears, and the Address List reappears.

Now you're ready to find anyone in your personal *Who's Who* faster than you can say, "Who?"

You probably noticed the downward-pointing triangle next to each phone number line. Whenever you see that character on a Palm screen, it means that a pull-down menu is hiding behind that button, where you can choose other options simply by tapping the triangle and then tapping your choice. Although every address record contains three phone number lines and an e-mail line, you can use any of the phone number lines to store any of seven different types of phone numbers or an e-mail address, as shown in Figure 5-4.

For example, if you want to save one person's work number and pager number but not his home number, simply tap the triangle next to Home and pick Pager from the list. Now the number that you enter is shown as a pager number.

If you have a list of names and addresses in another contact program on a desktop or laptop computer, then you can enter them in the desktop program as a list and then HotSync the whole bunch to your Palm device. As you can see, entering names and addresses in the Palm device is easy, but when you have a large collection of names, you can save time by letting your computers take care of the job. For more info about installing and operating the Palm desktop program, see Chapter 12.

Editing an address record

Some people, it seems, change their addresses more often than they change their socks. You can't very well tell them to stop moving, but you can keep up with their latest addresses by editing their address records in your Palm device. You may want to say something to them about their socks, though.

These steps help you to change an entry in the Address Book:

1. **With the Address List visible, enter in the Graffiti box the first few letters of the last name that you want to edit.**

   The letters that you enter appear on the Look Up line at the bottom of the display area. If the name that you're looking for is visible to start with, you don't have to look it up, of course.

2. **Tap the name of the person whose record you want to edit.**

   The Address View screen appears, as shown in Figure 5-6, showing details about the contact that you chose.

3. **Tap Edit at the bottom of the display area.**

   The Address Edit screen appears.

4. **Enter new information the same way that you entered info when you first created the address record.**

   (See the preceding section, "Adding a new name.")

   New information appears on the appropriate lines of the screen.

5. **If you want to replace existing information, select the text that you want to replace by drawing a horizontal line through it.**

   The text is highlighted.

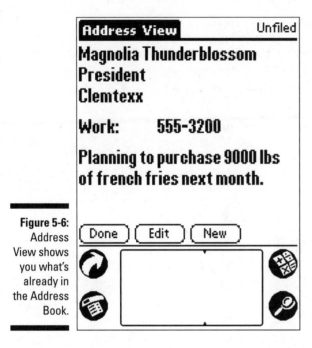

Figure 5-6:
Address
View shows
you what's
already in
the Address
Book.

6. **Enter new text in the Graffiti box at the bottom of the display area.**

   Just like your favorite word processor does, the text that you enter replaces the text that you selected. (For more info about entering text, see Chapter 2.)

7. **When you've made all the changes that you want to make, tap Done.**

   The Address Edit screen disappears and the Address List screen reappears.

A Palm device saves all your changes as soon as you tap Done; it has no Undo feature to put things back the way they were. If you want to change the person's address or other details back to the way they were originally, then you have to go through the whole editing process again.

Attaching a note to an address record

You want to know lots of things about a person — where she likes to go, what he said to you the last time you spoke to him, how much money she owes you — whatever. You can attach all sorts of information to a person's address record in the form of a note.

To attach a note to an address, follow these steps:

1. **With the Address List visible, tap the name of the person to whose record you want to add a note.**

   The Address View screen appears, showing details about the contact that you chose.

2. **Tap the Menu soft button at the bottom of the display area.**

   The menu bar appears at the top of the display area, as shown in Figure 5-7.

Figure 5-7:
You can
order from
the menu to
create a
note.

3. **Choose Record⇨Attach Note.**

   A blank note screen appears.

4. **Enter the note text in the Graffiti box at the bottom of the display area, or use the on-screen keyboard.**

   The text you enter appears on-screen, as shown in Figure 5-8.

5. **Tap Done at the bottom of the Note screen.**

   The Note screen disappears, and the Address View screen reappears.

6. **Tap Done again.**

   The Address View screen disappears, and the Address List reappears.

Thunderblossom, Magnolia

Planning to purchase 9000 lbs of
french fries next month.

[Done] [Delete...] ↑

Figure 5-8:
Enter plain
text in the
Note
screen.

If you enter information in a note and want to find the info again, you can use the Palm Find tool to search all the data on your Palm device. For example, if you add "drives a Studebaker" as a note to someone's record, then later on you can tap the Find soft button (in the bottom-right corner of the screen), enter the word *Studebaker,* and instantly find the record of the person who drives one.

Marking your business card

Now that everybody who's anybody has a Palm device (after all, you have one and I have one, and that's all that matters to me), we can take advantage of the Palm infrared port to exchange our business cards. But before you can beam your business card to anyone, you have to enter an address record containing your own name and contact information, as I describe in the section "Adding a new name," earlier in this chapter.

An infrared (IR) port is standard equipment on all current Palm models. The port was optional on much older PalmPilot models. The Infrared option lets you beam information from one Palm device to another. *Beaming* is the action of pointing two Palm devices at each other and then sending data through the air using an invisible beam of light over a distance of about three feet. (See Chapter 9 for more info about beaming.) You can even buy software that lets you change the channels on your TV with the Palm infrared feature (which sounds cool but doesn't really work that well). In the normal course of business, you can beam your business card (as well as other addresses, to-do items, memos, and appointments) to other Palm users.

When I send my business card to you via a Palm device, I'm really just beaming a name from my Palm device Address Book to the Address Book on your Palm device. The name that I send you just happens to be my own.

Here's how to set up your Palm device to send your business card:

1. **With the Address List visible, enter the first few letters of your last name in the Graffiti box.**

   The letters that you enter appear on the Look Up line at the bottom of the display area.

2. **Tap your name in the Address List.**

   The Address View screen appears, showing details about your contact record.

3. **Tap the Menu soft button at the bottom of the display area.**

   The menu bar appears at the top of the display area.

4. **Choose Record⇨Select Business Card.**

   The Select Business Card dialog box opens, as shown in Figure 5-9, and asks you if you want to make this name your business card.

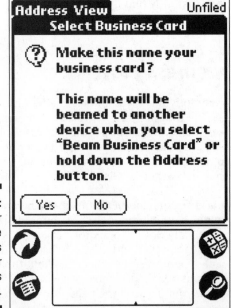

Figure 5-9: Mark your own name to serve as your business card.

Within the figure:

Address View — Unfiled

Select Business Card

(?) **Make this name your business card?**

This name will be beamed to another device when you select "Beam Business Card" or hold down the Address button.

[Yes] [No]

5. **Tap Yes at the bottom of the Select Business Card dialog box to close it.**

   A small icon that looks like a file card appears at the top of the Address View screen.

6. **Tap Done at the bottom of the display area.**

   The Address View screen disappears, and the Address List reappears.

 You don't absolutely have to mark a business card if you don't plan to use this feature. But if you use the beaming feature frequently, then you can save time by marking your business card because you don't have to spend time looking up your own name when you want to send a card. I owned a Palm device for several months before I ever beamed my business card, but I had my name marked anyway. If deep-space aliens had shown up á la *Independence Day,* I'd have been ready to beam them my friendly greetings — for all the good it would do (they probably all use Macs).

Using the Names That You Entered

I don't know anyone who has entered a whole list of names and addresses directly into their Palm device. Most people just create their Address List in a program on their desktop computer and then HotSync the list to their Palm device because it's a lot faster. (See Chapter 13 for more about HotSyncing.) So the first thing that you need to know is how to use a fully loaded Palm Address Book. Later in this chapter, I show you how to enter addresses on your Palm device if you need to add someone to your list in a pinch.

Finding Mr. Right (or whomever)

If you took the time to enter a bunch of names into your Palm device, then I guess that you probably want to find those names again. Call me crazy, but that's what I think.

Here's the quickest way to find a name in the Address Book:

1. **With the Address List visible, enter in the Graffiti box the first few letters of the last name that you want to find.**

   The letters that you enter appear on the Look Up line at the bottom of the display area, as shown in Figure 5-10.

 If you don't like messing with Graffiti, then you can press the hard scroll-down button at the bottom of the Palm device to scroll through your Address List. The Address Book can hold thousands of names, so if your list is long, scrolling can be laborious.

2. Tap the name of the person whose record you want to view.

The Address View screen appears, showing details about the contact you chose.

3. When you're finished, tap Done at the bottom of the display area.

The Address View screen disappears, and the Address List reappears.

Figure 5-10: Your Palm device figures out whom you're looking for when you enter the first few letters of a name.

If you want to make finding addresses easier, you can assign categories to names on the Address List. Then when you press the Address Book button several times, you cycle through the different address categories until you see the category that you want to use. For example, you can assign the category *Business* to some names, and you can assign the category *Personal* to other names. When you press the Address Book button the first time, you see all the names in your collection. The second time that you press the button, you see the names assigned to the Business category; and the third time that you press the button, you see the names assigned to the Personal category; and so on. On the other hand, you may be completely happy keeping all your names uncategorized, which is fine too.

To assign a category to any name in your list, open the record for editing, as I describe in the section "Editing an address record," earlier in this chapter, and then pick the category that you want to assign to your contact in the upper-right corner of the form. You can manage Address Book categories or define your own categories in exactly the same way that you manage categories of To Do items. (See Chapter 6 for more info about managing To Do item categories.)

The Quicklist category is preset in the Address Book to make room for the addresses you use frequently and need to find in a hurry. You can use this category for the most important people in your life.

Deleting a name

The main reason to add a name to the Address Book is to help you remember important things about a person. However, sometimes you'd rather forget some people in your list. I won't mention any names.

To delete an unwanted name from the Address Book, follow these steps:

1. **With the Address List visible, enter in the Graffiti box the first few letters of the last name that you want to delete.**

   The letters that you enter appear on the Look Up line at the bottom of the display area.

2. **Tap the name of the person whose record you want to delete.**

   The Address View screen appears, showing details about the contact you chose.

3. **Tap the Menu soft button at the bottom of the display area.**

   The menu bar appears at the top of the display area.

4. **Choose Record⇨Delete Address.**

   The Delete Address dialog box opens, as shown in Figure 5-11. The dialog box asks whether you want to delete the selected Address entry. You also see a check box for saving an archive copy of the item on your PC. (For more info about archived items, see Chapter 13.)

5. **Tap OK.**

   The Address List reappears, minus one name.

If you delete a name in a fit of pique and then want to bring it back, all is not entirely lost. If you haven't used HotSync between the time you deleted the name and the time you want it back, then you can find the name in the archive on your desktop computer. You can make a slight change in the address information and then resynchronize to make the (formerly) offending name a part of your list again. Then you can kiss and make up. I discuss synchronization in Chapter 12 and archiving in Chapter 13. Fractured friendships are another issue altogether.

Figure 5-11:
You can
easily delete
the names
of those
who no
longer
interest you.

Deleting a note from an address record

Sometimes the note you attached to someone's address becomes out-of-date.
You can change the contents of the note by using the same steps that you
used to create the note, or you can just delete the entire note.

Here's how to delete a note that is attached to an address:

1. **With the Address List visible, tap the name of the person from whose record you want to delete a note.**

   The Address View screen appears, showing details about the contact
   you chose.

2. **Tap the Menu soft button at the bottom of the display area.**

   The menu bar appears at the top of the display area.

3. **Choose Record⇨Delete Note, as shown in Figure 5-12.**

   The Delete Note dialog box opens.

4. **Tap Yes at the bottom of the Delete Note dialog box.**

   The Delete Note dialog box closes, and the Address View screen
   reappears.

Figure 5-12:
You can delete a note from a record, too.

5. **Tap Done at the bottom of the Address View screen.**

The Address View screen disappears, and the Address List reappears.

Zap! Your note is gone for good. (Well, not really for good; see Chapter 13 for details about how to recover items from your archive.)

Setting Address Book preferences

If you don't like the way the Address Book looks when it first opens, you can change its appearance . . . a little. I think the Address Book is just fine as it is, but if you simply must rearrange your list, here's how to do it:

1. **With the Address List visible, tap the Menu soft button at the bottom of the display area.**

The menu bar appears at the top of the display area.

2. **Choose Options⇨Preferences.**

The Address Book Preferences dialog box opens, as shown in Figure 5-13.

3. **From the List By box, choose between these options: Last Name, First Name or Company, Last Name.**

The choice you make is highlighted.

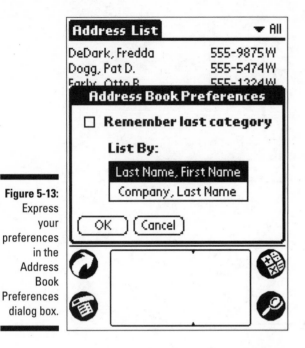

Figure 5-13:
Express
your
preferences
in the
Address
Book
Preferences
dialog box.

4. Tap the Remember Last Category box if you normally want the Address Book to open to the last category you used.

If you don't check the Remember Last Category box, then the Address Book always opens to show all names. I think it's better to leave the box unchecked, but that's a matter of personal preference.

Setting up custom fields

Sometimes you need to keep track of something about the people you know but you don't already have a line (or field) for it on your Address List. For example, if your job involves selling merchandise to retail stores, then your Address Book probably contains the names of all the store buyers to whom you sell. The Address Book includes four lines at the end of the Address Edit screen that you can rename to fit your needs. These four lines are called *custom fields*. You may want to set up one custom field to keep track of which type of merchandise that each buyer buys, such as housewares, appliances, and shoes. You can rename one of the custom fields to `Specialty` to show each buyer's area of interest.

To set up your custom fields, follow these steps:

1. **With the Address List visible, tap the Menu soft button at the bottom of the display area.**

    The menu bar appears at the top of the display area.

2. **Choose Options ⇨Rename Custom Fields.**

    The Rename Custom Fields dialog box opens, as shown in Figure 5-14.

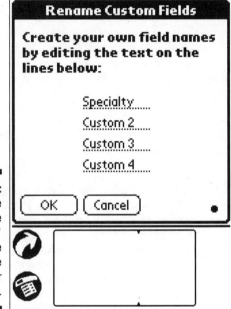

Figure 5-14:
Just replace the name
Custom 1
with the field name of your choice.

3. **Select the field that you want to rename.**

    The text that you select is highlighted.

4. **Enter the name that you want for the field with either the on-screen keyboard or Graffiti (see Chapter 2 for more info about entering text).**

    The text that you enter appears as the new field name.

5. **Rename the other custom fields by following Steps 3 and 4.**

    The text that you enter appears as the new field name.

6. **When you've renamed all the fields that you want to rename, click OK.**

    The Rename Custom Fields dialog box closes, and the Address List reappears.

You don't absolutely have to rename custom fields in order to use them. You can just enter information in the fields and remember that the field named `Custom 1` contains a certain type of entry. Renaming the custom fields just makes them a little more useful and easier to understand. When you rename a custom field, the field name is changed in all address records.

Alternate Address Books

Most people find that the built-in Palm Address Book suits them just fine. But if you're a Power Schmoozer who needs a super, turbo-charged address book, then you might consider replacing the Palm Address Book with a souped-up model. The following sections describe three programs that you can buy if you prefer supersonic schmoozing.

Key Contacts

A slight majority of all Palm owners (about 52%) synchronize their address book to Microsoft Outlook, a much more robust program with many more features than the Palm Address Book. Key Contacts replaces the Palm version with a whole new program that matches the oomph you get from Outlook, as shown in Figure 5-15. The program can track all the phone numbers you can store in Outlook — and sync to an unlimited number of different Contact folders. Key Contacts even overcomes the 15-category barrier that stymies all Palm programs, letting you assign a contact to any of up to 250 categories. To get the full scoop on Key Contacts, go to `www.palmpilotfordummies.com/keycontacts`.

Figure 5-15:
Key Contacts stores and shows all the phone numbers you have for each contact.

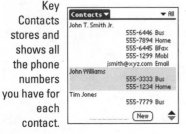

Action Names Datebook

Action Names from Iambic Software is one of the better-known Palm replace-ment programs. Not only can you link and sort more freely with Action Names than with the built-in programs, but you can also take advantage of your color display if your Palm device has one. You can also customize the display with your own collection of icons to make your Address Book easier to use. To find out more about the program, see www.palmpilot fordummies.com/actionnames.

Address Pro

AddressPro offers souped-up sorting and elaborate customization features but still uses the Palm device's built-in database so that your addresses still HotSync properly to your desktop. The program can also search and replace for situations like when a large group of your contacts get a new area code or company name. Find out more at www.palmpilotfordummies.com/addresspro.

Chapter 6

Doing It NOW with To-Dos

Do you have so much to do that you don't always know what to do next? Well, if you want to *do,* then *list* first; your Palm To Do List stands ready to keep you on track when you're on the fast track. I met a businessman recently who said that he never realized how much "down time" he had until he had a Palm organizer to help him stay productive. Whether your goal is to do more work or to get the work done sooner and take more vacations, you can make your minutes count with the To Do List.

The To Do List on your Palm device can help you keep a handle on all those little errands and projects that take up all your time. You can add a task when you think of it rather than wait to get back to your computer. By the time I get back to my desk, I usually forget that terribly important detail I have to take care of.

The first part of this chapter assumes that you're using a normal Palm device, exactly the way it comes out of the box. Although that's what most people do, it isn't your only choice. At the end of this chapter, I tell you about some programs that you can get to replace your To Do List. In fact, if you use a Handspring Visor, it has an optional DateBook+ program that manages appointments *and* to-dos. If you've replaced the To Do List with some other program (such as To Do Plus), then many of the instructions in this chapter won't work for you. I don't want to discourage you from trying other programs — lots of good ones exist — but unfortunately, I can't cover all the third-party software that's out there for Palm devices.

To call up your To Do List, just push the To Do List hard button (normally the second one from the right at the bottom of your Palm device, as shown in Figure 6-1). I say normally, because certain Palm organizers, such as the Palm i705, assign some other program to that button. In that case, you'll need to start the To Do List in a different way; tap the Applications soft button, then tap the To Do icon in the Applications list on the screen. Whichever way you start, you'll then be ready to do whatever you want to do with your to-dos!

Figure 6-1:
Press the
To Do List
button to
bring up
your list of
to-dos.

To Do List
hard button

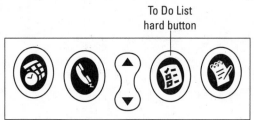

Adding New To-Dos

Adding items to the To Do List is as easy as you want to make it. If you want to keep track of short lists of simple projects, you can go a long way with the tools that come with a Palm device. If your planning process involves long lists of elaborate plans and projects, and goes beyond the capability of the Palm organizer's To Do List, then you may need some extra help in the form of extra software or a daily download from your desktop computer. You can always rely on a desktop program (such as ACT! or Goldmine) to do all the heavy lifting, and you can just HotSync your Palm device to your desktop every day to keep a handy portable copy of your information. For more info about HotSyncing your Palm device with third-party software, see Part IV.

Creating a to-do in the To Do List

You can take advantage of the powers of the To Do List only if you've entered the to-dos that you have to do. No voodoo is involved with To Do — just press a button, tap with a stylus, and you're in business.

Here's how to add a new item to the To Do List:

1. **With the To Do List open, tap New at the bottom of the To Do List.**

   A new, blank line appears on the To Do List.

2. **Enter the name of your task with either the on-screen keyboard or Graffiti.**

The name of the task that you enter appears on the new line, as shown in Figure 6-2. (See Chapter 2 for more info about entering text.)

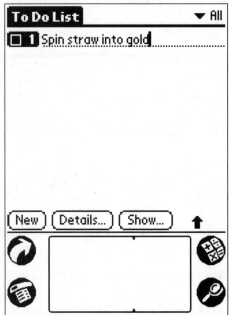

Figure 6-2:
Just tap a
line and
enter the
name of
your task.

3. **Tap any blank area of the screen or press the Scroll Down button at the bottom center of the case.**

   The highlighting next to your new item disappears.

Ta-da! It's a new task to call your very own.

You can use an even simpler way, of course, to enter a new to-do: Press the To Do List button and enter the name of your task by using either the on-screen keyboard, Graffiti, or an add-on keyboard. Your Palm device automatically creates a new to-do with the name that you enter.

Entering details for a to-do item

You may not be satisfied with a To Do List that keeps track of only the names of your tasks. Knowing what a productive, demanding person that you are (or could be, if you really wanted to), the To Do List enables you to assign priorities, categories, and due dates to each task.

To add details to your tasks, follow these steps:

1. **With the To Do List open, tap the name of the task to which you want to add details.**

Highlighting appears next to the name of the task you choose.

2. **Tap the word `Details` at the bottom of the display area.**

   The To Do Item Details dialog box opens.

3. **To set the priority of your item, tap one of the numerals (1 through 5) next to the word `Priority`.**

   The number you tap is highlighted.

   If the only detail you want to change about your task is the priority, then you can simply tap the priority number on the To Do List and then pick the priority number from the drop-down list.

4. **To assign a category to your task, tap the triangle next to the word *Category*.**

   A list of available categories appears. Although the option of assigning categories helps you organize your To Do List, you don't have to assign a category to a task. I explain how to use categories in the section "Viewing Items by Category," later in this chapter.

5. **Tap the name of the category you want to assign to your task.**

   The list disappears, and the name of the category you chose appears.

6. **To assign a due date to your task, tap the triangle next to the words *Due Date*.**

   A list appears, giving you these choices: Today, Tomorrow, One week later, No Date, and Choose Date. See Figure 6-3.

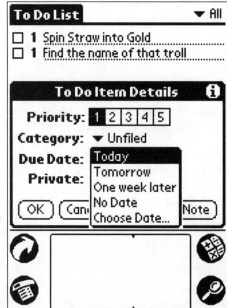

Figure 6-3: Pick the due date for your to-do item in the To Do Item Details box.

7. **Tap the name of the due date you want for your task.**

   The list disappears, and the date you chose appears, unless you tap Choose Date. Tapping Choose Date opens the Due Date screen, which looks like a calendar, as shown in Figure 6-4.

8. **If you tap Choose Date, then tap the desired due date for your task on the calendar on the Due Date screen.**

   The Due Date screen disappears, and the date you chose appears in the To Do Item Details dialog box.

Figure 6-4:
You can choose a date from the calendar.

9. **If you want to mark your entry as private, tap the check box next to the word *Private*.**

   A check mark appears in the check box to show that the task is private.

   Private entries normally appear with your other entries, but you can also hide your private entries. Just tap the Applications soft button to call up the Applications list, choose Security, and then tap the word *Hide*. (For more info about privacy and passwords, see Chapter 3.)

10. **Tap OK.**

    The To Do Item Details dialog box closes, and the To Do List re-appears with your changes made visible on the screen.

You may have noticed when you were creating a new task that the Details button was available on-screen the whole time. If you want to add all sorts of details while you're adding a new task, nothing can stop you. However, if you're in a hurry and just want to enter the task quickly, you can enter just the name of the task and then add details later.

Attaching notes to items

A popular book by Robert Fulghum tells us that we learn everything we need to know in kindergarten. That's okay, I guess, but if you didn't get past kindergarten, don't mention it in your next job interview.

In the same way, many tasks need a bit more explanation than a quick subject line can describe, so you may need to add a note to your task if you want to keep track of a detailed explanation along with a task.

Here's how to add a note to a to-do item:

1. **With the To Do List open, tap the name of the task to which you want to add a note.**

   The check box to the left of the item is highlighted to show which task you've selected.

2. **Tap Details at the bottom of the To Do List.**

   The To Do Item Details dialog box opens.

3. **Tap Note at the bottom of the To Do Item Details dialog box.**

   A blank Note screen appears.

4. **Enter your text by using either the on-screen keyboard or Graffiti.**

   The text you entered appears, as shown in Figure 6-5. (See Chapter 2 for more info about entering text.)

Figure 6-5: If you have more detailed instructions about your task, add a note.

Spin straw into gold

Find out the name of that little troll before tomorrow

[Done] [Delete...]

5. **Tap Done at the bottom of the Note screen.**

   The Note screen disappears and the To Do List reappears. A small, square icon appears to the right of the item you chose, showing that a note is attached. If you want to view a note attached to a to-do, just click the note icon to call up the Note screen.

The Note screen also has a Delete button that lets you delete a note after you read it. I discuss another way to delete notes attached to to-do items in the section "Deleting a note," later in this chapter, although deleting a note from the Note screen is as good a method as any.

If you create a note on the Memo List or attach a note to an entry in the Address Book, then you find that the general idea of creating notes stays the same throughout your Palm device. Unfortunately, notes attached to different types of Palm computing items don't have anything to do with each other. For example, you can't move a note from the Memo List to the To Do List or from the To Do List to the Address Book. Not now, at least — maybe in the future. (For more about the Memo List, see Chapter 7, and for more about the Address List, see Chapter 5.)

Viewing Items by Category

To-do items always belong to a category of one type or another. If you don't assign a category yourself, then your Palm device automatically assigns the category *Unfiled*. The name of the category you're viewing appears in the upper-right corner of the screen. When you first press the To Do List button, the word in the corner is *All,* which means you're viewing all your tasks, regardless of category.

Palm categories have two big limitations — you can't assign any item to more than one category, and you can't have more than 15 categories. Many people don't mind, but for me those things are problems.

One way I get around those limitations is to devise "codes" that I enter into the Note section of my To Do items. (This trick also works in the Date Book and Address Book.) After I enter my category code, I can use the Palm Find feature to find all the items containing that code. For example, my To Do items that involve this book all include the code *PFD* in a note (that stands for *Palm For Dummies*). When I just want to see items involving this book, I tap the Find button, enter **PFD,** and tap OK to see all the items about this book. Similarly, I use the code OLFD for items related to my other book, *Microsoft Outlook For Dummies.* Because I synchronize my Palm organizer with Outlook, I can use Outlook's Find feature to find items the same way I find items on the Palm. Palm categories are easier to use, but if you get stuck, this trick can help you get around the Palm's limitations.

You can change your view to a different category in two ways — the short way and the even shorter way. (The shortest way of all is to get someone else to do it. Hey, don't look at me! I'm busy!)

I start with the short way:

1. **With the To Do List open, tap the name of the category in the upper-right corner of the screen.**

    The list of available categories appears. The first time you use your Palm device, the list has four categories: All, Business, Personal, and Unfiled. After you have used your Palm device for the first time, a fifth option — Edit Categories — is available, as shown in Figure 6-6. I talk about that option later in this section.

Figure 6-6: To switch categories, just pick from the list.

2. **Tap the name of the category you want to display.**

    The To Do List changes to display only the items assigned to the category you chose. The name of the category you're viewing appears in the upper-right corner of the screen.

The shorter way to change the category you're viewing is — you guessed it — even shorter. Just press the To Do List button more than once. Each time you press the To Do List button, you see the next category for which you've created entries. The categories appear in alphabetical order, including any categories you may have added yourself (see the following section, "Adding categories"). Neat, huh?

Adding categories

People who use Palm devices are often busy people with scads of things to do. If you're usually juggling too many tasks to fit on one little screen, you'll find assigning categories to your tasks useful. You can look through them all with a few clicks of the To Do List button. Sooner or later, you'll want to create categories of your own.

Follow these steps to create a new category:

1. **With the To Do List open, tap the name of the category in the upper-right corner of the screen.**

   The list of available categories appears.

2. **Tap Edit Categories.**

   The Edit Categories screen appears.

3. **Tap New.**

   The Edit Categories dialog box opens.

4. **Enter the name of the category you want to add, using either your favorite keyboard or Graffiti (see Chapter 2 for more info about entering text).**

5. **Tap OK.**

   The name you entered appears in the Edit Categories dialog box, and the dialog box closes.

6. **Tap OK again.**

   The Edit Categories screen disappears.

 Remember that you're better off if you stick to a few well-used categories rather than dozens of categories you never look at. A To Do List should focus on things you really plan to do; otherwise, you could just call it a "Round Tuit" list — things you'll do if you ever get around to it.

Deleting categories

If you've gone hog-wild and created categories that you never use, delete some of them. You can also create a category for a special event and then delete that category when the event ends. I do that for trade shows sometimes; I create a category for things I have to do during the show, and delete the category when the show is over.

Follow these steps to delete a category:

1. **With the To Do List open, tap the name of the category in the upper-right corner of the screen.**

   The list of available categories appears.

2. **Tap Edit Categories.**

   The Edit Categories screen appears.

3. **Tap the name of the category that you want to delete.**

   The category that you tap is highlighted to show you've selected it.

4. **Tap Delete.**

   The Remove Category dialog box opens, warning you that all items in that category will be reassigned to the Unfiled category. If no items are assigned to the category you chose to delete, the Remove Category dialog box doesn't open.

5. **Tap Yes.**

   The Remove Categories dialog box closes and your category is deleted.

6. **Tap OK.**

   The Edit Categories screen disappears.

The All and Unfiled categories don't show up on the Edit Categories screen because they're not really categories. You can't get rid of the view that shows all your tasks (a mistake you probably wouldn't want to make anyway); finding things that you mistakenly categorized would be harder.

Renaming categories

What's in a name? Shakespeare's Romeo thought it didn't matter, but look what happened to him. Sometimes you want your categories to make sense, so you change the names to fit your style.

To rename a category, follow these steps:

1. **With the To Do List open, tap the name of the category in the upper-right corner of the screen.**

   The list of available categories appears.

2. **Tap Edit Categories.**

   The Edit Categories screen appears.

3. **Tap the name of the category you want to rename.**

   The name of the category is highlighted to show you've selected it.

4. **Tap Rename.**

   The Edit Categories dialog box opens.

5. **Enter the new category name you want to add, using either the on-screen keyboard or Graffiti (see Chapter 2 for more info about entering text).**

6. **Tap OK.**

   The name you entered replaces the preceding name of the category in the Edit Categories dialog box, and the dialog box closes.

7. **Tap OK again.**

   The Edit Categories screen disappears.

 Because your categories can be sorted and displayed in alphabetical order, you may want to pick category names that fall in line a certain way. Business tasks come before Personal tasks in more ways than alphabetical order. Also numbers come before letters; for example 1monkey comes before 2monkey. On the other hand, you can cycle through all your categories with a few clicks of the To Do List button so you can see all your tasks without much fuss.

What to Do with the To-Dos You Do

Even if you don't enter to-do items yourself, you may wind up with a collection of tasks on your list — whether they are sent to you by another person or by a program on your desktop computer. (See the following section and Chapters 9, 12, and 13 for more info about beaming your to-dos, and connecting your Palm device to a desktop computer.) After you have your to-dos, you need to know what you have to do. (Anybody else feel a little dizzy?)

Have I got a job for you? Beaming to-dos!

You don't have to keep your to-dos to yourself. You can also beam tasks to other people if they're similarly equipped (and amenable to the idea). Although beaming to-dos is reasonably safe and totally sanitary, beaming too many tasks at people can make them sick — that is, sick of all the tasks that you're sending. (You can read more in Chapter 9 about beaming.)

To beam a to-do item from one Palm device to another, follow these steps:

1. **With the To Do List open, tap the name of the task that you want to beam to another Palm device.**

   The check box to the left of the item is highlighted to show which task you've selected.

2. **Tap the Menu soft button at the bottom of the display area.**

   The menu bar appears at the top of the display area.

3. **Choose Record➪Beam Item, as shown in Figure 6-7.**

   The Beam dialog box opens.

Figure 6-7:
Your Palm
device lets
you beam
your tasks
away.

4. **Tap OK.**

   The Beam dialog box closes, and the To Do List reappears.

Remember that the beaming feature of a Palm device works just like the remote control for your TV. The two Palm devices have to be pointed at each other and reasonably close together, within three feet. If you want to beam a task to someone in the office building across the street, or even to a passenger on a passing train (as in that old Palm commercial), you're out of luck. (Hmm. Maybe *that's* why I haven't seen that ad in a while.)

Changing to-dos

The French have a saying, *"Plus ça change, plus c'est la même chose,"* which means, "The more things change, the more they're the same." Even if you don't speak French, you know that makes no sense, although it sounds terribly charming in French.

The charming thing about changing to-do items is that you do pretty much the same steps to change an item as you did to enter it in the first place.

To change the priority of a to-do item, follow these steps:

1. **With the To Do List open, tap the name of the task that you want to change.**

   The check box to the left of the item is highlighted to show which task you've selected.

2. **To change the priority of your task, tap the number next to the name of the task.**

   A list of numbers 1 through 5 appears, as shown in Figure 6-8.

Figure 6-8:
Set priorities to sort out what's *really* important.

3. **Tap the number for the new priority that you want to give your task.**

   The highest priority is 1; the lowest is 5. When you tap a number, the list disappears and the new priority number appears next to your task.

If you want to change the name of a to-do item, follow these steps:

1. **With the To Do List open, tap the name of the task that you want to change.**

   The check box to the left of the item is highlighted to show which task you've selected.

2. **Select the text that you want to change by drawing a horizontal line through it with the stylus.**

   The text is highlighted to show you've selected it.

3. **Enter new text with either the on-screen keyboard or Graffiti (see Chapter 2 for more info about entering text).**

   The selected text is replaced by the text you enter.

If you want to make further changes to a to-do item, follow these steps:

1. **With the To Do List open, tap the name of the task that you want to change.**

   The check box to the left of the item is highlighted to show which task you've selected.

2. **Tap Details at the bottom of the To Do List.**

   The To Do Item Details dialog box opens.

3. **Make whatever changes that you want in the To Do Item Details dialog box.**

   You can use the same methods for changing the details of your task that you used to enter the details in the first place (see the section "Entering details for a to-do item," earlier in this chapter).

4. **Tap OK.**

   The To Do Item Details dialog box closes and the To Do List reappears.

The one trick about changing to-do items is that the To Do List almost never displays *all* the things you can change about a task. If you change something that's not displayed, at first you may think that your changes didn't take. To find out how to show everything you want to see on-screen, have a look at the "Setting preferences for the To Do List" section (later in this chapter).

Undoing a mistake

If you make a mistake when you're changing the text in a To Do item, you can fix it in a jiffy by following these steps:

1. **With the To Do List open, tap the Menu soft button at the bottom of the display area.**

   The menu bar appears at the top of the display area.

2. **Choose Edit⇨Undo.**

   The text returns to the way it was before you changed it.

Undo only works when you change or replace text. You can't use the Undo command to recover a to-do item that you accidentally delete. If you have archived deleted items, then you can go to the archive on the Palm Desktop to recover the item. (See Chapter 13 for details about recovering items from the Palm Desktop archive.)

Marking the to-dos that you've done

As you finish the tasks that you've assigned to yourself, mark them as completed. Marking to-do items as completed does more than give you a feeling of satisfaction; it can also shorten that depressing list of things left to do. I say "can" because you can set up your Palm device to either display all tasks, completed or not, or to hide completed tasks. See the section "Setting preferences for the To Do List," later in this chapter for information about hiding tasks.

To mark a task as completed, tap the check box next to the name of the task you want to mark. A check mark appears in the check box to show that you've completed the item, as shown in Figure 6-9. If you told your Palm device in the To Do preferences not to show completed items, then the item disappears from the To Do List.

Figure 6-9:
When you finish a task, check it off.

Deleting a to-do

Perhaps you added a task to the To Do List and then lost your nerve and decided to erase any trace of it. If you've made it your task to tell what's-his-name that he's a dirty, rotten so-and-so, you may be wiser to delete the thing. If you end up telling him anyway, don't say I didn't warn you.

To delete a To Do List item, follow these steps:

1. **With the To Do List open, tap the name of the task that you want to delete.**

   The check box to the left of the item is highlighted to show which task you've selected.

2. **Tap the Menu soft button at the bottom of the display area.**

   The menu bar appears at the top of the display area.

3. **Choose Record⇨Delete Item.**

   The Delete To Do dialog box opens, as shown in Figure 6-10.

Figure 6-10:
If you don't want to complete it, delete it.

4. **Tap OK.**

   The Delete To Do dialog box closes and the To Do List reappears.

Some people like to delete tasks rather than mark them as completed because it keeps their list of tasks short. The reason not to delete completed tasks is so that you can brag about all the things that you've accomplished. That's a particularly useful approach if you have a job that gives performance reviews. It's up to you: Complete or delete.

The Delete Items dialog box offers to save to your PC an archive copy of each item that you delete. By doing so, you can dig up old deleted items through the Palm Desktop on your PC if you need them in the future. If you leave the box checked, each item is archived automatically. If you click once on the archive check box, it stays unchecked for every item that you delete until you check it again. (For more info about archived items, see Chapter 13.)

Deleting a note

After you've done a task a few times, you may not need a note telling you how to do the task anymore. You can delete a note attached to a to-do item without deleting the item.

To delete a note, follow these steps:

1. **With the To Do List open, tap the name of the task from which you want to delete a note.**

   The check box to the left of the item is highlighted to show which task you've selected.

2. **Tap the Menu soft button at the bottom of the display area.**

   The menu bar appears at the top of the display area.

3. **Choose Record⇨Delete Note.**

   The Delete Note dialog box opens, asking whether you're sure that you want to do this.

4. **Tap Yes.**

   The note is deleted, but the task remains.

When you delete a note, it's gone for good; notes are not archived separately, and the Undo command doesn't bring them back. So, be sure that you *really* want the note to be deleted.

Setting preferences for the To Do List

If you never change a thing about the To Do List, you still get plenty of mileage from your Palm device. Everybody works a little differently, though, so you may want to slice and dice the items on the To Do List in a way that works better for you.

To change the To Do List preferences, follow these steps:

1. **With the To Do List open, tap Show.**

   The To Do Preferences screen appears.

2. **Tap the triangle next to the words *Sort By* to set up your sort order.**

   Your choices, as shown in Figure 6-11, are

   - Priority, Due Date
   - Due Date, Priority
   - Category, Priority
   - Category, Due Date

Figure 6-11: You can sort your tasks in four different ways.

3. **Tap the check boxes that correspond to the elements that you want displayed on the To Do List.**

   The To Do Preferences screen has a half-dozen check boxes that set your display area to show completed items, due dates, priorities, categories, and other items. If you display everything, then your screen can get a bit crowded, but that's your choice.

If you check any of the following boxes, here's what happens:

- **Show Completed Items:** Tasks that you complete stay on the list until you delete them. This option is for people who would rather not forget what they did yesterday.

- **Show Only Due Items:** Tasks with due dates set in the future don't show; only tasks with no due date or with a due date set for today or earlier appear. This option is for people who like to wait until the last minute.

- **Record Completion Date:** The due date of a task changes to the date on which you mark the task as completed. For example, if I set the due date of a task for Friday but mark the task as complete on Wednesday, then the due date is automatically changed to Wednesday. (This one's for people who like to remember when things were really completed rather than when things should have been completed.)

- **Show Due Dates:** This option makes a due date appear on the screen along with the name of each task. It's for people who like to put first things first.

- **Show Priorities:** This option makes the priority number appear next to each task. It's for people who put the most important things first.

- **Show Categories:** Use this option to make the category of each task appear next to the name of the task. This one's for people who like to put everything in its place.

4. **Click OK.**

    The To Do Preferences screen disappears, and the To Do List reappears.

If you choose to sort by category or priority, displaying the category or priority is also a good idea. Otherwise, your screen may look confusing.

Looking up an address and phone number

Creating to-do items that involve other people is fairly common, even if the task is something as simple as calling someone on the phone. You can get your Palm device to look up a name from the Address List and plug that person's name and phone number into the to-do item. Phone Number Lookup can save you the trouble of looking up the person's number when it's time to make the call.

Here's how to look up a name and phone number from the Address Book:

1. **With the To Do List open, create, or begin to edit a To Do List item.**

    See the sections "Creating a to-do item" or "Changing to-dos," earlier in this chapter for more information on this step.

2. **Tap the Menu soft button at the bottom of the display area.**

   The menu bar appears.

3. **Choose Options➪Phone Lookup.**

   The Phone Number Lookup screen appears. If this screen looks like the Address Book, don't be surprised — that's where the phone numbers come from, as shown in Figure 6-12.

Figure 6-12:
Use the Phone Number Lookup feature to find important numbers.

4. **Tap the name of the person whose phone number you want to add to your to-do item.**

   The name is highlighted to show that you've selected it.

5. **Tap Add.**

   The name and phone number of the person whose name you chose appear as part of your to-do item. Bear in mind that the to-do item shows only the first phone number of the address record you pick, no matter how many phone numbers the address record contains.

Unfortunately, you can't get from the To Do List to the person's Address List entry to see other details about the person, such as his street address or other details. You have to press the Address List button and find the name.

Purging to-dos you've done

The reason for keeping a to-do list is to help you get things done. After you've done the things on your list, you have no reason to leave them hanging around. The Purge function automatically deletes items that you've marked as completed. You could delete all your completed items one by one, but the Purge function deletes them *en masse*.

To purge completed to-do items, follow these steps:

1. **With the To Do List open, tap the Menu soft button at the bottom of the display area.**

   The menu bar appears at the top of the display area.

2. **Choose Record⇨Purge.**

   The Purge dialog box appears. Make sure a check mark appears in the box that says `Save Archive Copy on PC`. Otherwise you won't have a record of all the things you've done.

3. **Tap OK.**

   The Purge dialog box closes, and the items you marked as completed disappear.

If you need to dig up a list of the things you've done to show your boss at review time or as dramatic courtroom testimony ("Just where were you the night of . . . ?"), you can go back to the archives of your to-do items, as long as you checked the archive box in the Purge dialog box. (For more info about retrieving to-do items from the archive, see Chapter 13.)

Also, if you synchronize your Palm device with a desktop program like Microsoft Outlook, you'll be better off using the Archive feature in Outlook rather than purging items from the Palm screen. That way all your archived items are still available for viewing through Outlook.

To Do Replacements

If the Palm To Do program doesn't cut the mustard for you, don't despair. Clever programmers have written scads of applications to replace your To Do List with something slicker or more muscular. Here are two popular choices:

ReDo

ReDo is a fairly simple To Do enhancement program that manages recurring tasks and recurring reminders. The program also adds alarms to your To Do items and gives you more flexibility in scheduling recurring tasks than the built-in Palm To Do program provides. (See Figure 6-13.) Whether you've done a task once or done it a thousand times, you'd do well to give ReDo a look at www.palmpilotfordummies.com/redo.

Figure 6-13:
ReDo gives
you more
flexibility
than the
built-in Palm
To Do
program
offers.

Change Repeat

Repeat every 1___ match(es)
From: ▼ Fri 3/28/97
To: ▼ No End Date
Where Dates are: 1-31
and Weeks are: [1][2][3][4][L]
and Days are: [S][M][T][W][T][F][S]
and Months are:
[J][F][M][A][M][J][J][A][S][O][N][D]
(OK) (Cancel)

ToDo Plus

Another popular program is ToDo Plus, which not only lets you add alarms to your To Do items to remind you when to do things, but it also has advanced sorting and filtering features to help you manage unusually long lists of tasks. Additionally, this program allows you to add drawings to your To Do items in case you need to include maps or diagrams. For true productivity enhancement, ToDo Plus lets you beam items to other people so that you can make *them* do your To Do items. (Tom Sawyer would be proud.) Find out more at www.palmpilotfordummies.com/todoplus.

Chapter 7

Thanks for the Memos

The Palm Memo Pad is my secret weapon. Most people don't use the Memo Pad much because either you need to be a good Graffiti writer (or you need to own a Palm-compatible external keyboard) to make the most of your Memo Pad. Like many writers, my best ideas always hit me when I'm farthest from my desk and least able to record them. Now I keep my Palm device nearby 24 hours a day, 7 days a week so that every Brilliant Flash of Insight, along with every Foolish Whim, gets recorded on my Memo Pad. At this point, the Foolish Whims outnumber the Brilliant Flashes by a long shot, but because I can change and delete a memo at any time, I can make myself look foolish less often. As you've probably noticed, I haven't yet figured out how to look brilliant.

The Mystery of the Fourth Button

The rightmost of the four buttons at the bottom of the Palm case has a split personality like Dr. Jekyll and Mr. Hyde (both of whom lurk in Figure 7-1). It actually has more than two personalities, so it's more like Dr. Jekyll and Mr. Hyde and Beavis and Butt-head. The button does different things on different Palm models. Some Palm devices show you the Memo Pad when you push the fourth button, others show something called the Note Pad (which sounds like the same thing, but isn't), and others bring up something totally different such as an e-mail program or a wireless online chat program.

Figure 7-1:
The rightmost button brings up your Memo Pad or Note Pad or . . . uh, something else!

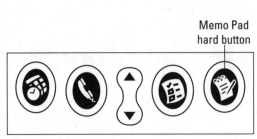

Memo Pad
hard button

Note Pad — A Simple Approach to Memos

At the time of this writing, most of the Palm devices (the m105, m125, m515, and so on) bring up the Note Pad program when you press the right-most application button. This program starts by displaying a blank screen with no lines. Just scribble or draw right on the screen, and the program stores your scribblings for later reference.

The main advantage to using Note Pad is speed. You don't have to learn Graffiti or add a keyboard. Just scribble off a note in your own handwriting. The disadvantage is that you can't transfer notes you've scribbled directly into a word processor or e-mail program. (If you want to use the regular Palm Memo Pad instead, you can reprogram the fourth button as I describe in Chapter 3.) Another shortcoming of the Note Pad is that it won't let you create a new Note on the desktop and HotSync the note to your Palm device; you can read and delete notes in the Palm Desktop program, but you can only create notes on your Palm device.

The Note Pad program has a New button at the bottom of the screen. When you tap the New button, whatever you've scribbled in a previous Note is saved and a new, blank screen appears, ready for more scribbling. You can scroll through the notes you've scribbled by pressing either of the scroll buttons at the bottom of the Palm case.

I've found that the fastest way to create a series of notes in the Note Pad is to press any application button *other* than the Note Pad button, and then press the Note Pad (rightmost) hard button. That has the same effect as tapping the New button on the screen, but it's a little quicker.

So the Note Pad is really a very simple program for a very simple purpose; it's a place to scribble things for later reference. Personally, I prefer the Memo Pad to the Note Pad because I can search for the information I've stored or copy it into e-mails or other documents.

Memos You'll Really Remember

If you use the Memo Pad, you can synchronize your Palm device with a desktop computer (as I describe in Chapter 12), and then copy and paste the text from your memos to regular word-processing programs. That's the best way to format, print, or e-mail the precious prose you've collected on the Memo Pad.

Take a Memo

If you plan to use the Memo Pad to write down large amounts of information while you're away from your desk, it really pays to understand how to use Graffiti. You can get by in all the other Palm Computing programs by using the little on-screen keyboard to tap out short pieces of text, but that gets tiresome quickly. (I discuss the keyboard and Graffiti in Chapter 2.) Even Graffiti can get a little tiring if you're used to the speed of a standard computer keyboard, but that little on-screen keyboard is even worse.

You can also take advantage of the Palm Portable Keyboard if you want to enter lots of text wherever you go. The Palm Portable Keyboard folds up like a James Bond-type gadget so it fits in your pocket, but when you lay it out, it's nearly the same size as a regular desktop computer keyboard. For only 99 bucks, the Palm Portable Keyboard is a good investment. I also love using the keyboard for sending wireless e-mail from a Palm i705 or other wireless Palm devices. (See Chapter 15 for more about wireless e-mail on your Palm device.)

Adding items

Many people don't enter memos on their Palm device's Memo Pad; they either enter data from the Palm Desktop program (see Chapter 12) or they ignore memos. Take your pick. As I've said, I'm a big fan of the Memo Pad, so I add stuff constantly.

To create a new memo, follow these steps:

1. **With the Memo List open, tap New.**

   A blank note screen appears.

2. **Enter your text by using either the on-screen keyboard or Graffiti (see Chapter 2 for more info about entering text).**

   The text you enter appears on the memo screen, as shown in Figure 7-2.

3. **Tap Done.**

   The memo screen disappears, and the Memo List reappears.

What I've just described is the prescribed way of entering a memo. An even easier way to enter a memo is to press the Memo Pad button and just start writing stuff in the Graffiti box. The Memo Pad just assumes you want to create a new memo and opens a new memo screen. You still have to tap Done to close the new memo.

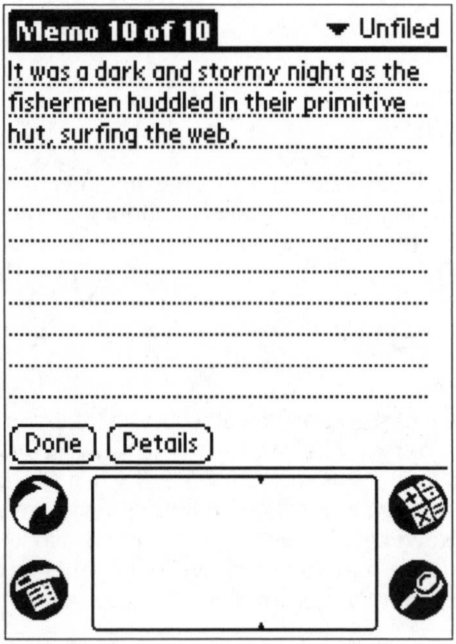

Memo 10 of 10 ▼ Unfiled

It was a dark and stormy night as the fishermen huddled in their primitive hut, surfing the web.

[Done] [Details]

Figure 7-2: Create memos by using the Memo Pad.

Reading memos

The word *memo* looks like someone started to write the word *memory,* but forgot to finish. You don't have to worry about forgetting how to read your memos, though — it's just a matter of press-and-tap. Here's how:

1. **With the Memo List open, tap the name of the memo you want to read, as shown in Figure 7-3.**

   The memo you selected opens.

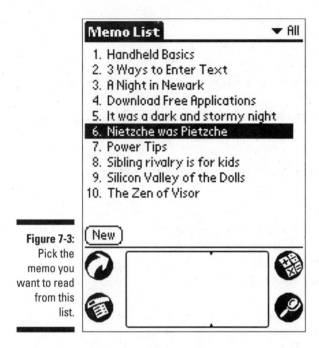

Figure 7-3:
Pick the
memo you
want to read
from this
list.

2. **Read your memo to your heart's content.**

3. **Tap Done.**

   Your memo closes.

The other sneaky thing I like about memos is that you can read them in the dark. Your Palm computer has a backlight, so you can read (or write) memos after the lights go out. It's just like being back in the days when you used to read comic books under the covers with a flashlight. If you want to turn on the backlight, hold down the power button for two seconds. Don't get caught, though.

Bear in mind that the backlight can drain your batteries rather quickly, so use the backlight sparingly.

Changing items

What's the difference between a Foolish Whim and a Brilliant Insight? Editing! (My editors certainly agree with me about that.) Editing your memos is just as easy as reading and creating them.

The simplest change you can make to a memo is to add new text. I have certain memos to which I add one or two lines every day. Adding more text to a memo takes only a second.

To add new text to a memo you've already created, follow these steps:

1. **With the Memo List open, tap the name of the memo you want to change.**

   The memo opens on your screen.

2. **Tap the spot in the memo where you want to add new text.**

   A blinking line, called the *insertion point,* appears at the spot where you tapped.

3. **Enter the text you want to add, using the on-screen keyboard, Graffiti, or an external keyboard (see Chapter 2 for more info about all the ways to enter text).**

   The text you enter appears in the spot you tapped.

4. **Tap Done.**

   Your memo closes.

Another common way to edit a memo is to change the text that's already there. When you select any text you've entered in your Palm device and then enter new text, the text you select is automatically replaced by the text you enter. Most Windows and Macintosh programs work in pretty much the same way, so you should be ready to edit memos in a flash.

To replace existing text in a memo, follow these steps:

1. **With the Memo List open, tap the name of the memo you want to change.**

   The memo opens on your screen.

2. **Select any text you want to replace.**

   The text you select is highlighted to show you've selected it, as shown in Figure 7-4. (For more info about selecting text, see Chapter 2.)

3. **Enter replacement text by using either the on-screen keyboard or Graffiti (see Chapter 2 for more info about entering text).**

   The text you enter replaces the selected text.

4. **Tap Done.**

   Your memo closes.

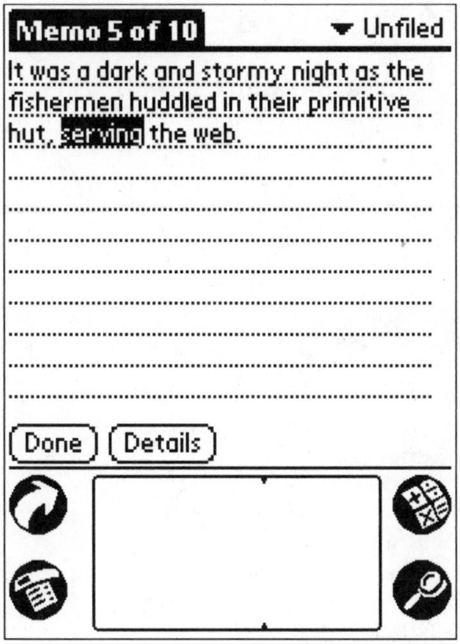

Memo 5 of 10 ▼ Unfiled

It was a dark and stormy night as the
fishermen huddled in their primitive
hut, serving the web.

(Done) (Details)

Figure 7-4:
Get rid
of pesky
typos by
highlighting
text to
change it.

If you want to select the whole memo and replace everything in it, you can
open the memo, tap the Menu icon, and choose Edit⇨Select All. If you're going
to go that far, though, you may as well just delete the memo and start over.

You may have noticed that only the first line of the memo shows up on the
Memo List. If you let your Palm device sort alphabetically, then the first word
of the first line determines where the memo turns up on the Memo List. You
can make sure that a certain memo always ends up at the top of the Memo
List by making 0 (zero) the first character in the memo.

Categorizing items

After you've created a large collection of memos, you may want to start organizing them so you can quickly find the information you want. You can assign
a category to each memo so it shows up alongside other memos with similar
content. Here's how:

1. **With the Memo List open, tap the name of the memo you want to
   categorize.**

   The memo opens.

2. **Tap the name of the category in the upper-right corner of the display area.**

   If your memo is uncategorized, the word *Unfiled* appears in the upper-right corner of the screen. When you tap the down arrow next to the category name or the name itself, a list of categories appears, as shown in Figure 7-5. (Categories work in pretty much the same way on the Memo Pad as they do on the To Do List, so see Chapter 6 for more information about dealing with categories.)

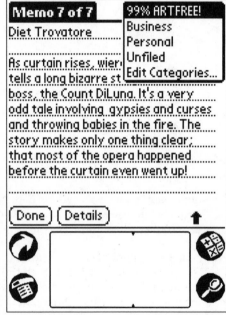

Figure 7-5:
Tap the name of the memo category and pick a new category.

3. **Tap the name of the category to which you want to assign your memo.**

   The list disappears, and the category you chose appears in the upper-right corner.

4. **Tap Done.**

   Your memo closes, and the Memo List reappears.

Making a memo private

If you want to be wise about recording your Foolish Whims, you can mark them all as Private so only you know what you've entered. This is a good way to keep from looking foolish if anybody else gets hold of your Palm device. I've thought about marking my sillier memos as Private, but I suspect that everybody already knows I'm foolish, so it's probably too late.

Follow these steps to keep private memos to yourself:

1. **With the Memo List open, tap the name of the memo you want to make private.**

   Your memo opens.

2. **Tap Details.**

   The Memo Details dialog box opens, as shown in Figure 7-6.

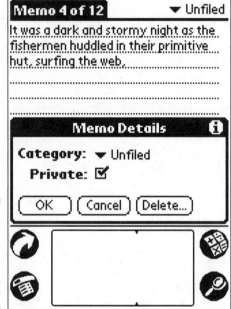

Figure 7-6:
This dialog box lets you keep your secrets safe.

3. **Tap the check box marked Private.**

   A check mark appears in the check box.

4. **Tap OK.**

   The Private Records dialog box appears if you haven't elected to hide private records. The Private Records dialog box warns you that marking this item Private doesn't matter until you choose to hide your private records. (I discuss hiding and showing private records in Chapter 3.) If you have elected to hide private records, the Memo Details dialog box simply closes.

5. **Tap OK in the Private Records dialog box.**

   The Private Records dialog box closes.

6. Tap Done.

Your memo closes, and the Memo List reappears. If you have chosen to hide your private records, then the memo you marked Private is no longer listed.

You can choose whether to show or hide all private items on your Palm device by going to the Security application and picking either Show or Hide. If you pick Show, all your items can be seen, private or not. If you pick Hide, the items marked Private seem to disappear. If you mark an item as Private while hiding items marked as Private, then the item seems to vanish, only to reappear when you go back to the Security application and pick Show Private Items. (For more info about hiding private items, see Chapter 3.)

You can also set up a password to protect your private items. That's one more way of keeping your private items private. (Check out Chapter 3 for more information about passwords.)

The tricky thing about items marked as Private is that nothing appears on the screen to tell you whether you're seeing them. One way to remind yourself whether your private items are showing is to create a memo with a first line that starts with a zero and states `0 PRIVATE ITEMS SHOWING`. This way, you're reminded to check for any items you marked Private.

Using What You Have

Even if you don't enter memos directly into your Palm device, you still want to read the memos you've accumulated and organize your memo collection in a useful way. The Memo Pad offers a range of organizing tools that are simple but useful. You can sort your memos in different ways, view different categories, and make your memos easier to read by changing the font that your Palm device uses for displaying text.

Deleting items

"When in doubt, throw it out." (I had a memo with the name of the person who made up that saying, but somebody threw it out.) Deleting a memo takes a few more steps than I wish it did, but not much mystery is involved.

To delete a memo, follow these steps:

1. With the Memo List open, tap the name of the memo that you want to delete.

Your memo opens.

2. **Tap the Menu icon.**

   The menu bar appears.

3. **Choose Record⇨Delete Memo.**

   The Delete Memo dialog box opens and asks whether you want to delete the current memo, as shown in Figure 7-7.

Figure 7-7:
You can delete a memo when you don't want it anymore.

4. **Tap OK.**

   The Delete Memo dialog box closes, and your memo is deleted. If you change your mind about deleting this memo, you can tap the Cancel button in the Delete Memo dialog box to call off the deletion. Be sure that a check mark appears in the box marked Save Archive Copy on PC. That's the only way your deleted memos can be recovered later. (For more info about archiving, see Chapter 13.)

Boom! The memo's gone.

Viewing memos by category

My, how memos multiply! In no time at all, you'll probably gather up dozens and dozens of memos, full of stuff that you're sure you want to keep handy at all times. Of course, the catch is this: The more memos you try to keep handy on your Palm device, the less handy they get because you have so doggone many of 'em.

Earlier in this chapter, I show you how to assign categories to your memos (see the section "Categorizing items"), although to really use categories, you need to be able to see which memos are in each category.

To view your memos by category, follow these steps:

1. **With the Memo List open, tap the name of the category in the upper-right corner of the screen.**

   The list of available categories appears. When you first use your Palm device, the list has four categories: All, Business, Personal, and Unfiled.

2. **Tap the name of the category you want to display.**

   The Memo List changes to display only the items assigned to the category you chose. The name of the category you're viewing appears in the upper-right corner of the screen.

If you want to really impress your friends with your Palm Computing prowess, you can whip through your memo categories even faster by clicking the Memo Pad button more than once. Each time you press the Memo Pad button, you see a different category. You can also create your own categories to assign to your memos. See Chapter 6 for more about creating your own categories.

Changing fonts

When you change the font on your Palm device, you change the size and style of the lettering that you see on the display area. The itty-bitty letters that the Palm device usually displays enable you to show a great deal of information on that tiny little screen, but if your eyes aren't so sharp or if the light isn't just right, your screen can be tough to read. Each new Palm model offers a few more choices in the type of font you can choose to display your text.

You can change the font on both the Memo List and in the text of your memos; just choose the font from the menu bar. Tap the Menu icon, choose Options➪Font, choose the font that you want to display from the Select Font dialog box, and tap OK. Your Palm computer lets you choose from among three fonts. You have to choose the font for your memo text and the Memo List separately. If you change the font for the Memo List, then you haven't changed the font that you see for the text of your memos. You have to open a memo to change the font for the body of memos. When you change the font for the body of one memo, all memos appear in that font until you pick another font.

Setting preferences to organize your memos

When it comes to organizing memos, I believe in freedom of choice — alphabetical or manual. You can let your Palm device organize your memos by the first letter of the first word in each memo. Or you can set up your Palm to let you drag the titles of memos around the Memo List, and then drop them off in the order you like. I prefer the alphabetical arrangement.

Follow these steps to let your Palm device know your preferences:

1. **With the Memo List open, tap the Menu icon.**

   The menu bar appears.

2. **Choose Options⇨Preferences.**

   The Memo Preferences dialog box opens, as shown in Figure 7-8.

Figure 7-8:
You have preferences. Your memos do, too.

3. **Tap the triangle next to Sort By.**

   A list appears offering you two choices: Manual and Alphabetic.

4. **Tap the choice you prefer.**

   The list disappears, and your choice appears.

5. **Tap OK.**

   The Memo Preferences dialog box closes, and the Memo List appears in the sort order of your choice.

If you choose to sort your memos alphabetically, you get the result you'd expect: All your memos line up in alphabetical order according to the first word in the memo. If you choose Manual sorting, then your memos appear in the order in which you created them so the last memo you created appears at the bottom of the list. When you sort your memos in manual order, you can also drag them to the point on the Memo List where you want them to appear. The category you're currently looking at doesn't matter when you set the preferences; the setting you choose applies to all categories.

If you've sorted your memos manually and then you switch to alphabetical sorting, your manually sorted arrangement is lost for good. The memos are still there, but you have to re-sort everything.

Beaming your memos

Yes, Virginia, there is a Santa Claus, and if he has a new Palm organizer next Christmas, you can write your gift list on your Palm device's Memo Pad and beam it directly to Santa. That way, of course, you don't get to sit on his lap.

Grownups have to go about it a bit more deliberately, but if you're in range and in the line of sight, you can beam nearly anything — not just memos — from one Palm device to another. (For more info about beaming, see Chapter 9.)

To beam a memo, follow these steps:

1. **With the Memo List open, tap the name of the memo you want to beam.**

   Your memo opens.

2. **Tap the Menu icon.**

   The menu bar appears.

3. **Choose Record⇨Beam Memo, as shown in Figure 7-9.**

   The Beam dialog box opens.

4. **Tap OK.**

   Your memo is magically sent to the other Palm device.

You have to set the Palm devices within about three feet of each other, of course, for the beaming process to work, which means you can't beam your list to Santa as he flies over. And remember that dreamy couple in the Palm commercial who beam their cards to each other from passing trains? Keep dreaming. You probably can't beam to someone 'til you see the whites of their eyes. Because the Palm devices must also be within line of sight of each other, you can't beam through walls yet; that's still a job for Superman. Rumor has it, though, that upcoming Palm organizers *will* be able to beam through walls. "It's a bird, it's a plane, no . . . it's my Palm computer!"

Figure 7-9:
Beam
memos to
another
Palm device
at the speed
of light.

Other Memo-rable Options

After you get in the habit of entering lots of text right into your Palm device, you may want to consider one of the fine third-party text-editing and management programs. Here are a few I like.

WordSmith

A company called Blue Nomad makes a surprisingly powerful Palm word processor called WordSmith. The program lets you do all sorts of fancy formatting and has many of the features you're accustomed to using on big desktop computers such as a thesaurus and a spell-checker. You can also set up WordSmith to automatically synchronize certain Microsoft Word documents on your desktop to WordSmith documents on your Palm device. You can find more information at www.palmpilotfordummies.com/wordsmith.

iambic Office

This suite of programs is designed to deal with a variety of standard business tasks, such as word processing, spreadsheets, and e-mail. It includes FastWriter, a powerful word-processing program that can do all kinds of fancy formatting — and deal with the most popular file types (including HTML documents, Microsoft Word files, and others). Details are available at www.palmpilotfordummies.com/iambicoffice.

Info Select

If you do research or if you need to store and organize lots of free-form text information, Info Select from Micro Logic Corporation is an amazingly flexible tool for the job. By *free-form,* I mean information gathered in dribs and drabs that don't always fit neatly into a series of memos or documents.

The program comes in two parts — one for your Palm device and another for your Windows-based desktop computer. Each part is sold separately, and you really need the Windows version to make good use of the Palm version. The Palm version can do basic searching and managing of your data, as seen in Figure 7-10, and the desktop version does fairly elaborate searches with blinding speed. To find out more, visit www.palmpilotfordummies.com/info select.

Figure 7-10:
Info Select
manages
free-form
text data in
a jiffy.

Chapter 8

The Date Game

*T*he Date Book may soon become your favorite Palm Computing feature. Everybody knows how powerful a computer can be at keeping track of your schedule. You probably use one at work to keep track of your appointments. A Palm device lets you carry that power around in your pocket and keep your schedule up-to-date while you're carrying it out. Then, when you return to your office or home, you can just HotSync to your desktop computer to keep the Date Book current. (For more info about performing a HotSync, see Chapter 12.)

To access the Date Book, just press the Date Book hard button, which is normally the far-left button at the bottom of your Palm device, as shown in Figure 8-1. Some Palm organizers assign the Date Book to one of the other four buttons, but it usually has some kind of icon that looks like a clock or a calendar. If you're not sure, you can press each of the four buttons and see which one makes a calendar pop up; then you can arrange your appointments however you like.

Date Book
hard button

Figure 8-1:
Opening the
Date Book
with the
program
button.

Date Book Views

The Date Book is pretty easy to use — after you've tried it a bit. The only tricky part about understanding the Palm Computing Date Book comes from the size of the screen. Your Palm device can't really show a whole calendar on that itty-bitty display area and still show what's going on each day, so the Palm device breaks the calendar into different views that show a day, a week, or a month.

Each view of your calendar includes three icons at the bottom of the screen that represent the three calendar views: day, week, and month. The icon for the view you're currently seeing appears darkened; if you want to switch to another view, tap a different icon. For example, when you look at Day view, the left icon is darkened. When you tap the middle icon, Week view appears.

Another way to switch between Date Book views is to press the Date Book button more than once. Each time you press the button, you see a different view of the Date Book — the Day, Week, or Month view. If you don't like the view you see, keep pressing the Date Book button until the view you want appears.

Day view

The first time you press the Date Book button, you see a daily schedule, as shown in Figure 8-2. It shows a line for each hour of the day, and any appointments you have on your schedule are listed in order of starting time.

Figure 8-2:
Checking
daily
appoint-
ments.

Your Palm device usually shows today's appointments first. If you want to see appointments for a date earlier or later in the week, tap the letter for the day of the week at the top of the screen. You can also move from day to day by pressing the scroll buttons on the case of your Palm device.

Week view

Week view, as shown in Figure 8-3, just shows a diagram of your schedule for the week. It shows a grid of days and times. Shaded bars represent blocks of time when you have appointments scheduled, but the bars don't tell you specifically what's scheduled. If you want to find out what you've scheduled at a certain time, tap the bar representing that scheduled item, and the information regarding the appointment appears at the top of the screen.

Figure 8-3:
Viewing
your
appoint-
ments over
the course
of a week.

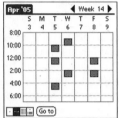

You can look at your weekly schedule for the future or the past by pressing the scroll buttons on the case, just like you can in Day view. You can also change the week you're looking at by tapping one of the triangles at the top of the screen.

Week view has one important feature that the other two views don't have: You can change an appointment to a different time in the week by dragging the bar representing the appointment time and then dropping it off at another time in the week. Figure 8-4 shows an appointment (represented by the box with the heavy border) being dropped in at 2 p.m. on September 10.

Figure 8-4:
Move
appoint-
ments
quickly by
dragging
and
dropping —
only in
Week view.

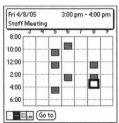

As you're dragging and dropping, the name and time of your appointment appear at the top of the display area to show you exactly when you've set the new appointment time. You have to be pretty steady with the stylus if you drag and drop this way, but it's the fastest way to change an appointment time.

If you've never done the drag-and-drop (no, it's not a dance step from the 1960s — that was the Watusi), don't fret. It's very simple:

1. **Put the tip of your stylus on the bar representing an appointment.**

2. **Slide the stylus tip along the screen to where you want the appointment to end up.**

   As you slide the stylus tip along the screen, a little box representing the appointment slides right along with your stylus, as though you were dragging the box along the screen. As you drag, the appointment listed in the banner at the top of the screen changes to show what the new appointment time will be if you "drop" the appointment at the current position by lifting your stylus.

3. **Lift up the stylus when the appointment is located where you want it.**

Now you're a drag-and-drop champ!

Month view

Month view, as shown in Figure 8-5, is the most familiar-looking view in the Date Book because it resembles a regular wall calendar. Unfortunately, Month view offers very little information about your schedule; only dots represent your appointments. The main advantage of Month view is the ability to navigate through your schedule easily. If you tap any date in Month view, you see Day view for that date.

Figure 8-5:
View the whole month to see which days have appointments.

Again, the scroll buttons change Month view from one month to the next. If you need to take a quick look at a date in the distant future (a year or more from now), tap Go To at the bottom of the Date Book screen and pick the date you want to see.

The Go To icon shows a calendar that enables you to tap the date you want to see. If you want to view a date later this month, tap Go To and tap the date you want to see. If you want to see a date in a different month of this year, tap the month you want from the list of months at the top of the screen, and then tap the day you want. If you want to look at a day in a different year, tap Go To, tap one of the triangles next to the year at the top of the screen (depending on whether you want to time-warp into the past or the future), and tap the month you want to see.

Making Dates

You can keep track of a surprising amount of detailed information in the Date Book. Thousands of appointments fit comfortably into the Date Book, along with reminders, notes, and other details. You don't have to enter your appointments directly into your Palm device if you don't want to. In fact, you can do most of the keyboard work on your desktop computer and then HotSync everything to your Palm device. In some situations, though, you may be better off entering appointments directly in your Palm device.

Adding appointments the simple way

Some folks are into dates; some aren't. You don't have to go crazy entering lots of details when you add an appointment to the Date Book. You can enter many types of appointments with very little effort.

Follow these steps to add a new appointment the simple way:

1. **With the Date Book visible, tap the line next to the hour when your appointment begins.**

   A blinking line, called the *insertion point,* appears on the line you tapped.

2. **Enter the name of your appointment by using either the on-screen keyboard or Graffiti (see Chapter 2 for more info about entering text).**

   The name of your appointment appears on the line you tapped, as shown in Figure 8-6.

3. **Tap the blank spot at the bottom of the screen to the right of Go To.**

   The insertion point disappears, and your appointment is set. (If you don't complete this step, nothing terrible happens; your Palm device just waits for you to do something else.)

Figure 8-6: Just write the name of your appointment in the appropriate time slot.

Adding appointments the complete way

If all your appointments start right on the hour and last exactly one hour, then the simple way to enter appointments (see the preceding section, "Adding appointments the simple way") suits you just fine. When you have appointments that start at odd times or don't last exactly one hour, you need to resort to the more complete method for entering appointments.

Follow these steps to enter detailed information about an appointment:

1. **With the Date Book visible, tap Go To.**

   The Go To Date dialog box opens.

2. **Tap the date for your appointment.**

   The Date Book appears in Day view, showing you the appointments you've scheduled for that date.

3. **Tap the hour closest to the starting time of your appointment.**

   The Set Time dialog box opens, as shown in Figure 8-7.

4. **Tap the hour and minute for the starting time of your appointment.**

   The hour and minute you tap appear in the Start Time box.

5. **Tap the End Time box.**

   The End Time box is highlighted to show you've selected it.

6. **Tap the hour and minute for the ending time of your appointment.**

   The hour and minute you tap appear in the End Time box.

7. **Tap OK.**

   The Set Time dialog box closes, and the Date Book screen reappears.

8. **Enter the name of your appointment by using either the on-screen keyboard or Graffiti (see Chapter 2 for more info about entering text).**

   The name of your appointment appears on the line next to the starting time.

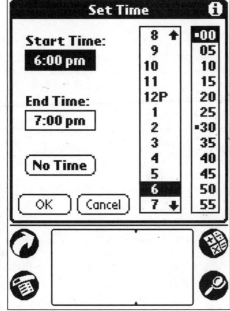

Figure 8-7:
Setting
more
accurate
times in the
Set Time
dialog box.

9. **Tap Details.**

   The Event Details dialog box opens.

10. **If you need to make any changes to the details of your appointment, tap the appropriate box and enter that information.**

    Because you've already entered the date and time, you probably don't need to change those details. I explain more about setting alarms, setting private appointments, and repeating appointments later in this chapter.

11. **Tap OK.**

    The Event Details dialog box closes, and the Date Book screen reappears.

There! You've done it! Isn't that satisfying? Okay, maybe not, but you've done all you can do, so take heart. If you didn't find this method helpful or efficient, you can enter your next appointment the simple way by following the steps in the preceding section.

The really super-duper fast way to enter a new appointment time is to write the time in Graffiti with the Date Book open to the Day view and no appointment selected. For example, if you run across someone right after lunch and decide to get together at 7:30 that evening, just press the Date Book button and write **7 3 0** on the number side of the Graffiti area. Tap OK and then enter the name of the person you're meeting. Presto! You've got a date!

Scheduling all-day events

Not everything on your schedule happens at a particular hour of the day. Birthdays and holidays, for example, just happen — all day long, even if it rains. If you want to enter an event without a time attached, just open the Date Book to Day view, and then enter the name of the event in the Graffiti box (I give more info about using Graffiti in Chapter 2), or use the Palm keyboard. Your new event appears at the top of the screen. You can also use the complete method of entering an appointment (see the preceding section) and tap No Time on the Set Time screen in Step 6.

Setting alarms

I'm the first to admit that I need lots of reminding. Fortunately, my Palm device is always around to gently pester me into doing what needs to be done — when it needs to be done. It's sort of a like an electronic mother-in-law. Even if your Palm device is turned off, the alarm wakes it up and makes a series of tiny beeps. You turn off the alarm by tapping OK on the screen.

Follow these steps to set an alarm:

1. **With the Date Book visible, tap the name of the appointment for which you want to set an alarm.**

   The insertion point appears on the line with your appointment's name.

2. **Tap Details.**

   The Event Details dialog box opens.

3. **Tap the Alarm check box.**

   A check mark appears in the check box, and the alarm setting appears to the right of the check box, as shown in Figure 8-8. Normally, the alarm setting is five minutes. That means the alarm will go off five minutes before the scheduled appointment time.

4. **If you want to change the alarm time, tap the word *Minutes*.**

   A list appears with the choices: Minutes, Hours, and Days.

5. **Tap your choice of Minutes, Hours, or Days.**

   The list disappears, and the choice you tapped appears.

6. **Enter the number of minutes, hours, or days before the appointment that you want the alarm to sound, using either the on-screen keyboard or Graffiti (see Chapter 2 for more info about entering text).**

   The number you enter appears next to the Alarm check box.

7. **Tap OK.**

   The Event Details dialog box closes.

Figure 8-8:
Check mark
the Alarm
option so
your Date
Book can
remind you
of an
important
appoint-
ment.

I usually check the Alarm check box *while* (rather than *after*) creating an appointment.

Adding notes to appointments

Every Date Book item can also contain a note explaining details about that appointment. Date Book notes work exactly the same way as the notes you can attach to to-do items. (See Chapter 6 for more info about attaching notes.)

Using Address Book Lookup

Another feature shared by the Date Book and the To Do List is the ability to look up a name in the Address Book and then automatically copy that person's name and phone number into the appointment. To look up a name, tap the Menu soft button at the bottom-left corner of the Palm screen and choose Options➪Phone Lookup. When the Address Book appears, tap the name you want to include in the appointment, and then tap the Add button.

Setting up repeating appointments

You certainly don't want to forget that important weekly meeting of Electronics Shoppers Anonymous. Rather than enter each of those meetings individually, you can set up a repeating appointment.

To mark an appointment as a repeating appointment:

1. **With the Date Book visible, tap the name of the appointment you want to set up as a repeating appointment.**

   The insertion point appears on the line with your appointment's name.

2. **Tap Details.**

   The Event Details dialog box opens.

3. **Tap the Repeat box.**

   The Change Repeat dialog box opens, as shown in Figure 8-9.

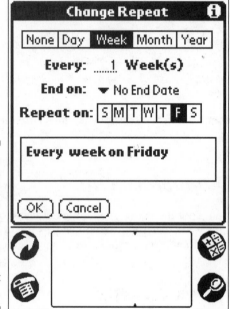

Figure 8-9:
Y'all come back, now! Set up recurring appointments in the Change Repeat dialog box.

4. **Tap one of the interval pattern buttons to set the frequency you want.**

   Your choices are None, Day, Week, Month, and Year. When you tap one, the screen changes to show intervals that are suitable to your choice. If you choose nothing, your Palm device assumes you mean None.

5. **Enter a number to indicate how often you want the appointment to repeat.**

   If you enter nothing, your Palm device assumes that the number is 1, meaning that the appointment occurs every day, week, month, or year, depending on which frequency you chose. If you change that number to the number 2, your appointment occurs every two days, two weeks, two months, or two years.

6. **If your appointment repeats until a certain date, tap the End On box.**

   Some appointments repeat for a certain period of time. If you go to night school, for example, your class may occur once a week for ten weeks. When you tap the End On box, a menu appears, giving you two choices: No End Date and Choose Date.

7. **Tap Choose Date from the End On box.**

   The Ending On screen appears.

8. **On the Ending On screen, tap the end date you want to appear on the calendar.**

   The Ending On screen disappears, and the date you chose appears in the End On box.

9. **Tap the appropriate box to indicate other information about your repeating appointment.**

   You have one other choice to make if your appointment repeats on either a weekly or monthly basis. You can set weekly appointments to recur on several days of the week (such as Monday, Wednesday, and Friday) by simply tapping the various days. Notice that the days are set on a *toggle* — meaning you must tap them again to deselect them. If you're setting up a monthly appointment, tap either Day (for example, the third Monday of every month) or Date (for example, the 15th of every month).

   When you make any of these choices, a line of text describing your recurrence pattern (such as "The third Monday of every month") appears in the box at the bottom of the Change Repeat dialog box. Keep an eye on this text to be sure you've set up your appointment correctly.

10. **Tap OK.**

    The Change Repeat dialog box closes, and the Event Details dialog box opens.

11. **Tap OK again.**

    The Event Details dialog box closes.

When you create a repeating appointment, each instance of the appointment looks like a separate item, but the occurrences are all connected in the mind of your Palm device. If you change or delete one occurrence of the appointment, then your Palm device wants to know whether you're changing every occurrence or just that one. When it asks, just tell it what you want.

Marking items as Private

You can enjoy the thrill of a secret rendezvous with your Palm device. I suppose you can enjoy the rendezvous without your Palm device, too, but it does help you remember the rendezvous while keeping it a secret from anyone else who looks at your Palm device:

1. **With the Date Book visible, tap the name of the appointment you want to make private.**

   The insertion point appears on the line with your appointment's name.

2. Tap Details.

The Event Details dialog box opens.

3. Tap the check box next to Private.

A check mark appears in the check box to show you've marked the appointment as Private.

4. Tap OK.

The Event Details dialog box closes. If you didn't choose to hide all Private Records, then you see a dialog box telling you how to hide all Private Records. (In case you forgot, see Chapter 3 for more info about hiding private items.)

Of course, there is such a thing as too much secrecy. If you mark an appointment as Private and then tell your Palm device to hide all Private Records, the appointment doesn't show on the screen, so *you* can't even see your Private Records. That's a problem. To prevent keeping your secrets secret from yourself, tap the Applications icon, choose the Security icon, and then pick Show Private Records.

Putting Appointments in the Past

You may be the type of person who rarely enters anything directly into your Palm device. If you enter everything via a HotSync from your desktop computer, you still want to be able to delete existing appointments and to set up your Palm device to suit your fancy.

Deleting appointments

Sooner or later, all your appointments become history. Perhaps you want to save all your appointment records for posterity. Perhaps you think posterity is baloney, and you want to get rid of the appointments after they're over. I go for the second choice.

Here's how to delete an appointment:

1. With the Date Book visible, tap the name of the appointment you want to delete.

The insertion point appears on the line with your appointment's name.

2. Tap the Menu soft button at the bottom-left corner of the Palm screen.

The menu bar appears at the top of the display area, as shown in Figure 8-10.

Record Edit Options
New Event ✓N
Delete Event... ✓D
Attach Note ✓A
Delete Note... ✓O
Purge... ✓E

1:00
2:00 Staff meeting
3:00
4:00
5:00
6:00

(New) (Details) (Go to)

Figure 8-10: Want to delete an appointment? Choose Delete Event from this menu.

3. **Choose Record⇨Delete Event.**

   The Delete Event dialog box opens.

4. **Tap OK.**

   The Delete Event dialog box closes, and your appointment disappears. Simple as that. If you check the box that says Save Archive Copy on PC, a wonderful thing happens: The next time you HotSync, the HotSync Manager saves a copy of the deleted item on your desktop computer. Who'd have thunk it? (For more information about archived items, see Chapter 11 or 12; for more about HotSyncing, see Chapter 11.)

Another way to delete an appointment is to tap the appointment name, then tap Details, and then tap Delete. You get the same result either way: No more appointment.

Setting preferences

You can change your Date Book in two ways: the range of hours it displays for each day, and the type of alarm. Some people like to display only a few hours on their daily calendar to keep the calendar from looking cluttered. If you feel compelled to customize the Date Book, here's how to do it.

_____

To set Date Book preferences:

1. **With the Date Book visible, tap the Menu soft button at the bottom-left corner of the Palm screen.**

   The menu bar appears at the top of the display area.

2. **Choose Options⇨Preferences.**

   The Preferences screen appears, as shown in Figure 8-11.

Figure 8-11:
Express
your
preferences
in the
Preferences
screen.

3. **To change the start time, tap one of the triangles next to the Start Time box.**

   Tapping the top triangle makes the start time later. Tapping the bottom triangle makes the start time earlier.

4. **To change the end time, tap one of the triangles next to the End Time box.**

   The End Time box works just like the Start Time box (see Step 3).

5. **To change the default alarm preset, tap the Alarm Preset check box.**

   A check mark appears in the check box, and the alarm setting appears to the right of the check box. Normally, the alarm setting is five minutes.

6. **If you want to change the Alarm preset time, tap the word *Minutes*.**

   A list appears with these choices: Minutes, Hours, or Days.

7. **Tap your choice of Minutes, Hours, or Days.**

   The list disappears, and the choice you tapped appears.

8. **Enter the number of minutes, hours, or days before the appointment you want the alarm to sound with either the on-screen keyboard or Graffiti (see Chapter 2 for more info about entering text).**

   The number you enter appears next to the words `Alarm Preset`.

9. **To change the type of alarm sound you hear when the alarm goes off, tap the triangle next to the words `Alarm Sound`.**

   A list of all the available alarm sounds appears.

10. **Tap the type of the alarm sound you want.**

    You have several squeaks and squawks to choose from. The sound you tap plays, and its name appears in the Alarm Sound box.

11. **Tap the Remind Me box to choose the number of times you want to be reminded of your appointment.**

    A list appears, offering choices ranging from Once to 10 Times.

12. **Tap the number of times you want to be reminded.**

    The choice you tap appears in the Remind Me box.

13. **Tap the Play Every box to choose how often to replay the Alarm.**

    A list appears, offering choices ranging from 1 to 30 minutes.

14. **Tap the choice you want to appear in the Play Every box.**

    The choice you tap appears in the Play Every box.

15. **Tap OK.**

Maybe I'm boring, but I've never changed my Date Book preferences. Maybe you're different. If I can get the alarm to play "Tea for Two," I may change my mind.

Purging the Date Book

Your Palm device can hold as many as 10,000 appointments. That sounds like a great deal, but sooner or later, you'll want to clear out some space and make room for more items. The fastest way to make room in your Palm device is to purge old Date Book items. The Purge feature removes appointments that are too far in the past. Purging the Date Book is quick and easy, and it doesn't hurt a bit.

To purge the Date Book, follow these steps:

1. **With the Date Book visible, tap Menu soft button at the bottom-left corner of the Palm screen.**

   The menu bar appears at the top of the display area.

2. **Choose Record⇨Purge.**

   The Purge dialog box opens, as shown in Figure 8-12. By default, your Palm device is set to purge appointments older than one week. If you want to change the age at which your Palm purges appointments, tap the words 1 Week and choose from the list that appears.

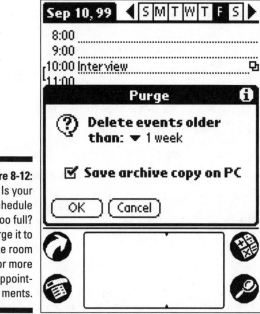

Figure 8-12: Is your schedule too full? Purge it to make room for more appointments.

3. **Tap OK.**

   The Purge dialog box closes.

Now you're rid of all the great things you've done, and you can move on to the great things you're going to do. Isn't that inspiring?

Using Alternate Datebooks

If the Palm datebook doesn't suit your fancy, don't be glum. You can always buy yourself a spanking-new add-on program that fulfills your datebook dreams.

SilverScreen

SilverScreen isn't really a datebook. It's a type of Palm program called a *launcher,* which pulls all your appointments, to-dos, and other important tidbits into a single, easy-to-use package. SilverScreen has won all kinds of awards for being useful and cool and is one of the most popular add-on programs in the entire Kingdom of Palm. Check it out at `www.palmpilotfor dummies.com/silverscreen`.

DateBk5

DateBk5, which is shown in Figure 8-13, is the supercharged grandchild of your regular Datebook. This critter has split screens, linked views (which let you see how different items connect to each other), pop-up menus, and just about everything but whitewall tires and chrome hubcaps (those are optional). Some Palm-powered devices, such as the Handspring Visor ship with a copy of a light version of this product called DateBk+. Find out more about DateBk5at `www.palmpilotfordummies.com/datebk`.

Figure 8-13:
DateBk5 enhances your calendar experience with several new ways to view your appointments.

DayNotez

DayNotez goes way beyond the regular Datebook features and adds spell check, auto correct, and multiple views to give you different ways to organize your information. The package also includes a companion Windows program for your desktop to make it easier to enter and manage data. If you need to keep notes on activities as they happen, take a look at `www.palmpilot fordummies.com/daynotez`.

Action Names Datebook

This souped-up day planner from Iambic, Inc, gives you an attractive, full-color, icon-based view of your appointments. It also provides links between appointments and contacts and advanced filtering, sorting, and grouping features. You can also create your own colorful icons to help give your schedule some pizzazz and personality. For more information, go to www.palmpilotfordummies.com/actionnamesdatebook.

Part III
Palm Organizers and the Outside World

The 5th Wave   By Rich Tennant

Although Phil enjoyed owning a multi-function PDA, he wished the vibrating pager had been more elegantly designed.

CLAK
CLAK
CLAK
CLAK

In this part . . .

Your Palm device isn't meant to be left all alone in the world. You have to hook it up to a regular desktop or laptop computer to take full advantage of a Palm device's features. In this part, you find out how to help your Palm device and your regular computer carry on a meaningful relationship.

Chapter 9

Beaming Data

· ·

· ·

You've seen the commercial: Two attractive, love-struck riders on passing trains lock eyes and instinctively reach for their Palm organizers. They oh-so-lovingly beam their addresses to one another as the music swells and the lights fade. We can only guess what happens after the commercial ends, but they both look so very happy! So who would want to quibble over whether you can *really* beam your address between passing commuter trains? (Actually you can't — not yet, anyway — but okay, I can pretend it's possible.) TV make-believe aside, even if you don't use the beaming feature to find Mr. or Ms. Right, you can impress your friends in many ways by exchanging a friendly beam.

The Beaming Thing

Beaming is a Palm Computing feature that enables you to send information from one Palm device to another by directly pointing the two units at each other. As long as the units are within about three feet apart with no obstacles between them, the process is quick and simple. My informal tests show that two Palm devices lose sight of each other when they're four feet apart, and they also have some trouble communicating if they're closer than three inches or so. However, at a typical conference table, you should have no trouble beaming information to a Palm device across from you.

The Palm beaming feature uses *infrared* (or *IR*) light, which is what TV remote controls use. Computer manufacturers include IR communications on laptops and printers. You also can find IR capability on certain pagers and cellular telephones.

Not all applications can use the beaming feature. Even the built-in programs, such as Palm Mail and Expense, can't beam items. But as time goes on, more and more Palm add-on programs include a beaming feature. In the following sections, I show you how to beam individual items, categories, and even applications.

Sending an item

Whenever you beam information between a pair of Palm devices, the data you send remains on your unit and is duplicated on the second unit. Think of the process as sending a fax. Before you send a fax, only you have a copy of the information, and after you're done, you and the receiver both have a copy (and a week later neither of you can find either copy).

Here's how to send an item:

1. **Make sure both Palm devices are turned on and pointed at each other.**

   Keep the two Palm devices within three feet of one another.

2. **Select the item you want to beam.**

   The item appears on your screen. You can send a memo, an address, a To Do item, or an appointment.

3. **Tap the Menu soft button at the bottom-left corner of the Palm screen.**

   The menu bar appears.

4. **From the menu bar, choose Record⇨Beam.**

   The menu shows Beam Event for a Date Book appointment (as shown in Figure 9-1), Beam Address for an Address Book entry, and so on.

   The Beam dialog box opens for a short time, first telling you that it's preparing to beam and then that it's searching for another Palm device. After your Palm device finishes beaming the item, the dialog box closes.

If all goes well, both Palm devices beep to let you know that the item reached its destination. Your recipient actually knows more about the transfer than you do because dialog boxes pop up on her Palm device to say what the device has received. If the transfer fails, your Palm device displays a message saying something's wrong and that you should try again.

If you enter your own address in your Palm Address Book and mark it as your business card, all you need to do when you want to beam your business card is hold down the Address Book button for about two seconds until the beaming process starts. See Chapter 5 for details about beaming your business card.

```
┌─────────────────────────────────┐
│ Record  Edit  Options           │
│ New Event        ╱N ············ │
│ Delete Event...  ╱D ············ │
│ Attach Note      ╱A ············ │
│ Delete Note...   ╱O ············ │
│ Purge...         ╱E ············ │
│ Beam Event       ╱B ············ │
│ ─────────────────────────────── │
│ 2:00 ··························· │
│ 3:00 ··························· │
│ 4:00 ··························· │
│ 5:00 Big Whoop! ·············· │
│ 6:00 ··························· │
│ ─────────────────────────────── │
│ ▪ ⋯▦  (New) (Details) (Go to)  │
└─────────────────────────────────┘
```

Figure 9-1:
This event
will move
through
the air.

Receiving an item

Just because you're receiving an item rather than sending one doesn't mean you can just stand there and do nothing. You can stand there and do *almost* nothing. Just watch the screen and tap Yes when the time comes, like this:

1. **Make sure both Palm devices are turned on and pointed at each other.**

   The two Palm devices should be within three feet of one another.

2. **When your friend sends an item to you, wait for the Beam dialog box to open.**

   The Beam dialog box tells you what someone is beaming to you and asks whether you want to accept the item.

3. **Tap Yes or No.**

   If you tap No, the Beam dialog box closes, and that's the end of the process. If you tap Yes, the application to which the beamed item belongs opens and shows you details of the item. For example, if the beamed item is someone's business card, your Address Book screen appears, showing the new address record that you're about to add to your Address List.

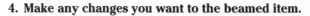
4. **Make any changes you want to the beamed item.**

You may want to change the category of the item or just make a note about when or where the beamed item originated. For example, if someone beams you her business card at a trade show, you may want to make a note of the trade show at which you met.

5. **Tap Done.**

The item closes, and you see the main screen of the application to which the beamed item belongs.

In theory, people can beam unsolicited items to you, but you can always refuse them by tapping No. My only gripe about how the routine works is that after you say Yes, your Palm device buries the item in the list of items in the Unfiled category. If I want to go through the items I received today, I have to guess which item came and when. If you assign categories or add a note to everything promptly, you don't have trouble figuring out what's new. (For more info about using categories, see Chapter 6.)

Sending a category

You don't have to beam items one at a time; you can send an entire category. You're limited, of course, to sending bunches of items that can handle categories. For example, because the Date Book has no categories, you can beam only one appointment at a time. (For more info about using categories, see Chapter 6.)

To beam an entire category, follow these steps:

1. **Make sure both Palm devices are turned on and pointed at each other.**

Keep the two Palm devices within about three feet of one another.

2. **Display the category you want to beam.**

The category appears on your screen.

3. **Tap the Menu soft button at the bottom-left corner of the Palm screen.**

The menu bar appears.

4. **From the menu bar, Choose Record⇨Beam Category, as shown in Figure 9-2.**

The Beam dialog box opens for a moment and then closes.

Before the Beam dialog box closes, it tells you very briefly the name of the category you're sending. A little Cancel button in the dialog box enables you to cancel the transfer if you've sent the wrong thing, but the dialog box closes so quickly that you really can't stop the transfer. Therefore, be sure you really want to send the items you're beaming.

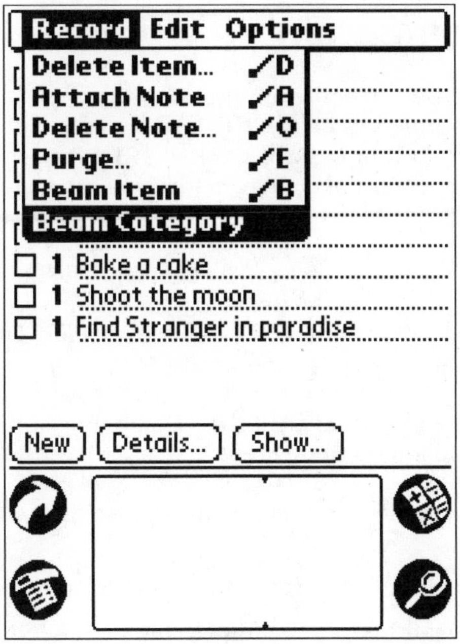

Figure 9-2:
Beam a
whole
category of
tasks for
someone
else to do.
That's how I
spell relief.

Receiving a category

The process of receiving a whole category of items works just like receiving a single item. (See the section "Receiving an item," earlier in this chapter.) Receiving a category of items is a problem, however, for two reasons:

✔ **When you tap Yes to accept incoming items, the Palm device opens only one of the items you received.** You can categorize only the first incoming item. The others get mixed up with your unfiled items, so you have to dig them out one by one. Because you have no way of knowing exactly which items the other person sent, you may have trouble figuring out who sent which items.

✔ **The category markings are removed from incoming items, which are all marked Unfiled.** The reason for that is simple: A Palm device can handle only 15 categories. If you were able to accept categorized items from lots of different people, you'd end up with a messy collection of categories. On the other hand, if someone sends you a category, you logically expect to get that category. I figure the Palm people will address this issue in a future upgrade.

Sending an application

Believe it or not, you can beam an entire application from one Palm device to another. Frankly, beaming programs between Palm devices is much easier than installing programs from your desktop computer. You have to install the program first on your Palm device, of course, before you can share it with anyone else.

Some Palm Computing applications refuse to be beamed. The little padlock next to the standard applications on the Beam list, for example, means you can't beam those programs because they're locked. Many Palm Computing programs are locked the same way to prevent software piracy.

At the moment, though, you can beam most Palm Computing software between Palm devices by following these steps:

1. **Make sure both Palm devices are turned on and pointed at each other.**

   Keep the two Palm devices within about three feet of one another.

2. **Tap the Applications soft button, the upper spot on the left side of the Graffiti box.**

   The Applications screen appears.

3. **Tap the Menu soft button at the bottom-left corner of the Palm screen.**

   The menu bar appears.

4. **From the menu bar, choose App⇨Beam.**

   The Beam screen appears, as shown in Figure 9-3, listing all your applications. The applications with a little padlock next to them are locked and can't be beamed.

5. **Tap the name of the application you want to beam.**

   The application you tap is highlighted to indicate you selected it.

6. **Tap Beam.**

   The Beam dialog box opens, indicating which program you're sending. If you change your mind, tap Cancel.

Because programs normally take longer to beam than individual items, keep the Palm devices pointed at each other until the Beam dialog box closes, indicating that the process is complete. Programs take longer to beam because they're bigger, and bigger programs take longer to beam than smaller ones. You can see how big a program is by checking the number next to the name of the program on the Beam screen. I've never seen the process of beaming a program between Palm devices take more than a few minutes.

Figure 9-3:
The locks
show the
programs
you can't
beam.

Receiving an application

The process of receiving a beamed application is just like receiving anything else (see the section "Receiving an item," earlier in this chapter, for details). After you agree to receive the application by clicking Yes in the Beam dialog box, your display area switches to the Applications screen, showing the new program.

Here's the big catch to beaming applications: Only the actual program is copied to the receiving Palm device. Files that the program has created or used don't come over with the program. For example, if you beam AportisDoc (a document-reading program) from a Palm device that has several text files in AportisDoc, those files aren't copied: only the program itself is. You can't beam AportisDoc files; you have to install the documents from a desktop through the regular Palm Install Tool.

Infrared HotSync

If you take advantage of IR HotSync, you can HotSync your Palm device to a laptop computer without lugging around a cradle or cable. This feature uses the same infrared (IR) light that beams your business card to another Palm device, but in this case it's connecting your Palm organizer to a laptop computer. (Desktop computers only rarely include an IR port, but you can almost always find an IR port on a laptop.)

Beaming ahead

Plenty of people want to write Palm programs that take advantage of the capability to sling data through the air, and several are available already. A couple of products I've tried are pretty interesting.

PalmPrint (www.palmpilotfordummies. com/palmprint) enables you to print through infrared to any suitably equipped printer. You can print from all built-in Palm applications as well as most of the popular add-on programs for the Palm organizer. At this point, HP, Canon, and other companies have printers with IR capability. With the PalmPrint program, you can point your Palm device at a printer and print a memo, task, or appointment on the spot.

OmniRemote Pro (www.palmpilotfor dummies.com/omniremote) turns your Palm organizer into the brainiest remote control your TV or VCR has ever seen. If OmniRemote Pro were any smarter, it wouldn't let you watch the junk you sit through. There's only one short-coming to using OmniRemote Pro software; the tiny Infrared light on your Palm device isn't strong enough to reach your TV from more than about three feet away. If you watch TV from a healthier distance, like your mother said you should, OmniRemote may be a bit cumbersome.

Using IR to perform a HotSync is a lot less reliable than beaming a business card or other small piece of information because the HotSync process moves a large amount of information in both directions between your Palm device and the computer. I've found that the IR HotSync process fails fairly often, so if you're planning to rely on IR HotSync while on a crucial business trip, test everything out before you leave.

You need to configure both your Palm organizer and your laptop for IR HotSync to make the process work. Let's start with the Palm side.

Follow these steps to set up your Palm device for an IR HotSync:

1. **Tap the Applications soft button at the lower left corner of the screen.**

   Your list of applications appears.

2. **Tap the HotSync icon.**

   The HotSync application appears.

3. **Tap the word Local near the top of the screen, just above the HotSync icon.**

   Local is highlighted to show you've selected it.

4. **Tap the triangle just below the HotSync icon in the center of the screen.**

   A drop-down list appears. One of the choices is IR to PC/Handheld. (If that choice isn't available, your Palm device can't use IR HotSync. Sorry.)

5. **Tap IR to PC/Handheld.**

   The choice you tapped appears next to the triangle to show you've selected it.

Now you'll need to set up your laptop. Every laptop is different, so you may need to check with the manufacturer of your laptop for details. But here's the basic lowdown on setting up your Windows-based laptop for IR HotSync:

1. **Right-click the HotSync Manager icon in the lower right corner of the screen.**

   A shortcut menu appears above the HotSync Manager Icon.

2. **Choose Setup.**

   The Setup dialog box appears.

3. **Click the Local tab.**

   The local settings page appears.

4. **Click the scroll-down button next to Serial Port.**

   A list appears.

5. **Choose either COM3 or COM4.**

   The choice you make appears in the Serial Port box.

6. **Click OK.**

   The Setup dialog box disappears.

How do you know you chose the right COM thingy? Well, okay, you don't. You have to try one and see whether it works. If it doesn't, repeat this process and try the other COM thingy. How do you test to see whether you did it right? By doing a HotSync, like this:

1. **Tap the Applications soft button at the lower left corner of the screen.**

   Your list of applications appears.

2. **Tap the HotSync icon.**

   The HotSync application appears.

3. **Tap the HotSync icon in the middle of the screen.**

   The words `Connecting with the desktop using IR to PC/Handheld` appear.

4. **Place your Palm device within three feet of your laptop so that the tiny dark red window (normally found at the top of the Palm case) points directly at a similar-looking red window on the laptop.**

   Laptop manufacturers put those little windows at different places on the laptop; sometimes it's on the back, sometimes right in front of the keyboard.

If the stars are aligned just right and you have good karma, your Palm device and your laptop makes cute little beeping and booping sounds, and a few minutes your Palm organizer and laptop are synchronized.

Isn't that romantic? If it works, maybe. If not, you can always go back to using your Palm HotSync cradle.

Chapter 10

Doing Business Everywhere with Documents To Go

1 f you're like most working people, you have a collection of documents on your desktop computer that you just can't live without: that essential price list, the summary of company policies, or that standard invoice form you use over and over. After you get used to using your Palm organizer to knock off essential work on the spur of the moment, you naturally want to keep your favorite desktop documents on your Palm device and at the ready as well.

To make it possible to have these documents at hand, most Palm devices you can buy include a free copy of a program called Documents To Go. This program allows you to carry copies of your most important documents on your handheld computer so you can work on them anywhere, anytime. You can also buy a more powerful edition of Documents To Go called the Professional Version, which includes support for presentations, e-mail, pictures, and Adobe Acrobat files. If your Palm device doesn't include a copy of Documents To Go, you can find out where to buy yourself a copy at `www.palmpilot` `fordummies.com/desktoptogo`.

Documents To Go Basics

Remember those old commercials about the candy mint that was also a breath mint? Of course not, you're too young. But you may remember the Saturday Night Live sketch about the dessert topping that doubled as a floor wax. Documents To Go is a similar, two-in-one deal. The program has two parts; one part lives on your Palm device and does the work of displaying and organizing your documents and helping your edit those documents. You'll find other part of the program on your desktop computer, doing the work of converting your documents to a Palm-friendly format, sending those documents to your Palm device and making sure that the desktop versions of your documents stay the same as the handheld versions.

Remember how I said that Documents To Go is really two programs, not just one. Okay, so I lied — it's really *four* programs, cleverly disguised as two programs. And if you pay a little extra, you can get six programs disguised as four programs. Huh? Ok, I know it sounds like a Groucho Marx routine, but when you actually see the whole system in action, it's pretty easy. If I were to explain how a bicycle is built it might sound confusing, too, but after you start pedaling you'd understand in an instant.

The main parts of Documents To Go on the Palm device are as follows:

- ✔ Word To Go: This program manages your word processing documents.
- ✔ Sheet To Go: This program handles your spreadsheets.
- ✔ Slideshow To Go: This program lets you view your presentations.

The fourth, hidden function of Documents to Go is the ability to read electronic books in the DOC format that is popular among Palm ebook fans. You can use Documents To Go with the types of files that most people use most frequently (word-processing documents, spreadsheets, and PowerPoint presentations). However, the program can't handle less popular types of files such as database files created in Microsoft Access or files created in special-purpose programs written especially for your business.

Sending an Office document to your Palm device

Documents To Go lets you keep identical copies of your favorite documents on both your Palm device and your desktop computer. I recommend being selective about which files you decide to carry around to avoid overloading your handheld or making things needlessly confusing. To transfer a document from your computer to your handheld, follow these steps:

1. **Click the Documents To Go icon on the main screen of your desktop computer.**

   The Documents To Go screen appears, as shown in Figure 10-1.

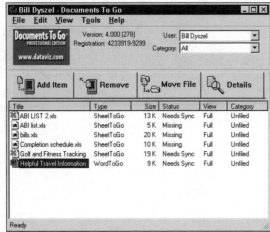

Figure 10-1:
The Documents To Go screen shows the documents you've selected to carry on your Palm device.

2. **Click the Add Item button on the Documents To Go toolbar.**

   The Open dialog Box appears, showing the files in your My Documents folder.

3. **Double-click the name of the file you want to send to your Palm device.**

   The My Documents screen closes and the file you chose appears in the list of files being managed by Documents To Go.

4. **Perform a HotSync to send a copy of the document you chose to your Palm device.**

After you send a file to your Palm device via Documents To Go, you end up with two documents, one on the desktop and one on the Palm device. If you make changes to one of the two, you need to perform a HotSync to make the two match. If you make changes to both the desktop copy and the Palm copy before performing a HotSync, Documents To Go creates a second copy of the document on each platform, in which case you have *four* copies of the document.

Opening a file on your Palm device

If you know how to open a document on your desktop computer, the details of opening that same document in Documents To Go are a bit different, but the basic idea is the same:

1. **Tap the Applications soft button.**

   Your list of applications appears.

2. **Tap the Documents To Go icon.**

   The Documents To Go application appears, showing a list of your documents, as shown in Figure 10-2. If you have a particularly long list of documents, you may need to press the scroll-down button at the bottom of your Palm device to scroll through your list until you find the document you're looking for.

Figure 10-2:
All the documents you've sent to your Palm device are listed in the main Documents To Go screen.

3. **Tap the name of document you want to view or edit.**

   Your document opens.

Don't be surprised if a document looks very different on your Palm device than it looks on your desktop computer. Remember, that tiny Palm screen only shows a little bit of your document, often just the upper-left corner. If you tried to display the whole document on your Palm screen like you do on a desktop computer screen, the letters would be too small to read (unless you have incredible vision). Chances are you'll need to scroll around your document to see what you want to see.

Changing a file on your Palm device

Changing the contents of a file on your Palm device is pretty similar to making changes to documents on the desktop. Naturally, some things differ because the screen is so much smaller and because you have no mouse and often no keyboard.

✔ **Add text:** To add text tap the spot where you want the new text to appear, then enter text using your favorite keyboard or Graffiti.

✔ **Select text:** To select text, drag your stylus across the text you want to remove, keeping the stylus tip on the surface of the screen; it's just like "dragging" your mouse over text you want to select on a desktop computer.

✔ **Delete text:** To delete text, tap immediately to the right of the letters you want to delete, then enter the Graffiti backspace character or press the backspace key on your favorite keyboard. You can also select some text, then enter the backspace character.

Closing a file on your Palm device

After you finish viewing or editing a document on your Palm device, you can just tap the Done button at the bottom of the screen to tell the program to close your document. If you've made no changes, the document closes right away. If you've made any changes at all to the document you're closing, the Save Changes? dialog box appears containing four question buttons. A four-button screen seems to imply complex choices to make, but don't worry — you just choose from four simple but slightly different possibilities:

✔ **Save Changes:** This means your document stays the way it now is, including the changes you just made.

✔ **Save As:** This button invites you to create a new document under a new name that reflects your changes, leaving the old document unchanged.

✔ **Don't Save Changes:** Tapping this button closes the screen and throws your changes away. This is an especially welcome choice when you get a document all messed up. It's like saying "Oh, never mind!"

✔ **Return to Document:** This choice sends you right back to where you were before you tapped the Done button, leaving you to make even more changes or to double-check the accuracy of your document before you close it.

Remember, the changes you make to documents on your Palm device don't take effect on your desktop until you perform a HotSync

Bookmarks in Word To Go

Getting from the beginning to the end of a Word To Go item is simply a matter of holding down the Scroll Down button at the bottom of the Palm case until the end of your text appears. If you're dealing with a document that's more than a few hundred words long, you may find the scrolling tedious, so you may want to take advantage of the bookmark feature. Bookmarks are just little hidden "milestones" that you can add to a document to help you find your way around more quickly.

Creating Word To Go bookmarks

Follow these steps to add a bookmark:

1. **Open a document in Documents To Go on your Palm device.**

   The contents of your document appear on the screen.

2. **Tap the spot where you want to place a bookmark.**

   The insertion point (a blinking bar) appears at the spot you tapped.

3. **Tap the Bookmark List triangle at the bottom center of the screen.**

   That little triangle at the bottom of the Word To Go screen has no label, so you might not think to tap it, but that's where the bookmarks are hidden. When you tap the triangle to the right of the Find button you'll see a list of your bookmarks (if you've created any) and the two lines that say Add Bookmark . . . and Edit Bookmarks . . . (as shown in Figure 10-3).

Figure 10-3: Tap the name of a bookmark to jump to a different part of your document.

4. **Tap the words "Add Bookmark . . ."**

   The Add Bookmark dialog box appears.

5. **Enter the name you want to give your bookmark using either Graffiti or your favorite keyboard.**

   The name you enter appears in the Add Bookmark dialog box.

6. **Tap OK.**

   The Add Bookmark dialog box closes.

Congratulations! You've now made your bookmark. Another way to add bookmarks to your documents is to use the Bookmark feature in Microsoft Word on your desktop. Just click the spot in your document where you want to place a bookmark, then choose Insert⇨Bookmark.

Using Word To Go bookmarks

Whether you created bookmarks on the Palm device or the desktop, they work the same way. Let's say you want to jump from the beginning of a document to a bookmark a spot about three quarters of the way into a document. Just choose the bookmark

1. **Tap the Bookmark List triangle at the bottom center of the screen.**

   Your list of bookmarks appears.

2. **Tap the name of the bookmark to which you want to jump.**

   The text you want to jump to appears.

Most people don't bother to use the Bookmark feature of Microsoft Word because they don't really need to on a desktop computer. On a Palm device, bookmarks let you get around documents a lot more easily.

Advanced Word To Go

Most people who use Documents To Go will never create (or even edit) a document on their Palm devices, but they'll be delighted that they can keep important documents handy for reference. For the three of you who get around to trying out the more advanced features, here are some things do:

- ✔ **Formatting text.** You can apply bold, underline, or italics to text by selecting the text, and then tapping the formatting buttons at the top of the screen. You're probably used to doing exactly the same thing on your desktop computer. You can also change the size of the typeface from small to large by selecting some text, tapping the Menu button, and then choosing Edit ⇨Font.

- ✔ **Creating new documents from old ones.** If you have a standard form letter or proposal that you use over and over, you can create a fill-in-the-blanks sample document to use as a template. To create a new document from your sample document, just open the sample document, tap the Menu soft button, and then choose Options⇨Save As and enter a new name for your document.

- ✔ **Creating new documents from scratch.** In most cases, you'll create your Documents To Go files on your desktop computer and then HotSync them to your Palm device. To create a new file in Documents To Go, tap the New button on the main screen of Documents To Go, enter a new file name, and then tap OK.

Spreadsheet Specialties

Somebody smarter than me once said, "Figures don't lie, but liars sure can figure." You never know when you'll need to out-figure somebody, so you'll be glad if you have Sheet To Go loaded and ready to figure out who's lying and who's going by the numbers.

Sheet To Go is designed to work seamlessly with popular spreadsheet programs like Microsoft Excel. In this chapter, I'm going to presume that you know how to use that program, but if you don't; I'd like to suggest an excellent book called *Office XP 9 in 1 Desk Reference For Dummies* by Peter Weverka (Wiley Publishing, Inc.) for a more complete explanation.

Navigating spreadsheets

Chances are that you'll be creating your spreadsheets on your desktop computer, using Microsoft Excel, most likely. But even if you don't create spreadsheets on your Palm device, you need to know how to get from one cell to another. Here are several ways to navigate in a Sheet To Go:

- **Tap a cell.** Yep, just tap any cell you see and (presto!) you select that cell. What you tap is what you get.

- **Scroll up or down.** As usual, the up and down scroll buttons at the bottom of the Palm case move the information on the screen up or down so that you can see more cells.

- **On-screen scroll buttons.** At the bottom of the Sheet To Go screen there are a bunch of triangles. One points up, one points down, two point left, and two point right. Tapping any of those triangles moves your view up or down, left or right.

- **The Go button.** When you tap the Go button at the lower right corner of the screen, the Go dialog box opens, which you can see in Figure 10-4. This dialog box offers two ways to change your location:

  - The simplest is to enter the cell you want to move to (such as D27) and tap the Go button in the dialog box.

  - You can also jump to any bookmark in your spreadsheet by tapping the word Bookmarks in the Go dialog box and then tapping the name of that bookmark in the list that appears.

- **Switch pages.** If you're viewing a spreadsheet with multiple pages, you can change the page you're viewing by tapping the page name in the upper-right corner of the screen to show the list of all page names, as shown in Figure 10-5, and then tapping the name of the page you want to view.

Figure 10-4:
You can
jump to any
cell in your
spreadsheet
by tapping
the Go
button.

Figure 10-5:
You can see
a list of all
the sheets
in your
workbook
by clicking
the sheet
name in the
upper-right
corner of
the screen.

When you tap a cell, that cell is selected, which means that you can then change the contents of that cell. You can select multiple cells by dragging your stylus over a range of cells.

An easy way to move around a Sheet To Go page is to drag your stylus to the edge of the screen in the direction of the cell you want to view. Technically, dragging your stylus selects a range of cells, but it also moves the display, so you end up moving around the sheet pretty quickly. Just drag until you see the cell you want to see, then tap the cell once to select it.

Entering spreadsheet data

One valuable reason to keep spreadsheets on your Palm device is to help you collect data in the field. Well, you don't actually have to be out in a field; you could be at a building site or at a warehouse or on the street. Any time you want to collect information outside the office and you still need to use it in the office, you'll probably save time by entering it into a spreadsheet.

You can enter several different types of information in several different ways in Sheet To Go:

- ✔ **Entering text and numbers:** To enter either text or numbers in a cell, just tap on a cell to select it, and then enter the information you want in that cell by using Graffiti or your favorite keyboard. When you've finished entering your information, tap any other cell in the spreadsheet.

- ✔ **Creating formulas:** To begin entering a formula, tap the f×️ button at the bottom of the screen. Tapping this button enters the equal sign that begins your formula and opens the toolbar with buttons for entering the plus sign, parentheses, and all the other mathematical operators.

- ✔ **Formatting cells:** You can apply formatting to any cell by tapping that cell to select it, and then tapping Menu⇨Format⇨Cell. To format a number, tap the cell containing the number, and then tap Menu⇨Format⇨Number and choose the kind of number you want (currency, date, time, percent, and so on).

If you have a spreadsheet that you view frequently in Sheet To Go, you may want to consider rearranging the cells for better viewing on your Palm device. Since most of us read from top to bottom and left to right, we often put important summary information, such as price totals, at the bottom or right-hand side of a spreadsheet. That's fine when you're looking at the numbers on paper or on a big screen, but because Palm programs only show you the top-right corner of spreadsheets when you start, you may end up missing the "bottom-line" numbers you really want to see. Consider building your spreadsheets with totals at the top and left side of the sheet.

Presentation Power

You may not believe you could do a PowerPoint presentation on a palm-sized computer, but if you have Documents To Go on one of those slick Sony Clie models with those amazing color screens, you may want to start thinking about palm-sized presenting when you're presenting to only one or two people at a time. The following reasons for using Slideshow To Go may apply to you:

- ✔ If you keep a PowerPoint presentation on your Palm device, you can review your presentation and even rehearse a bit before delivering it.

- ✔ Sometimes you can't fire up your laptop to check your presentation, but you might want to sneak a discreet peek at your Palm device.

One thing you can't do with the Slideshow To Go program is actually feed a presentation to a projector from your Palm device. Palm accessories do exist for that purpose, but the Documents To Go developers aren't aiming at that market.

When you open a presentation on Slideshow To Go, you can view your presentation several different ways, just like you can in PowerPoint. The three icons at the top of the screen let you switch among views:

- ✔ **Outline view:** The leftmost icon shows you the Outline view of your presentation. That's the view you use to change the text of your presentation.

- ✔ **Slideshow view:** The center icon shows you the Slideshow view. This is the view you use when you want to show your slides to someone else on your Palm device.

- ✔ **Notes view:** The right-most icon shows your Notes view for referring to the notes you use for giving your speech.

You can advance your presentation from one slide to the next just like you can in PowerPoint by pressing one of the scroll buttons at the bottom of the Palm case. If you want to skip between slides rather than advancing one by one, tap the triangle at the top-right corner of the screen to reveal a drop-down list of all your slides, listed by title. Just tap the name of the slide you want to see.

That tiny Palm screen can make your slides pretty tough to read, especially for those of us whose eyesight isn't as keen as it used to be. You can get a magnified view of your slides by tapping the button containing the plus sign at the bottom of the screen in the slide view. Or you could buy a magnifying glass like Sherlock Holmes. Elementary!

Beaming to Others

After you get the hang of the convenience of having Documents To Go on your Palm device, you'll wish everybody else did too. Well, you can! Just beam it to them. You can't beam the actual Documents To Go program to other people, but when you beam items from Documents To Go, the program sends a free viewer program along with the document so that your recipient can read the file.

If you look at the Documents To Go main screen, you notice that each document name displays an icon to the right, containing the letter I. If you tap that icon, the Document Details dialog box appears; then you see the Beam button at the bottom of the screen. Tapping the Beam button opens another dialog box, inviting you to Beam Application and Document (that is, both Documents To Go *and* the document) or just the document. If the persons to whom you want to beam your masterpiece don't already have Documents To Go, just beam the application to 'em, and *then* send your document. That'll knock their socks off.

Chapter 11

Using the PalmModem

You may already know this, but a *modem* is a little gizmo that connects a computer to a telephone line so it can connect to the Internet. Because you can connect your Palm device to nearly anything but your Mixmaster, you won't be surprised to find that you can connect your Palm organizer to the phone, too, by using a palm-sized modem designed to hang off the back of your Palm device.

However, it's become so easy to connect your Palm device to the Internet wirelessly that you may ask, "Why would I want to connect my Palm device to a telephone line?" The answer is simple: "You probably don't." I've met thousands of people with Palm computers over the years, and I probably haven't met a dozen who have ever used a Palm device with a modem even once.

There are very specific circumstances for giving your Palm device a wired connection to the Internet, particularly situations where you need to connect from a remote location beyond the range of wireless networks. If you happen to be in that kind of situation frequently, this chapter is for you. Some companies in the modem business totally stopped selling modems for handheld computers. That's a hint — go wireless if at all possible. For more about wireless connections, see Chapter 15 of this book.

PalmModem Basics

If you've just purchased a shiny, new, store-bought Palm device and a PalmModem, making them work together is fairly simple. When you see the Palm device and its modem together, you instinctively know how to attach them to one another. Just set your Palm organizer in the modem the same way you place the Palm device in its cradle and plug a phone line into the modem. The two work together seamlessly right from the get-go. After you've used your Palm organizer for a while, however, you may need to change some settings. This section gives you the nitty-gritty details about the PalmModem.

Each type of Palm organizer connects to a different type of modem. Devices from the Palm m100 and m500 series use one kind of modem, older Palm III and VII series units use a different kind of modem, the Palm V uses yet another, and the Handspring Visor requires an entirely different kind of modem. The Palm m100 doesn't accommodate a modem at all. Usually the people who sold you your Palm device can also sell you the right kind of modem. And if that's not confusing enough, you can get wireless modems that connect your Palm device to the Internet via radio, just like a cell phone. In this chapter, I'm just talking about regular modems that connect to a telephone wire. For more about wireless connections for your Palm device, see Chapter 15.

Setting up your modem

Your PalmModem doesn't need much attention. You can set it up in a snap. Here's the routine:

1. **Connect your Palm device to the modem.**

   The Palm device makes a slight snapping sound as it fits snugly into the modem, and a Visor modem snaps into the back of the Visor case.

2. **Plug a phone line into the modem.**

   The phone line snaps into your modem the same way it does when you plug it into your phone.

You need to plug a telephone line into your modem, of course. The jack, which looks just like the jack on your home telephone, is located on the case. Simply unplug the wire that goes into your telephone, and then plug the wire into your modem.

Not all phone lines are alike. Your home phone line is the right type of phone line to use with your modem. It's an *analog* line, the old-fashioned kind of phone line. Offices and hotels often use digital lines. Do not plug your modem into a digital line! In some cases, plugging your modem into a digital line can damage the modem. Many hotels now have phones with a special jack on the side labeled *modem* or *data* in which you can safely plug your modem. If you're not sure whether a certain line is analog or digital, just ask. You can feel fairly confident that a phone line in a private home is safe. In an office, a phone line attached to a fax machine is also a good bet.

Setting up your Palm device to use the modem

After you connect your Palm device to the modem and plug in a suitable phone line, you're connected. Just tell your Palm device the type of modem you're attaching and then enter the settings for the kinds of things you want to do.

To set up your Palm device to work with a PalmModem, simply plug your Palm device into the modem. The factory settings on a new Palm device enable it to run the PalmModem quite nicely. If your Palm device isn't factory-new, however, someone may have changed the settings. To adjust the modem settings (or to make sure your current settings are correct), follow these steps:

1. **Tap the Applications soft button to the left of the Graffiti area.**

   The applications list appears, showing icons for all the programs installed on your Palm device.

2. **Tap the Prefs icon.**

   The Preferences screen appears.

3. **Tap the pull-down menu in the upper-right corner of the screen.**

   The list of preferences categories appears.

4. **Tap Connection.**

   The Connection Preferences screen appears, as shown in Figure 11-1.

5. **Tap the word PalmModem in the list of available connections.**

   The word PalmModem is highlighted to show you've selected it.

6. **Tap Edit.**

   The Edit Connection screen appears. Make sure the first three settings read as follows:

   - Connect to: Modem

   - Via: Cradle/Cable

   - Dialing: TouchTone (Unless you are certain that the phone line you're using only supports rotary or pulse dialing. In that case, tap the word TouchTone; then tap the word Rotary from the drop-down menu.)

   - Volume: Low (You can set this to whatever volume you want; it won't affect the performance of the PalmModem.)

7. **Tap OK.**

Figure 11-1:
To reconfigure your
modem, go
to the
Connection
Preferences
screen.

 You can fiddle around with your modem settings a little bit without causing big problems with the way your modem works, but be careful about changing too much. Modems have a way of getting fussy during those precise moments when you can't call someone for help, so after you get things working, leave the settings alone.

Setting Up Your Palm Device for a Modem HotSync

The main purpose of the PalmModem is to enable you to HotSync your Palm device with your desktop computer via a phone line. To successfully HotSync over the telephone, you have to set up your desktop computer (as well as your Palm device) in advance.

If you plan to take your Palm device on your voyage to Mongolia and HotSync from there, you need to run a Local HotSync before you go. Also, don't forget your passport and some sensible shoes. If you haven't completed the Local HotSync process at least once, the HotSync Manager doesn't know what to do when it picks up the phone to do a Modem HotSync. Doing an initial Local HotSync is important because the HotSync Manager asks you to assign a username to your Palm device and then creates a set of files and folders dedicated to your Palm device. After you've completed a Local HotSync, the HotSync Manager knows which Palm device it's dealing with and where to store information. For more info about how to HotSync and set up your Palm Desktop program, refer to Chapter 14.

Entering your Modem HotSync phone number

When you perform a Modem HotSync, your Palm device calls your desktop computer on the phone and then runs the HotSync program. The most important information you have to supply is the phone number that your desktop computer answers.

To enter the HotSync phone number:

1. **Tap the Applications soft button to the left of the Graffiti area.**

   The applications list appears, showing icons for all the programs installed on your Palm device.

2. **Tap the HotSync icon.**

   The HotSync screen appears. If you've never entered a HotSync phone number, the box below the Modem Sync icon says `Enter Phone #`; otherwise, the phone number you've already entered appears there.

3. **Tap Enter Phone #.**

   The Phone Setup screen appears, as shown in Figure 11-2.

4. **Enter the phone number to which your desktop computer is connected by using either the on-screen keyboard or Graffiti. (Refer to Chapter 2 for more info about entering text.)**

   The number you enter appears on the `Phone #` line.

5. **If the phone system you're calling from requires you to dial a prefix before making a call, tap the Dial Prefix check box and enter the prefix after Dial Prefix.**

   Some offices and hotels require you to dial an 8 or a 9 before making a call. Enter the number your system requires on the `Dial Prefix` line.

Figure 11-2:
On the
Phone
Setup
screen,
enter the
phone
number that
you want
the HotSync
program to
call.

6. **If you're using a calling card, tap the Use Calling Card check box and enter your calling card number and PIN after the four commas on the line below Use Calling Card.**

   The four commas make the modem wait a few seconds before dialing the calling card number, just like you do when you dial the calling card number yourself.

7. **Tap OK.**

   The Phone Setup screen closes.

Disabling call waiting

I don't understand why call waiting is so popular; I hate interruptions during my phone conversations. Half the time, the people interrupting my calls are selling products I don't want.

Computers hate being interrupted by call waiting even more than I do. They often do crazy things when the little call-waiting beep sounds, but they never buy things from telemarketers. Fortunately, you can program your Palm device so it disables call waiting before a HotSync begins.

Follow these steps just once to tell your Palm device to turn off call waiting:

1. **Tap the Applications soft button to the left of the Graffiti area.**

   The applications list appears, showing icons for all the programs installed on your Palm device.

2. **Tap the HotSync icon.**

   The HotSync screen appears. The box below the Modem Sync icon displays either `Enter Phone #` or the last phone number you entered.

3. **Tap the box below the Modem Sync icon.**

   The Phone Setup dialog box opens.

4. **Tap the box next to Disable Call Waiting.**

   A check mark appears in the box to indicate you selected it.

   To the right of `Disable Call Waiting` is the number `1170`, which is usually the code you dial to turn off call waiting. If the number used to turn it off in your area is different, select the number that appears on-screen and then enter the number that does the trick in your locale.

5. **Tap OK.**

   The Phone Setup dialog box closes.

Setting up the Palm Desktop for a Modem HotSync

Doing a HotSync over the telephone has the same result as running a HotSync directly from your desktop computer: It makes the contents of your Palm device identical to the contents of your Palm Desktop. If you have e-mail messages on your desktop computer, copies of those messages are transferred to your Palm device.

When your Palm device performs a Modem HotSync, it dials the phone number of your desktop computer. Your desktop computer then has to answer the phone when the Palm device calls. To be able to answer that call, your desktop computer must

✔ Have a modem

✔ Be connected to a phone line

✔ Be running when you call

✔ Not be running any other communications program

✔ Be configured to accept your call

After that, it's easy! Because so many types of computers are out there, I can't tell you how to configure yours to accept your call. Refer to your owner's manual for that. But here's how to configure your computer to wait for your Modem HotSync call:

1. **Start the Palm Desktop by clicking the Palm Desktop icon.**

   The Palm Desktop appears.

2. **Choose HotSync➪Setup from the main menu on the Menu Bar.**

   The Setup dialog box opens.

3. **Click the Modem tab.**

   The modem settings page appears, as shown in Figure 11-3.

Figure 11-3:
On this tab, tell the HotSync program where your modem is installed so it can answer the phone.

4. **On the Serial Port list, choose the port to which your modem is assigned.**

   You can check which port your modem uses in Windows 95 or later by clicking the Start button, choosing Settings➪Control Panel, and then double-clicking the Modems icon. After the Modems dialog box opens, click the Properties button. The properties page tells you which port your modem uses. The ports are named COM1 through COM4.

   If you use Windows XP, choose Control Panel from the Start Menu, then click on the Phone and Modem icon, which will open the Phone and Modem options dialog box. Click on the Modem tab; you'll see what type of Modem is installed and which port it's using.

5. **In the Speed box, choose As Fast As Possible.**

   I don't know why you'd want to pick anything else. The speed you choose appears in the Speed box.

6. In the Modem box, choose the type of modem you're using.

You can check what type of modem you're using in Windows in the Control Panel, just like you checked the port in Step 4. If in doubt, Hayes Standard should work. The modem you choose appears in the Modem box. The setup string for the modem you pick automatically appears in the Setup String box. The *setup string* is the series of commands your modem uses to configure itself, so don't mess with the string.

7. Click OK.

The Setup dialog box closes.

8. Right-click the HotSync Manager icon on the Windows taskbar.

The HotSync Manager icon is in the lower-right corner of your screen; it is the little circle containing a red arrow and a blue arrow pointing in opposite directions. When you right-click the icon, the HotSync Manager menu appears.

9. If no check mark appears next to Modem, choose Modem.

A check mark appears next to Modem, as shown in Figure 11-4, and then the menu disappears.

Figure 11-4:
Click the HotSync icon on the Windows taskbar; then choose Modem.

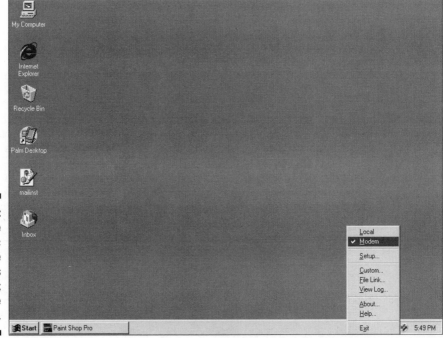

Now just leave your computer turned on and go your merry way.

I have both good news and bad news. The good news is that after you set up the HotSync Manager for a Modem HotSync, you can call up your desktop computer at any time to update your Palm device. The bad news is that nobody can receive phone calls on the phone line that your computer is connected to because the HotSync Manager answers *all* incoming calls. And you can't attach an answering machine to that computer. The HotSync Manager hogs the phone line whether your computer is running Windows or the Mac OS.

The Modem HotSync trick is best for people who call phone numbers that are totally dedicated to taking calls from computers, like the phone numbers many corporations have. If you need to HotSync by modem frequently, you may want to consider getting an extra phone line.

So why bother doing a Modem HotSync at all? Because doing a HotSync — at any time, anywhere — backs up your data. After you're completely addicted to your Palm device (admit it — you're hooked already), you depend on the collection of information you've amassed. If your Palm device falls from a gondola or gets rammed by a rhino in the course of your adventures, you can replace the little critter with a wave of your credit card, but you can lose months while trying to re-create the data you lost.

Palm Computing on the Internet

With the PalmModem or the Visor Modem, you can connect to the Internet and do two of the things that make the Internet so popular: exchange e-mail and browse the Web. I won't pretend that the little Palm device navigates the Internet as easily or impressively as your mighty desktop computer. The tiny gray screen shows you only so much. But like someone once said about a talking dog, no matter how well the trick is done, seeing it done at all is amazing.

Although you need some extra software to be able to exchange e-mail messages or browse Web pages, the foundations that enable you to access the Internet and take advantage of what it offers are already on your Palm device. The Palm operating system includes *TCP/IP*, the language that all computers connected to the Internet speak. You never actually see TCP/IP, but if you try to connect a computer to the Internet without it, nothing happens.

Setting up your Internet connection

Before you do anything on the Internet, you have to get connected. You need an ISP, or Internet service provider. An *ISP* is a company (such as Netcom or CompuServe) that gives you a phone number to dial when you want to connect to the Internet. You may be able to use the same ISP that you use to connect your desktop computer to the Internet. Just enter the same information in the Network Preferences program on your Palm device, and you're on your way. Check with your ISP to see whether you can connect your Palm device to the Internet through your ISP's servers.

When you set up your Internet connection, you also have to set up your modem as I describe in the section "Setting up your Palm device to use the modem," earlier in this chapter.

To set up your Palm device to dial your ISP:

1. **Tap the Applications soft button to the left of the Graffiti area.**

   The applications list appears, showing icons for all the programs installed on your Palm device.

2. **Tap the Prefs icon.**

   The Preferences screen appears.

3. **Tap the pull-down menu in the upper-right corner of the screen.**

   The list of preferences categories appears.

4. **Tap Network.**

   The Network Preferences screen appears, as shown in Figure 11-5.

Figure 11-5: On the Network Preferences screen, tell your Palm device how to connect to the Internet.

5. **Tap the triangle next to Service.**

   A list of the services with which the Palm device is ready to connect appears.

6. **Tap the name of the Internet service provider you use.**

   The name of the service you tap appears next to the word *Service*.

   If your ISP doesn't appear, call up your ISP's tech-support area and ask what the folks there recommend.

7. **Enter your username on the User Name line by using either the on-screen keyboard or Graffiti. (Refer to Chapter 2 for more info about entering text.)**

   If the User Name line is blank, just tap the line and enter your username. If temporary text appears on the User Name line, select the text and then enter your username.

8. **Tap the box next to Password.**

   The Password dialog box opens, as shown in Figure 11-6.

Figure 11-6:
Enter your
Internet
password
in the
Password
dialog box.

9. **Enter your password.**

   The password you enter appears in the Password dialog box.

10. **Tap OK.**

    The Password dialog box closes.

11. **Make sure the Connection line shows the name of the type of connection you're planning to use (most likely PalmModem).**

    If the Connection line doesn't show the type of connection you want, tap the triangle next to the word Connection and choose from the drop-down list.

12. **Tap the box next to Phone.**

    The Phone Setup screen appears.

13. **Enter the phone number of your Internet Service Provider by using either the on-screen keyboard or Graffiti. (Refer to Chapter 2 for more info about entering text with Graffiti or a keyboard.)**

    The phone number you enter appears on the Phone # line. You can also set up a dial prefix and a calling card number exactly the same way that I describe earlier in this chapter.

14. **Tap OK.**

    The Phone Setup screen closes.

After you set up your network preferences, you probably won't have to mess with them again except to change the ISP phone number when you're traveling. Because many ISPs have toll-free 800 numbers you can use everywhere, you can travel anywhere in North America without changing the phone number.

The Connect button at the bottom of the Network Preferences screen makes the modem dial the phone number you've entered and connects you to the Internet. You usually don't need to tap the Connect button because most e-mail programs and Web browsers connect you automatically. In a pinch, though, you can return to the Network Preferences screen and tap Connect to force your Palm device to connect to the Internet. After you're connected, that same button says Disconnect, so you can tap the Disconnect button to force your Palm device to disconnect from the Internet.

Tapping the Details button displays a screen showing some nitty-gritty details that your Palm device needs to know to connect to the Internet. I can't think of any reason why you'd change those settings, so leave them alone.

Browsing the Web

So you can't believe you can surf the Internet on your Palm device? Well, it's true. Granted, most Web sites look poor on that teensy little screen. But, you can find a great deal of text on the Internet, too, and text looks fine on an itty-bitty screen.

There's a catch, of course. Before you can surf the Web with your Palm device, you need two things: an Internet connection and a Web browser. In the "Setting up your Internet connection" section, earlier in this chapter, I show you how to connect to the Internet. You also have to get a Web browser and install it on your Palm device.

My favorite browser at the moment is Blazer from Handspring, the people who make the Visor and Treo handhelds. Blazer is a zippy, full-color Web browsing program that does a nice job of reformatting Web pages to make them look decent on a small screen. Many handheld computers offered by Handspring include a free copy of Blazer (and so do certain Handspring accessories). If you didn't get a free copy, you can buy one from Handspring and run it on any Palm-powered device.

International incidentals

Like a hair dryer or an electric razor, the PalmModem is designed for use in the United States and Canada. If you want to connect your PalmModem to telephone systems outside North America, you may have to buy adapters and make special arrangements because the telephone lines and electrical outlets outside North America sometimes don't work with American electronics. I know of one company, iGo, that specializes in supplying gear to people who travel with computers. Check out the company's Web site, at www.igo.com, for details about equipment that enables you to hook up a computer in any country on Earth.

Part IV

Making the Palm Connection to Bigger Things

The 5th Wave   By Rich Tennant

"Most of our product line is doing well, but the expanding touch pad on our PDA keeps opening unexpectedly."

In this part . . .

A lot of punch is packed into that little Palm device, but a whole world of possibilities opens up when you hook your Palm device to something bigger (say, your desktop computer, company network, or the Internet). In this part, I show you how to connect your Palm organizer to the wider online world — and how to make that connection pay off.

Chapter 12

Operating the Palm Desktop Program

In This Chapter

▶ Understanding the Palm Desktop interface

▶ Organizing your appointments in the Date Book

▶ Setting up your Address Book

▶ Tracking your to-dos

▶ Working with memos

*Y*ou may ask, "If a Palm device is so great, why use a desktop computer at all?" Now take a breath. I know how enthusiastic people get about their handheld computers, but the little critters were never intended to send your desktop computer the way of the dinosaur. Not yet, anyway. The people who designed the Palm organizer intended the two to work as a team, so you need a program for your desktop computer that talks to your Palm device and makes entering and retrieving information from such a tiny gadget a little easier.

In this chapter, I tell you all about the Palm Desktop program for Windows that comes with your Palm device. It's a perfectly good program for keeping track of appointments, addresses, and the other stuff that most people keep on their Palm devices, but you may decide not to use the Palm Desktop for several good reasons:

✔ **You use Microsoft Office 97, 2000, or XP for Windows.** You may already be keeping track of names and dates in Microsoft Outlook because it's included with Microsoft Office. Outlook is a rich program; so rich that I've written an entirely separate book to cover it. Check out *Outlook 2002 For Dummies* (published by Wiley Publishing, Inc.). Outlook thinks the same way your Palm device does and ties in with Office so well that it only makes sense to use Outlook instead of Palm Desktop. Also, the Palm installation program automatically links your Palm handheld to Outlook if it finds Outlook on your computer. So using Outlook is by far the easiest way to go.

✔ **You use a Macintosh.** As with many other Mac programs, the Palm Desktop program for the Mac is a different critter than its Windows counterpart. While the general ideas of using the Mac version are similar, the details differ. However, Mac partisans swear it's much easier to use on the Mac (but then, they always do).

✔ **You use ACT!, Goldmine, or one of those other highfalutin' contact managers.** A number of other programs for managing names and dates are available, and you may be deeply attached to one of them. Your current preference is probably okay because you can connect your Palm device with most personal information managers.

If your program doesn't connect with a Palm device without help, you should consider using a program called Intellisync from Puma. Intellisync can make your Palm device talk to nearly anything but the ghost of Jimmy Hoffa, Sr. (and he ain't talkin'). Check out `www.palmpilotfordummies.com/intellisync` for more information.

A Palm device does an amazing amount of work for a little gizmo with a tiny screen and a half-dozen buttons. But there's nothing like a big old computer with an old-fashioned keyboard and mouse for whipping off appointments, memos, to-dos, and addresses in a flash. Remember, though: You can use both the Palm Desktop and your Palm device to enter your data — whatever suits your fancy. In this section, I give you an overview of the Palm Desktop interface and take you on a tour of the basic applications of the Palm Desktop.

Understanding the Palm Desktop Interface

Interface is a techie term that computer geeks use to describe what you see on your computer screen after you open a program. The Palm Desktop's interface is made up of the same elements that most programs' screens contain, plus the elements of the Palm device screens. You can see the name of the program in the upper-left corner of the screen, in the title bar area. Below that is the menu bar, which works just like the menu bar in other computer programs. Below the menu bar sits the toolbar, as shown in Figure 12-1, containing a row of icons you can click to perform tasks easily.

On the left edge of the Palm Desktop screen is a column of buttons named *launch bar*. The names of the buttons correspond to those of the standard Palm organizer applications: Date, Address, To Do, and Memo. Clicking any of these buttons launches the corresponding application.

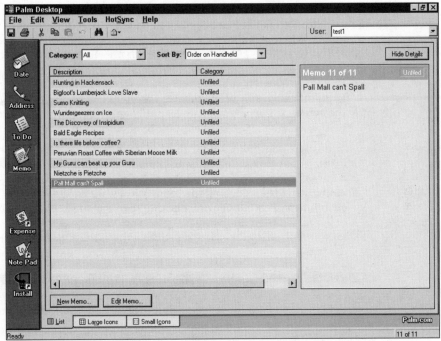

Figure 12-1:
The Palm
Desktop
toolbar.

Below the four application buttons are two more buttons labeled Expense and Install. The Expense button starts up the special Microsoft Excel spreadsheet that's filled with data from your Palm Expense application (if you use it). If you don't have Excel on your computer, the Palm Desktop Expense button does nothing, although you can still see it.

The Install button launches the Palm Install Tool for installing programs on your Palm device. Just one click launches the program for you. (For more info about installing Palm applications, see Chapter 13.)

Arranging Appointments in Your Date Book

The Date Book on the Palm Desktop has many of the same parts as the Date Book screens on your handheld, but the Palm Desktop organizes things a bit differently because your computer screen has more room to display items than your Palm device screen does.

To open the Date Book, click the Date icon on the left side of the screen. Along the bottom of the Date Book, you can see three tabs labeled Day, Week, and Month. When you click any of those tabs, the view on the screen changes to the view you clicked. Here's the lowdown on what you see in each view:

✔ **Day view:** The left side of the Palm device in Day view shows a list of appointments for a single day, as shown in Figure 12-2. The right side of the screen shows a miniature monthly calendar. When you click a date on that calendar, the list of appointments for that date appears.

The small monthly calendar that appears on the right side of the screen displays the current month and the following month. You can switch to a different month by clicking the name of the month to reveal a list of months and then clicking the month you want to see. You can also switch to a different year by clicking the year to show a drop-down list of years and then choosing the year you want to see from that list. You may end up using Day view more than the other views (at least I do).

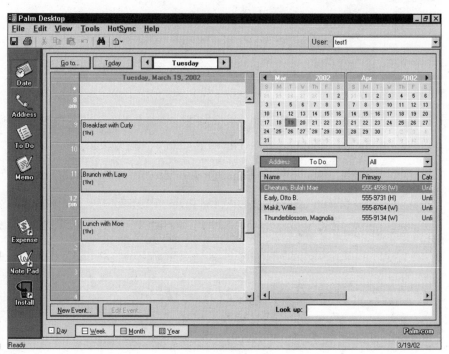

Figure 12-2: Why, I oughta check my date book!

✔ **Week view:** Whenever you want to see how your week is shaping up, Week view shows a grid representing the whole work week. Week view works just like it does on your Palm device, although Palm Desktop shows you the names of your appointments, whereas your Palm device shows you only bars representing the appointments.

✔ **Month view:** If you like to think ahead, Month view shows you what you're doing for the whole month. In this view, Palm Desktop gives you more detail than your Palm device because your computer screen is larger.

✔ **Year view:** When you need to see the really big picture, click the Year tab and see how much longer you have to wait for that hefty year-end bonus. (I spent mine already; I got *two* gumballs.) If you double-click on a date in the year view, details for that date appear.

For more info about using the Date Book on your Palm device, see Chapter 8. To bring up your Date Book in Palm Desktop, just click the Date button on the left side of the screen or choose View⇨Date Book from the menu bar, and then continue to the following sections.

Adding appointments

Entering appointments in your Palm Desktop is undoubtedly faster than entering them on your Palm device itself, as long as you're sitting at your big computer. If you're out in the field or at a meeting, the story is different.

While you're sitting at the keyboard, follow these steps to add an appointment to the Palm Desktop:

1. **With the Date Book visible, click the Day tab on the right edge of the screen (or press Alt+D).**

   Daily view of your Date Book appears.

2. **Click the date of your appointment on the calendar, which is on the right side of the screen.**

   The Date Book shows the appointments scheduled for that date.

3. **Click the line next to the hour when you want your appointment to begin.**

   A box opens where you clicked, and a blinking bar (an *insertion point*) appears. The first line of Daily view, next to the black diamond, has no time assigned to it; you can click there to enter events that last all day or that have no specific time assigned.

4. **Type a subject for your appointment.**

   The subject appears on the schedule.

5. **Click any other part of the screen (or press Tab).**

   Your appointment appears shaded to show you entered it.

I describe the method of adding appointments to Daily view of your calendar on the Palm Desktop because it is most similar to the way you add appointments on the Palm device. You have more flexibility in how you enter appointments on the desktop, though. For example, Palm Desktop enables you to add appointments in Weekly view and Monthly view — something you can't do on a Palm device. To add an appointment in Weekly view, just follow Steps 3 through 5 in the preceding example.

You may have noticed the New Event button at the bottom of the Day view screen. That's the button that opens the New Event dialog box. You can always use the New Event dialog box for entering a new appointment, which is frankly the most complete and detailed way to enter information, but I think it's a little cumbersome. You can read more about the Edit Event dialog box in the following sections.

Repeating appointments

Anything worth doing is worth doing at least once a week — that's my opinion. Especially days off. Try to make a habit of those, won't you? And note them in your Palm Desktop, like this:

1. **With the Date Book visible, click the Day tab on the right edge of the screen (or press Alt+D).**

   The Daily view of your Date Book appears.

2. **Click the date of your appointment on the calendar, which is on the right side of the screen.**

   The Date Book shows the appointments scheduled for that date.

3. **Click the appointment you want to repeat in your Date Book.**

   The appointment's shaded box appears shadowed to show that you selected it.

4. **Click Edit Event at the bottom of the screen (or choose Edit➪Edit Event from the menu bar).**

   The Edit Event dialog box opens.

5. **Click the Repeat tab in the Edit Event dialog box.**

   The Repeat page appears, as shown in Figure 12-3.

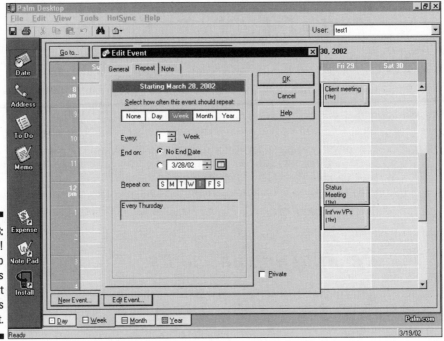

Figure 12-3:
Do it again!
Set up
appointments
that repeat
as often as
you want.

6. **Click the name of the repeat pattern you want.**

   The name you choose is selected, and options for that pattern appear.

7. **Enter the choices you want for the repeat pattern you chose.**

   The choices you make appear in the Change Repeat dialog box. The text box at the bottom of the dialog box confirms your choices. You can choose from a variety of daily, weekly, and monthly repeating patterns.

8. **Click OK.**

   The Edit Event dialog box closes, and a little circle appears next to your appointment to show it repeats.

One tricky thing about repeating appointments is that every time you change one, the Palm device asks if you're just changing this one appointment or the whole series. Don't be alarmed; just click the All button if you want to change all instances of the appointment, or click Current if you just want to change this instance of the appointment.

Making appointments private

Private appointments work pretty much the same way as private memos do except the check box is on the main screen, not hidden. See the "Making a memo private" section, later in this chapter. To find the hidden check box that makes an appointment private, click the appointment to select it and then click the Edit Event button at the bottom of the screen. That action opens the Edit Event dialog box, which contains the Private check box.

Whenever you mark an appointment as private, a tiny lock appears in the upper-left corner of the appointment box. You can hide all private records by choosing View⇨Hide Private Records from the menu bar. When you hide private records, a lock appears on the toolbar. You can show private records again by choosing View⇨Show Private Records.

Deleting appointments

Sometimes, you may tell a person that you can "pencil him in," which implies that you may erase him, too. All appointments on your Palm device are "penciled in" in a way because erasing them is so easy.

Take these steps to delete an appointment from your Palm Desktop:

1. **With the Date Book visible, click the Day tab on the right edge of the screen (or press Alt+D).**

   The Daily view of your Date Book appears.

   You can also click the Week tab. If you prefer to view your whole week at a glance, jump ahead to Step 3.

2. **Click the date of your appointment on the calendar on the right side of the screen.**

   The Date Book shows the appointments scheduled for that date.

3. **Click the appointment that you want to delete.**

   The appointment's shaded box opens, and the shadowing shows you selected it.

4. **Press the Delete key (or choose Edit⇨Delete from the menu bar).**

   The Delete Date Book Items dialog box opens.

5. **Click OK if you want your appointment to disappear, or click Cancel if you have a change of heart.**

   If you leave the Archive box checked in the Delete Date Book Items dialog box, the appointment isn't lost forever. It automatically moves to an archive file, where you can look it up later. You can find out more about archiving in the next chapter.

Arranging Entries in Your Address Book

Keeping that little black book on a pocket computer is wonderfully efficient and amazingly quick, but it has one big drawback: What if you lose the thing? Yikes! Losing a contact lens is nothing compared to losing your personal organizer.

Fortunately, you can maintain the whole mess on your desktop computer, where it's all safe and sound and backed up. What are the chances of losing both your desktop computer and your Palm device at the same time? Do you really want to find out? I didn't think so.

To bring up your Address Book, just click the Address button on the left side of the screen, or choose View⇨Address Book from the menu bar and continue to the following sections. You won't have a problem making sense of the Address Book. When you open it, a list of names appears on the left side of the screen, and full details of the person you select from the list appear on the right.

Adding a new Address Book entry

You can keep track of as little or as much information as you want about each person in the Address Book. Just fill out the form.

To add a new entry to your Address Book on the Palm Desktop, do the following:

1. **With the Address Book visible, click New Address at the bottom of the screen (or choose Edit⇨New Address from the menu bar).**

   The New Address dialog box opens.

2. **Type the last name of the contact in the Last Name text box.**

   The text appears in the Last Name text box, as shown in Figure 12-4.

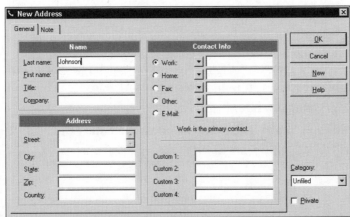

Figure 12-4:
To add a new address, fill out the form, please.

3. **Enter the contact's first name, title, and company in the appropriate boxes.**

4. **Enter the contact's telephone number in the appropriate phone number box.**

   Your choices for telephone number are Work, Home, Fax, Other, and E-Mail. I explain how to use and customize these fields later in this chapter.

5. **Click the radio button to the left of the phone number you want shown on the Address List.**

6. **In the Address section, type the Street address of your contact.**

   The person's street address appears in the Address box.

7. **Enter the contact's City, State, Zip code, and Country in the appropriate boxes.**

8. **Click OK.**

   The New Address dialog box closes.

 Although you can enter plenty of information in an Address Book entry, you can get away with just filling in one blank. If you enter just a phone number and not the name of the person at that phone number, of course, you don't get much benefit other than a way to start a weird party game. (It depends on what kinds of parties you go to. I probably won't be there, thanks.)

Editing an address record

I think most people who carry Palm devices are upwardly mobile, and so are most of the people they know. Don't you? Of course. We both carry Palm devices. What else would we think?

As you would expect, all these upwardly mobile people are continually moving to better jobs and addresses, so plan on making lots of changes to your Address List. And, please, don't forget the little people.

These steps show you how to edit an address in your Palm Desktop:

1. **With the Address Book visible, double-click the name of the person whose record you want to change.**

   The Edit dialog box opens.

2. **Add new information the same way you entered it originally.**

   For more information, see the preceding section, "Adding a new Address Book entry."

3. **Select any information you want to change and type the new information.**

   The text you enter replaces the information you selected.

4. **Click OK when you finish.**

   The Edit dialog box closes.

A big advantage to making your changes on the Palm Desktop rather than on the Palm device is that you can save the old address in your archive. Just select the address record and press Ctrl+C to copy it. Pressing Ctrl+V pastes the info to the same list of addresses, and then you have two identical records. With the old address safely stored for posterity, you can change the one that's left. To dig an old address from your archive, see the section about archiving in the next chapter.

Attaching a note to an address record

"Always tell the truth," a wise person said. "It's the easiest thing to remember." If you can't always recall what you said to whom, you could probably benefit from keeping track of what you say along with a record of who you say it to. The perfect way to store these gems is in the form of notes in your Address Book. That way, you won't get caught.

Follow these steps to attach a note to an address record on your Palm Desktop:

1. **With the Address Book visible, double-click the record you want to annotate.**

   The Edit Address dialog box opens.

2. **Click the Note tab.**

   The Note page of the Edit Address dialog box appears, as shown in Figure 12-5.

3. **Enter the text of your note.**

   The text you type appears in the Note box.

4. **Click OK when you finish.**

   The Edit Address dialog box closes. To view your note, just click the person's name on the Address List; the note appears with the other contact information in the box on the right side of the screen.

If you still can't remember what you said, keep your fingers crossed.

Figure 12-5:
Notes have
their own
page in the
Edit Address
dialog box.

Finding the name you want

If you need to find a person's vital statistics quickly, you can just type the first few letters of the person's last name in the Look Up text box at the bottom of the screen. When you type a letter or two in the Look Up text box, the Palm Desktop highlights the first name on the list that starts with those letters. If that's not the exact name you're looking for, the one you are looking for probably isn't far away. Keep typing letters until the name you want to find is highlighted. You can open that person's address record by double-clicking her name.

Deleting a name

Some names just don't make your list anymore. It's sad but true. To gently but firmly remove the name of someone who is no longer close to your inner micro-processor, just click her name on your Address List and press Delete. A dialog box opens to make sure you really want to do the deed; if you're sure, click OK.

If you change your mind, you can always restore any address record you saved in an archive. See the section about archiving in the next chapter for details.

Setting Up Custom Labels

If you keep track of lots of people who have a few important things in common, setting up special places in your Address Book to help you keep track of information is useful. If you're a teacher, for example, you may want to keep track of each student's age or grade level. If you're a Realtor, you may want to distinguish buyers from sellers and renters from landlords. Every address record in the Palm desktop program includes four spaces for personalized information that you can label as you see fit. Techies call spots like this "custom fields." Whatever you call them, it's good to know you can customize four of the blanks in the Address Book for your own use. You can create custom fields from either the Palm Desktop or the Palm device; the result is the same.

These steps help you set up custom labels in the Palm Desktop:

1. **With the Address Book visible, choose Tools⇨Options.**

   The Options dialog box appears.

2. **Click the Address tab.**

3. **Type the name you want to assign to the first custom label.**

   The name you type appears in the Label 1 box, as shown in Figure 12-6.

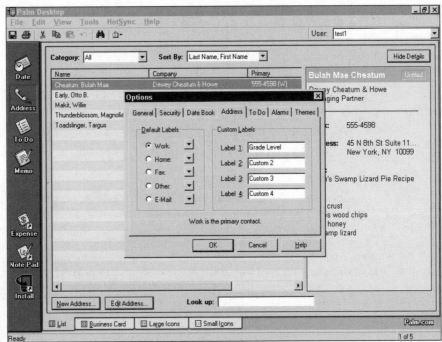

Figure 12-6: You can customize four of the blanks in your Address Book.

4. **Press Tab and type the name you want to assign to each successive custom label.**

5. **Click OK.**

After you define the name of a custom label, all your address records have a label by that name. For example, if you rename a field as Grade Level, every record on your address list has a label by that name, even if the records aren't for students.

Working with To Dos

Knowing what to do isn't enough if you don't remember to do it. The To Do List lets you add the items you need to do to your Palm device so the Palm device can remind you to do them.

To bring up your To Do List, just click the To Do button on the left side of the screen or choose View➪To Do List from the menu bar. Then, continue to the following sections. The list of your to-dos appears on the left side of the To Do screen, much like the Palm device To Do screen. The right side shows details of a To Do item you select.

Creating a To Do item

Nothing could be easier than entering a task on your To Do List. If only doing the tasks were so easy!

1. **With your To Do List visible, click New To Do at the bottom of the screen (or choose Edit➪New To Do from the menu bar).**

   The Edit To Do dialog box appears, as shown in Figure 12-7.

2. **Type what you need to do in the To Do text box.**

3. **Click OK.**

   The name of your task appears on the To Do List on the left side of Palm Desktop screen.

Of course, you can also set the Priority of your To Do item as you create the item. Just choose the priority number you want before clicking OK, and your task will show up as a top priority (or as a bottom priority or somewhere in between; whichever you want).

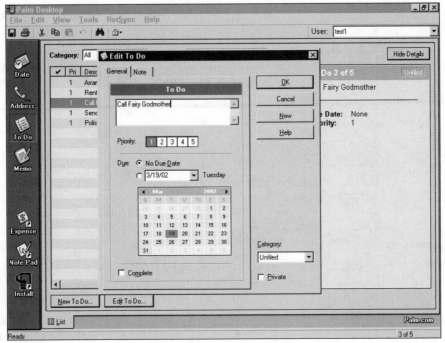

Figure 12-7:
Whatever
you type
appears
in the
rectangle.

Setting the priority for a To Do item

With so many important things on your To Do List, how do you know what to do first? You need to set priorities. You have only the numbers 1 through 5 to assign as the priority for each task, but that's enough to make sure you get to the important things first.

Here's how to set the priority of a To Do item:

1. **With your To Do List visible, double-click the name of the To Do item for which you want to set a priority number.**

2. **Click one of the numbers next to Priority.**

   The number you click is shaded to show which number you selected.

3. **Click OK.**

   The priority you assign appears next to your To Do item.

Another trick you can try is to simply click the priority number on the To Do List. Clicking a priority number makes a list of priority numbers appear, as shown in Figure 12-8. You can choose the number you want by picking it from the list with a single mouse click.

Figure 12-8:
Some tasks
are more
important
than others.

Having more than one To Do with the same priority is okay. You can make every task your top priority or your bottom priority — whatever you like.

Assigning a category to a To Do item

Another way to keep track of what task you need to do next is to assign categories. For example, you must do some tasks at home and do other tasks at work. When you're at the office, you don't need to remind yourself to mow the lawn (although if it gets you out of the office early, it's worth a try).

To assign a category to a To Do item, follow these steps:

1. **With your To Do List visible, click the name of the To Do item to which you want to assign a category.**

2. **Click the Category box in the lower-right corner of the screen.**

   The drop-down list of available categories appears.

3. **Click the category you want to assign to your To Do item.**

   The category you click appears in the Category text box.

4. **Click OK.**

   The category you assign appears next to your To Do item.

Adding categories

You can maintain your collection of categories on either your Palm device or the Palm Desktop. Every time you HotSync your data, the categories you set up on your Palm device are mirrored on the Palm Desktop and vice versa.

Follow these steps to create a new category:

1. **With your To Do List visible, click the arrow next to Category in the upper-left corner of the screen.**

   The drop-down list of available categories appears.

2. **Click the words Edit Categories.**

   The Edit To Do Categories dialog box opens.

3. **Click New.**

   The New Category dialog box opens.

4. **Enter the name of the category you want to add.**

   The name you enter appears in the New Category dialog box.

5. **Click OK.**

   The new category appears in the Edit To Do Categories dialog box.

6. **Click OK again.**

   The Edit To Do Categories dialog box closes.

You can have no more than 15 categories on your Palm device or on the Palm Desktop. If you try to exceed 15 categories, the program adamantly (but nicely) refuses to add new categories.

Deleting categories

If you went wild and added some categories that you now regret, you can just zap your excess categories and get back to basics.

Follow these steps to delete a category:

1. **With your To Do List visible, click the arrow next to Category in the upper-left corner of the screen.**

   The drop-down list of available categories appears.

2. **Click the words Edit Categories in the drop-down list.**

   The Edit To Do Categories dialog box opens.

3. **Select the name of the category you want to delete.**

   The category you click is highlighted to show you selected it.

4. **Click Delete.**

   The Delete Category dialog box opens, asking whether you want to move all items in the category to the Unfiled category or delete all items.

5. **Choose either Move All Items to Unfiled or Delete All Items.**

   The circle next to the choice you click appears darkened to show you selected it.

6. **Click OK.**

   The Delete Category dialog box closes, and your category is deleted.

7. **Click OK.**

   The Edit To Do Categories dialog box closes.

 At least when you delete a category on the Palm Desktop, you can either delete all the items in the category or send them all to the Unfiled category. (On the Palm device, you can only send everything to Unfiled.)

Renaming categories

Did you know that Whoopi Goldberg changed her name from Caryn Johnson? Go figure. Changing the names of your categories is easier than changing your name for show business, but it won't make you a star.

To rename a category, follow these steps:

1. **With your To Do List visible, click the downward-pointing arrow next to Category in the upper-left corner of the screen.**

   The drop-down list of available categories appears.

2. **Click the words Edit Categories in the drop-down list.**

3. **Click the name of the category you want to rename.**

   The name of the category is highlighted to show you selected it.

4. **Click Rename.**

   The Rename Category dialog box opens.

5. **Enter the new name of the category you want to change.**

   The name you type replaces the old name in the Rename Category dialog box.

6. **Click OK.**

   The name you entered replaces the preceding name of the category in the Edit To Do Categories dialog box.

7. **Click OK again.**

   The Edit To Do Categories dialog box closes.

In case you're interested, Hal Linden started off as Harold Lipshitz, and Peter Marshall was originally named Pierre LaCock. But that's a totally different category.

Assigning a due date to a To Do item

Your To Do List can do more than tell you what tasks to do; it also helps you remember when to do them.

Follow these steps to assign a due date to a To Do item:

1. **With your To Do List visible, double-click the name of the To Do item to which you want to assign a due date.**

   The Edit To Do dialog box appears.

2. **Click the date you want to assign to your To Do item.**

3. **Click OK.**

   The Edit To Do dialog box disappears, and the date you chose appears in the Due text box.

Unfortunately, the To Do List doesn't have reminders that pop up and nag you to do the things on your list, so you have to remember to look at your list from time to time.

Marking a To Do item private

You may have things to do that some other people shouldn't know about. Shhh! Keep them under your hat — or at least under a password.

These steps show you how to mark a To Do item private on the Palm Desktop:

1. **With your To Do List visible, click the name of the To Do item you want to mark as private.**

2. **Click the Private check box on the right side of the screen.**

3. **Click OK.**

   A little lock appears next to your item on the To Do List to show it's now marked as private, as shown in Figure 12-9.

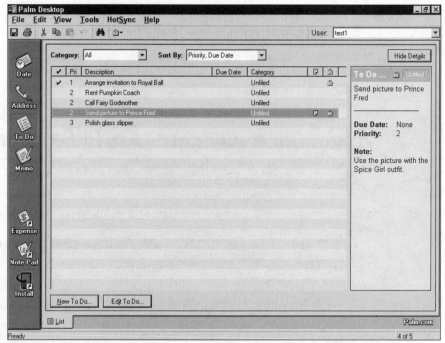

Figure 12-9:
Those little
locks mark
your private
tasks.

If you want your private items to remain private, you should choose, of course, View⊏⟩Hide Private Records from the menu bar. That action makes your private items invisible until you choose View⊏⟩Show Private Records. If you want to password-protect your private items, you have to set your password on your Palm device. For more info about setting up passwords, refer to Chapter 3.

You'll see another option for keeping items secret when you choose View⊏⟩ Mask Private Records. *Masking* a record means that a shaded box appears in place of the item you marked Private. That way, you know there's a To Do item that needs your attention, but other people won't know exactly what your To Do item is.

Attaching a note to a To Do item

You know what you need to do and when you need to do it, of course, but do you always remember how or why? Perhaps you just need a more detailed explanation of some part of the task, such as driving directions or a secret formula. If you need some elaboration on your task, add a note.

To add a note to a To Do item in the Palm Desktop, follow these steps:

1. **With your To Do List visible, click the name of the To Do item to which you want to attach a note.**

2. **Click the Note tab.**

   The Edit To Do dialog box opens, as shown in Figure 12-10.

3. **Type the text of your note.**

   The text you type appears in the Note dialog box.

4. **Click OK.**

   The Edit To Do dialog box closes, and the same little piece of paper that's on the Note button appears next to the name of your To Do item to show that the item has a note attached.

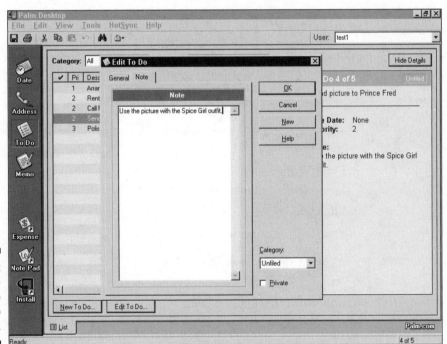

Figure 12-10:
Make a note
of what to
do in your To
Do item.

You don't have to type lots of text into the note if you don't want to. You can always copy text from another document on your desktop or from a Web page and paste the text into the Edit To Do dialog box. When you want to read the note, click the Note icon next to the name of the To Do in your list.

Viewing items by category

If you make the effort to assign categories to your tasks, you get some real mileage from that feature by viewing your tasks according to the categories to which they belong. The name of the category you're viewing is always shown at the top of the To Do List. If you click the name of the category you're viewing, a drop-down list of the other categories appears. Just choose the category you want to see.

Deleting a To Do item

Some tasks become unnecessary before you even do them. If you had planned to water the lawn and it rains, you're in luck.

Follow these steps to delete a To Do item on the Palm Desktop:

1. **With your To Do List visible, click the name of the To Do item you want to delete.**

2. **Press Delete.**

   The Delete To Do Items dialog box opens.

3. **Click OK.**

   Your To Do item is deleted.

The check box in the Delete To Do Items dialog box enables you to send deleted items to the archive for storage. I discuss how to deal with archived items in the next chapter.

If you actually do a task, your best bet, of course, is to mark the task as complete. The little check box next to the name of the task is put there for that very reason. One click, and you're the hero! Mission accomplished!

Setting preferences for your To Do List

Setting preferences is, well, a matter of preference. You don't need to make any changes in your To Do List preferences if you don't want to. But if you like your To Do List just so, you can change several little things.

To set your To Do List preferences on the Palm Desktop, follow these steps:

1. **With your To Do List visible, choose Tools⇨Options.**

   The Options dialog box appears.

2. **Click the To Do tab.**

   The To Do options page appears.

3. **Click the check boxes next to the options you want for your To Do List.**

   The first two of the three options only affect how many items appear on the To Do screen. If you uncheck the Show Completed Items box, each To Do item disappears from the view as soon as you mark it complete. If you check the Show Only Due Items box, you see only items that are due today or uncompleted items that were due before today.

   Checking Record Completion Date makes the Due Date entry for each item reflect the day you actually mark an item complete. If you enter a Due Date for an item and then mark it complete sooner, the Due Date is replaced by the actual completion date. If you didn't enter a Due Date, the completion date appears in place of the due date.

4. **Click OK.**

   The Options dialog box closes, and your To Do List reflects the preferences you set up, as shown in Figure 12-11.

Figure 12-11:
What you
see is what
you set.

If you set up your preferences and then decide you'd prefer something else, just change everything again.

If you want to change the way your To Do list is sorted, just click the box next to Sort By at the top of the screen and choose a different arrangement.

Working with Memos

The best reason to enter memos on the Palm Desktop rather than use Graffiti is that memos usually contain lots of text, and typing is much faster than scribbling with Graffiti or punching in individual letters on the Palm device's on-screen keyboard. You can also copy and paste text to a memo from other desktop programs, such as your word processor.

To bring up the Memo Pad, just click the Memo button on the left side of the screen or choose View➪Memo Pad from the menu bar.

Creating a memo

Sometimes, you need certain information that's not exactly an appointment and not exactly a To Do item, but you still need it on your Palm device. The simplest way to keep miscellaneous information on hand is to create a memo. Nothing could be easier.

Use these steps to create a new Memo on the Palm Desktop:

1. **With the Memo Pad visible, click New Memo button at the bottom of the screen (or choose Edit➪New Memo).**

   The New Memo dialog box appears.

2. **Type the text of your memo.**

   The text you type appears in the memo area, as shown in Figure 12-12.

3. **Click OK.**

   The title of your memo appears on the list of memos on the left side of the screen.

If you hate to type, you can also copy and paste text into your Memo Pad, too. Just select text from a word-processing document or even from the World Wide Web, press Crtl+C to copy the text, start the Palm Desktop Memo Pad, and then press Ctrl+V to paste the text directly into the memo. You don't even need to create a new memo; the Palm Desktop figures out that you want a new memo and creates one automatically.

Figure 12-12:
Type or copy
whatever
you like into
a memo.

Reading a memo

You may not want to hang around reading your memos on the Palm Desktop because you can send them all to your Palm device and then go read them in the park. Even so, you may need to check what you put in your memos now and again, and, fortunately, I can show you a way to do just that.

To read a memo, all you have to do is click the Memo Pad button on the left side of the screen (or choose View➪Memo Pad from the menu bar) and then click the memo you want to see. Read away!

If you need to read through all the memos on your desktop quickly, you can whip through the whole list by pressing the down-arrow key. Each time you press the down-arrow key, the next memo on the list appears in the memo area, which is on the right side of the screen.

Printing a memo

Another big thing you can do from the desktop is to print things. Yes, some people out there have clever schemes for beaming their Palm organizer data to especially well-equipped printers. However, the whole scheme is still tricky, and most printers aren't up to the job. You probably have a printer hooked up to your desktop computer, so printing from the desktop is the quickest way to see your data on paper.

To print a memo from the Palm Desktop, follow these steps:

1. **With the Memo Pad visible, click the title of the memo you want to print.**

   The text of the memo you clicked appears in the memo area, which is on the right side of the screen.

2. **Choose File⇨Print from the menu bar (or press Ctrl+P).**

   The Print dialog box opens.

3. **Click OK.**

   Your memo prints.

Palm Desktop doesn't let you do any fancy formatting with your memos; it's all plain vanilla. If you need to format and fiddle around with your text, you can copy the memo you want to work with, paste it into your favorite word processor, and beautify your memo as you please.

Editing a memo

If you use memos often, as I do, you certainly want to change a few of them now and then. The biggest advantage to keeping memos in an electronic form is that the text is so easy to change.

Follow these steps to edit a Memo on your Palm Desktop:

1. **With the Memo Pad visible, double-click the title of the memo you want to edit.**

   The Edit Memo dialog box appears.

2. **Make any changes you want to the memo.**

3. **Click OK.**

If you replace a large amount of the text in a memo, the text you replace is ordinarily gone for good. Normally, that's fine by me, but sometimes you may want to save a copy of the original memo. One thing you can do with memos on the Palm Desktop that you can't do on the Palm device is copy whole memos and then just change one of them. To copy a whole memo, click the name of the memo to select it, press Ctrl+C to copy the memo, and then press Ctrl+V to paste it. You then have two identical memos in the same list. Just change one, and you have two different memos.

Categorizing a memo

Categories are particularly useful after you've collected more than a few dozen memos. Categorizing not only makes memos easier to find but also lets you see your memo collection more easily on your Palm device because that little screen can show only 11 memos at one time.

Follow these steps to assign a category to a memo on the Palm Desktop:

1. **With the Memo Pad visible, click the title of the memo you want to categorize.**

   The text of the memo you clicked appears in the memo area on the right side of the screen.

2. **Click the category name to the right of the memo text and choose the category you want.**

   The category you choose appears below your memo text.

If you want to create several memos in the same category, switch to that category and then create the new memos. For example, if you switch to a view of your business memos and start creating new memos, all the new memos are automatically assigned to the business category.

Making a memo private

I'm sure you have some things you don't want just anybody to see, but you don't want to forget them yourself. You can mark certain memos as private to protect them from prying eyes.

To mark a memo private in the Palm Desktop, follow these steps:

1. **With the Memo Pad visible, double-click the title of the memo that you want to mark as private.**

   The text of the memo you clicked appears.

2. **Click the Private check box in the lower-right corner of the Edit Memo dialog box.**

   A check mark appears in the Private check box to show that this memo is private. A lock also appears to the right of the subject of any memo that's marked as private, as shown in Figure 12-13.

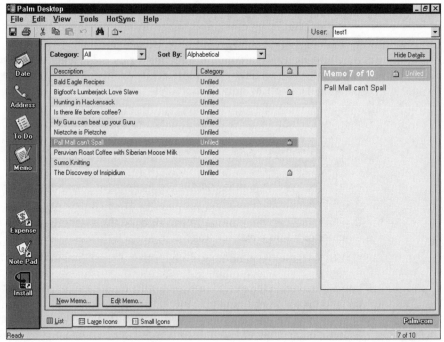

Figure 12-13:
Do you have
a secret?
Shhh! Mark
it private.

You can make all your private items disappear by choosing View⇨Hide Private Records from the menu bar. If you want to make them reappear, choose View⇨Show Private Records. Presto! If you prefer, you can choose View⇨Mask Private Records, which obscures private items but doesn't hide the fact that they exist. If you want to be sneaky, you can set a password on your Palm device to keep anyone from seeing your private records unless they know your password. For more information about setting passwords, refer to Chapter 3.

Deleting a memo

You know how memos are — easy come, easy go. Especially go. Follow these steps to make your memos go away:

1. **With the Memo Pad visible, click the title of the memo you want to delete.**

   The text of the memo you clicked appears in the memo area on the right side of the screen.

2. **Choose Edit⇨Delete from the menu bar (or press Delete).**

   The Delete Memo Pad Items dialog box opens. If you put a check mark in the box next to Archive Deleted Memo Pad Items, your memo is stored in an archive file.

3. **Click OK.**

Poof! Your memo is gone.

If you left the Archive box checked, you can go back and find the deleted memo later. See the section on archiving, in the next chapter, for more information.

What Does That Expense Button Do?

Your Palm device includes an application called Expense that can help you track how much money you spend as you spend it. When you perform a HotSync, the information you've gathered is pulled into a file on your desktop. Frankly, the program is limited and is best for people who need to track business spending in order to file expense reports. Even for those people, the program has major drawbacks. It requires you to choose a description for each expenditure from a noncustomizable list (its 28 choices range from Airfare to Telephone). Expense may not be useful if you can't enter the exact types of expenses you incur.

To start Expense on your Palm device, tap the Applications soft button, the upper spot on the left side of the Graffiti box, and then tap the Expense icon. Write in the amounts you spend; pick the description that you think fits each one best. The program automatically assigns the current date to each expenditure unless you tap the date and pick another one from the calendar.

The Expense button on the Palm Desktop for Windows automatically starts a special Excel spreadsheet. The spreadsheet captures data that you've entered in Expense on your Palm device. If you don't have Excel installed on your Windows PC, the button is still present, but it doesn't do anything. Plenty of Palm device users have complained that Expense is too weak. In fact, the Palm people have dropped Expense entirely from a number of Palm models, so they seem to think so, too. I hope that future versions of Expense are more useful. In the meantime, you might take a look at any of the replacement programs for the Expense application, such as ExpensePlus, which you can check out at www.palmpilotfordummies.com/expense.

There's also a Memo Pad button in the Palm Desktop program that shows the handwritten notes you may have scribbled in the Memo Pad program on your Palm device. You can't create Memo Pad entries in the Palm Desktop program; you can only create them on your Palm device. (For more about the Memo Pad, see Chapter 7.)

Chapter 13

Managing Palm Data

- -

In This Chapter

▶ Managing memory

▶ Installing and deleting applications

▶ Backing up and restoring your data

▶ Managing archived items

▶ Setting up multiple users

- -

"*W*hat if I lose my Palm organizer?" That's the first question I usually get from Palm newbies. Relax. You can replace a lost Palm device with the wave of a credit card. What's important is the information you've stored on your Palm device. You can replace that easily, too, if you've synchronized your Palm device regularly to your desktop computer. If you take a few minutes to manage the data on your Palm device now and again, you don't need to worry about losing all your precious personal data.

Furnishing Your Palm Device

What is a home, after all, without some furnishings? You may have a lovely breakfast nook, but eventually you want a dinette, at least. You can furnish your Palm device as lavishly (or as sparingly) as you furnish your home. A few games, a spreadsheet — who knows what may strike your fancy?

Checking memory

Before you start adding things to your Palm device, you'd better make sure you have room for the stuff. After all, most Palm devices only have 8MB of memory, and some bargain models (and older models) still only offer 2MB to store your precious data. So, unlike my hall closet, which I seem to be able to cram anything into, your Palm device protests if you try to put too much stuff on it.

You can see how much space is available on a Palm III or later model by following these three steps:

1. **Tap the Applications soft button, the upper spot on the left side of the Graffiti box.**

    The applications list appears.

2. **Tap the Menu soft button at the bottom-left corner of the Palm screen.**

    The menu bar appears.

3. **Choose App⇨Info from the menu bar.**

    The Info screen appears. The line at the top of the Info screen says something like `Free Memory: 7974K of 8064K`, as shown in Figure 13-1.

Figure 13-1:
Before you install a new program, check your memory to see whether you have enough room.

Most Palm organizer applications are small, so as long as you have a few hundred kilobytes of memory (computer geeks use the abbreviation *K*), you should be okay. Remember, though, that every time you add an item to one of the standard applications, like the Address Book or the Date Book, you tie up a bit more memory. So leave yourself some breathing room. You can free up some memory by either deleting applications, as I describe later in this chapter, or by deleting bunches of items from the standard Palm organizer applications. The easiest way to delete records en masse is to use the Palm Desktop, as I describe in later sections of this chapter.

If you're still using a PalmPilot Professional or earlier model, the process for checking memory is a bit different because earlier Palm devices have a separate Memory application. To check how much memory is available on those models, tap the Applications soft button and tap Memory.

Installing applications

Remember that the Palm Install Tool doesn't install applications; it *prepares* applications for installation. After picking an application with the Palm Install Tool, you have to perform a HotSync. Just place the Palm device in its cradle and press the HotSync button. (For more info about HotSyncing, refer to Chapter 14.)

To install Palm organizer programs by using the Palm Desktop, follow these steps:

1. **Launch the Palm Desktop.**

2. **Click the Install button on the left side of the screen or choose View⇨Install from the menu bar.**

   The Palm Install Tool dialog box opens.

3. **Click Add (or press Alt+A).**

   The Open dialog box opens, as shown in Figure 13-2.

4. **Click the name of the file you want to install.**

   The filename you click is highlighted to show you selected it.

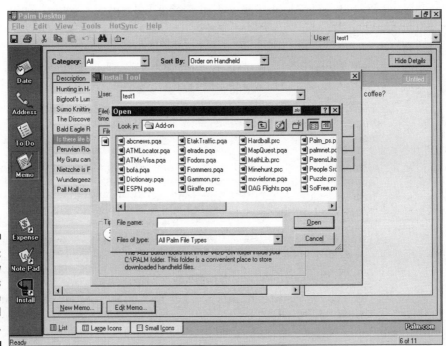

Figure 13-2:
Add new programs with the Palm Install Tool.

If you downloaded the application from the Internet or are installing applications from the CD, browse until you find the application you want to install.

5. **Click Open.**

The Open dialog box closes, and the filename you picked is now listed in the Palm Install Tool dialog box.

6. **Click Done.**

Another dialog box opens, telling you that the applications will be installed the next time you HotSync.

7. **Click OK.**

The Palm Install Tool closes.

8. **Put the Palm device in its cradle and press the HotSync button.**

The HotSync process begins, and the program is installed on your Palm device.

You have an even easier way to install Palm applications if you're comfortable dealing with files in Windows. Just find a Palm application file in Windows Explorer. (Palm files end with .prc, .pdb, or .pqa.) Double-click the name of the file when you find it with Windows Explorer, and the Palm Install Tool opens, already showing the name of the file you double-clicked. Just click OK in the Palm Install Tool dialog box, and your program will be installed on your next HotSync.

Deleting applications

Eventually, you may tire of your once-fashionable furnishings. I mean, orange shag carpet? Lava lamps? Please! Your decorator would send you straight to Lord & Taylor!

Discarding unwanted applications from your Palm device is even easier than dumping those old Woodstock posters. You'll also be less embarrassed if someone catches you at it. You don't need to launch Palm Desktop to delete applications, either.

1. **Tap the Applications soft button, the upper spot on the left side of the Graffiti box.**

The applications screen appears.

2. **Tap the Menu soft button at the bottom-left corner of the Palm screen.**

The menu bar appears.

3. Choose App⇨Delete from the menu bar.

The Delete screen appears, as shown in Figure 13-3.

Figure 13-3: Clear out the clutter by deleting unwanted applications.

4. Tap the name of the application you want to delete.

The name you tap is highlighted to show you selected it.

5. Tap Delete.

The Delete Application dialog box opens, as shown in Figure 13-4.

6. Tap Yes if you're sure. If you change your mind, tap No.

If you tap Yes, the application is deleted, and its name disappears from the list of applications on the Delete screen. If you tap No, the dialog box closes, and the application is still there.

7. Tap Done.

The Delete screen closes.

There you are! And there it isn't! Your unwanted application is gone like platform shoes. Oops, I guess platform shoes *have* made a comeback. Well, you can always reinstall the applications by using the same procedure shown in the "Installing applications" section, earlier in this chapter.

Figure 13-4: Throw out old, leftover programs from this dialog box.

Protecting Your Turf

Sometimes the worst does happen; your little Palm device gets lost, stolen, or destroyed. You can always buy a new Palm device — that's the easy part. But what about all your data? You're in luck — the Palm Desktop makes reinstalling all your precious data easy.

Restoring Palm organizer data

In the best of times or in the worst of times, you may need to restore all your Palm organizer data. The best of times may be when you upgrade to a new Palm organizer model; the worst of times may be when you replace a lost, stolen, or destroyed Palm device. Either way, you can restore everything that was on your old Palm device with a simple HotSync:

1. **Put your Palm device in its cradle.**

   Nothing happens. Surprise!

2. **Press the HotSync button on the Palm device's cradle.**

   The HotSync Manager on your desktop PC is launched, and the Users dialog box opens on your desktop PC's screen.

3. **Click the name of the user whose data you want to install on the Palm device, which is probably your name.**

   The name you click is highlighted to show you selected it, as shown in Figure 13-5.

4. **Click OK (in the Users dialog box).**

   The HotSync Progress dialog box opens. After a few minutes, the dialog box closes, your Palm device plays some tinny little fanfare, and a button labeled Reset appears on the Palm screen.

5. **Tap the Reset button on the screen of your Palm device.**

   The General Preferences screen appears on your Palm device. You don't need to do anything in the General Preferences screen after a reset; you can either turn off the Palm device or go right on and use any application.

If you use one desktop computer to synchronize more than one Palm device, don't assign the same username to more than one Palm device. The HotSync program can get confused and send the wrong data to the wrong Palm device or, worse, make data disappear.

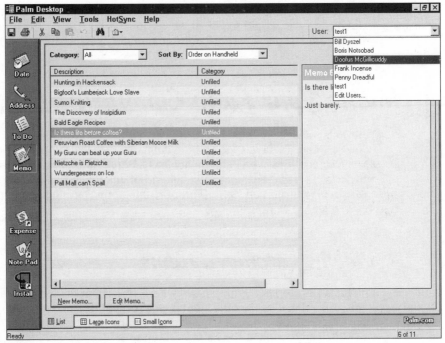

Figure 13-5:
Pick the
name of the
user whose
data should
go on this
Palm
device.

Backing up your data

If you only use the programs that come in the box with your Palm device and
you HotSync regularly to keep your data current, you're covered. Your data
from all standard Palm computing applications gets saved and archived by
Palm Desktop every time you HotSync. It's a good idea, of course, to back up
the data on the desktop machine regularly.

On the other hand, if you install programs that don't come preinstalled on
your Palm device, those programs may not automatically back themselves up
like your standard Palm computing apps do, so you need a backup program
to keep those files safe. You can buy a hardware expansion module called the
Backup Module, which automatically copies everything on your Palm device
for safekeeping. Just pop the module in your Palm organizer now and again,
and your precious data is protected from harm.

There's also a software program called Backup Buddy that can help you back
up your nonstandard programs automatically. To find out more, see the manufacturer's Web site at `www.palmpilotfordummies.com/backupbuddy`.

If all you've added to your Palm device are a few games, you probably don't
need to worry about backing up your data. You primarily need to be concerned with backups if you've added programs that add data themselves,

such as spreadsheets, databases, or time and billing applications. If your Palm device was issued to you at work, you should check with your system administrator about whether you should do anything special with backups.

Archiving Your Palm Computing Stuff

Your Palm device can hold only a fraction of the information your desktop computer can. To save space on the Palm device, clearing things out regularly is a good idea. The Palm device has a Purge function in the Date Book and To Do List that automatically gets rid of unneeded items and moves them to an archive file, if you want. (For more info about purging Palm organizer items, refer to Chapter 6.)

Viewing archived items

The Palm Desktop is the only place where you can open and view archived items. Even if you use another personal information manager, such as Microsoft Outlook or Lotus Organizer, to put items into your Palm device, you still need to look in the Palm Desktop to view your archived items.

These steps show you how to view your archived items on the Palm Desktop:

1. **Choose the type of archived item you want to look at from the buttons on the left side of the screen (or from the View menu).**

   Calendar items are archived separately from items deleted from the Address Book, To Do List, or Memo Pad, so you need to open the part of the Palm Desktop that handles the type of item you want to see.

2. **Choose File⇨Open Archive from the menu bar.**

   The Open Archive dialog box opens, as shown in Figure 13-6.

3. **Click the name of the archive file you want to view.**

   Usually, only one file appears on the archive list. If more than one archive file is listed and the archive you open doesn't contain the item you want, repeat Steps 2 and 3 until you find the archive containing the item you want.

4. **Click OK.**

   The items in the archive you picked appear as a new list of items on your Palm Desktop.

If you're looking at the archive of items assigned to categories, the archive files are organized by category — personal, business, or whatever you assign.

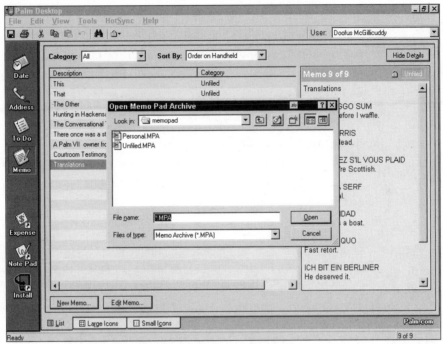

Figure 13-6:
Find those
old, deleted
files by
opening an
archive file.

Returning an archived item to your Palm device

Another benefit of keeping archive files is to help you get back items you accidentally delete. Don't be embarrassed — it happens to everybody.

To recover an item from an archive on the Palm Desktop, follow these steps:

1. **Choose the type of archived item you want to recover from the buttons on the left side of the screen (or from the View menu).**

   Pick either Date Book, Address Book, To Do List, or Memo Pad.

2. **Choose File⇨Open Archive from the menu bar.**

   The Open Archive dialog box opens.

3. **Click the name of the archive file you want to view.**

   The file you click is highlighted to show you selected it.

4. **Click OK.**

   The items in the archive file you picked are listed on the Palm Desktop.

5. **Click the item you want returned to your Palm device.**

   The item you click is highlighted to show you selected it.

6. **Choose Edit⇨Copy from the menu bar (or press Ctrl+C).**

   The item is copied to the Clipboard. Nothing happens on the screen.

7. **Choose File⇨Open Current.**

   Your collection of current items appears.

8. **Choose Edit⇨Paste (or press Ctrl+V).**

   The item appears as part of your collection of current items.

9. **Place your Palm device in its cradle, and press the HotSync button on the cradle.**

   The HotSync dialog box opens and shows the progress of your synchronization.

The whole reason for archiving items is to save space on your Palm device — so don't load old items back on your Palm device unless you really need them.

Accommodating Multiple Users

Most people use a Palm device in conjunction with a desktop computer in order to simplify data entry and keep the data on their Palm devices safe. But you don't have to limit yourself to one Palm device per computer. The Palm Desktop enables you to synchronize Palm devices with different users. The first time you HotSync your Palm device, the HotSync Manager asks for your username. The Palm device username you enter (or choose) is added to the list of usernames on the Palm Desktop. Each time you put a Palm device in the cradle attached to that desktop computer, the program recognizes which Palm device is in the cradle when you press the HotSync button. After you've set up a computer to HotSync a particular Palm device, the desktop computer always knows which Palm device it's dealing with and synchronizes to that particular person's information.

If you don't use the Palm Desktop program, setting up multiple users on the same computer isn't a good idea. You can make your Palm device information synchronize to other programs, such as Microsoft Outlook or Act!, but you could encounter some confusion if you try to synchronize more than one Palm device to one of those programs. Using several Palm devices with those programs is possible, but everything won't necessarily work right if you do it all through the same computer. If you want to host several Palm devices on the same desktop PC or Mac, your best bet is to stick with the Palm Desktop.

The Palm Device Name Game

Although all Palm devices look pretty much alike in those little tiny boxes, each one has one important difference: the name of the user. You can find out which name is assigned to the Palm device you're using by tapping the Applications soft button, the upper spot on the left side of the Graffiti box, and then tapping HotSync. The HotSync screen displays the name of the user assigned to it in the upper-right corner of the screen. Also, when you perform a HotSync by placing the unit in its cradle and pressing the button on the cradle, the name of the user whose data is being synchronized appears in the HotSync Progress dialog box. You determine the Palm device username the first time you perform a HotSync. If you try to HotSync a Palm device to a computer that hasn't ever seen a Palm device with that username, the HotSync Manager asks whether you want to set up a new account for that user.

Chapter 14

Installing and HotSyncing to the Desktop Program

· ·

· ·

*I*n theory, you can use your Palm device all by itself, with no other computer involved. But if you're only interested in doing things the easiest way possible (my favorite way), then the Palm Desktop program may be the best way to put things in your Palm device. Then, you can carry your Palm device around to read your saved data and fiddle with it a little bit, as you see fit. Although I still prefer to enter most of my Palm Computing data by using Graffiti, most people I know don't. (Refer to Chapter 2 for more information on using Graffiti.) Among the many clever ways you can put information into your Palm device, Palm Desktop is the simplest and most understandable method for anyone who has used a computer. In this chapter, I show you how to install the Palm Desktop program, and I tell you all you need to know about HotSyncing your Palm device to your desktop computer. In Chapter 12, I show you how to do all that cool Palm Computing-type stuff on your desktop computer.

Installing Palm Desktop for Windows

Each time a new, improved Palm product comes out, the details of how you install it change a tiny bit. But one thing stays the same: It's very simple. You need do only three things to install desktop software for your Palm device:

1. **Plug the Palm HotSync cradle into your computer.**

2. **Put the Palm software CD-ROM into your computer.**

3. **Follow the directions on the screen.**

That's it! The directions in the rest of this chapter show how a basic Palm installation happens, but what you see when you install the exact Palm device you own may differ slightly. Don't worry; just follow the instructions on the screen, and you'll be fine.

Connecting the cradle to your PC

Typically, you can simply plug your Palm cradle into the only plug — known as the USB port — on the back of the PC in which it fits. If you can plug the cradle into the back of your PC easily, you've got it made. Just shout "Hooray," pass Go, and collect $200 (or jump ahead to the next section).

If you can't plug the cradle right in, you may not have a USB port on your computer. If that's the case, you need to get a Serial Cradle. A Serial Cradle will synchronize your data just as well as the standard USB cradle. Some people think the USB cradle is faster, but you probably can't tell the difference. Check with www.palm.com to find the Serial Cradle for your particular Palm device.

Now, you get to install Palm Desktop

Palm Desktop for Windows enables your computer to talk to and work with your Palm device through a process called *HotSyncing*. You only have to install the desktop software once, and then you're through. After you install the Palm Desktop program, all you need to do is place your Palm device in the cradle and press the HotSync button on the cradle every day or so to keep the data on your handheld and your computer in sync. (I discuss HotSyncing in more detail later in this chapter.)

After you connect the cradle to your computer, you can install Palm Desktop by following these steps:

1. **Put the CD that came with your Palm device in your CD-ROM drive.**

   The Palm Desktop Installer Menu appears, as shown in Figure 14-1. If for some reason the screen doesn't appear automatically, use the Start⇨Run option to browse the CD for the setup.exe file, then double-click that file to start the setup process.

2. **Click Install Palm Desktop.**

   The Setup screen appears and tells you what's about to happen, as shown in Figure 14-2.

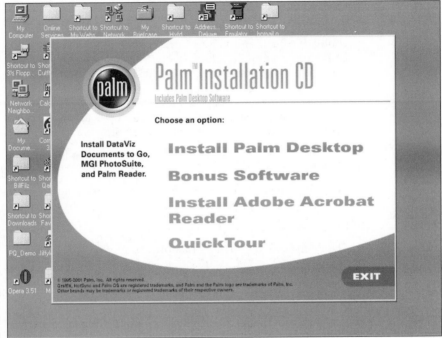

Figure 14-1:
The Palm
Desktop
Installer
kicks off the
installation
process.

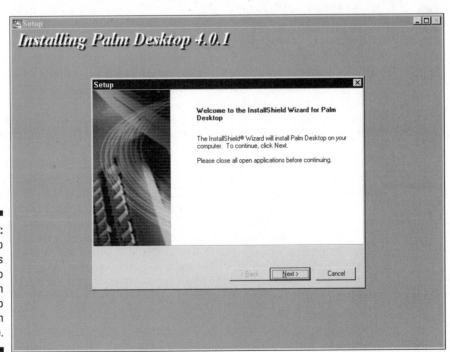

Figure 14-2:
The Setup
screen tells
you what to
do to begin
setting up
your Palm
device.

3. **Click Next.**

   The License screen appears, asking you to agree to a bunch of legal gobbledygook that involves turning over all your worldly possessions and first-born child to Palm Computing, Inc. Just kidding! It's the usual legalese about not doing anything nasty with the software.

4. **Click Yes.**

   The Destination dialog box appears, asking whether you want to store the Palm desktop files in the usual place (that is, the `C:/Palm` folder). Sure you do!

5. **Click Next.**

   The program spends a few seconds copying files, and then the Install Complete screen appears.

6. **Click Finish.**

   The Palm Desktop Installer disappears.

At this point, the Installer program may invite you to perform your first HotSync or install some optional software, depending on which Palm model you're using and what you've installed before.

To HotSync or Not to HotSync . . . Just Do It

When you install Palm Desktop, you end up with a good tool for tracking all your to-dos, addresses, memos, and appointments. That's fine if you're always at your desk. But if you divide your time between sitting at your desk and being on the go (and who doesn't, nowadays?), then keeping track of the data on two different machines can be a real pain. That's where HotSyncing comes in.

HotSyncing your Palm device with your desktop computer is blindingly simple. All you do is make sure your desktop computer is running, put the Palm device in the cradle, and push the HotSync button. That's it. The HotSync button is the only button on the cradle and has two arrows pointing at each other, so you can't go wrong. You don't even have to launch Palm Desktop. Pressing the HotSync button calls the HotSync Manager into action, which coordinates the whole process of swapping data. The HotSync Manager automatically turns on your Palm device, compares the data on it and on your desktop computer, and updates each machine with the most current info. After a few minutes, you end up with the same data on two different machines.

Most of the time, you don't need to know how the HotSync process works. However, every once in a while, you have to deal with HotSync problems, which happen most often when you synchronize your Palm device with other personal information managers, such as Microsoft Outlook, Goldmine, or Act! Then, you need to mess around with something called a *conduit,* which moves data between your Palm device and non–Palm Computing programs. I say more about conduits in Chapter 16.

Part V
Going Outside the Box with Your Palm

The 5th Wave   By Rich Tennant

"So much for the Graffiti handwriting system."

In this part . . .

You can't stop Palm computing progress. (Who would want to?) The list of new features and functions for Palm devices is growing, and you'll certainly want to keep up with the latest developments. In this part, I also tell you about some cool stuff — both software and hardware — that you can add to your Palm device to make it even more productive.

Chapter 15

Wireless Wonderland

· ·

· ·

*I*f anything's better than a pocket-sized computer, it's a pocket-sized computer that can connect wirelessly to all those big computers out on the Internet. Right now lots of CEOs are betting their companies on the idea that pocket-sized devices offering advanced wireless services are going to be the next big thing. You can be sure that you'll soon see a whole range of devices that can do some amazing things:

✔ Find a new airline flight when the one you're about to board gets cancelled.

✔ Send an e-mail or instant message to someone you've just met within minutes of first meeting them.

✔ Find the address of someone you need to meet while you're traveling to meet them.

Some of these companies have products in the pipeline that look like little computers and others that look like big cell phones, but all of them aim to help you get through your hectic work life in a jiffy and move on to important things like weekends and vacations. That's reason enough for me.

The Ways of the Wireless Warrior

If you're ready to do battle with the latest weapons, you have a bewildering array to choose from. Each path has its plusses and minuses. Table 15-1 gives you a list of choices, starting with the simplest.

Table 15-1	Picking the Best Wireless Connection for You		
If You Want	*Get*	*Pros*	*Cons*
A simple, one-piece solution for getting organized and connecting to the Internet.	Palm i705	You don't have much to fuss with. Just charge the batteries, enter your information, and get to work.	Can only reach a few hundred of the mil lions of sites on the Internet (although they're the best ones). Wireless service only available in major cities.
A combined Palm device and cell phone with Internet access	Any of the growing list of Palm-powered cell phones, including the Samsung i300, Kyocera 7135, or the Handspring Treo	Only one gadget to fuss with.	You must learn a little bit more than with a Palm i705, and con-nection charges can be a bit higher if you check the Web a lot.
Full-fledged Internet access you can use with either your laptop or your Palm device with *no* extra cables.	An IR-equipped phone, an IR-equipped laptop, and any compatible Palm device	You can use many Palm devices, including the Palm m135 with a color screen or the sleek Palm m515 (the best of all worlds). Service is available anywhere your cell phone works.	Much more fuss. You need to know whether your phone is IR-equipped and whether your cellular service can handle Palm connections.
Full-fledged Internet access (including e-mail) you can use with either your laptop or your Palm device *with* extra cables.	A cell phone, laptop, Palm device, and the appropriate connection kit for the phone and Palm device	Same as above, plus you can choose from a wider range of Palm devices.	Also more fuss. You have to carry around more wires.

Table 15-1 lists the leading choices as of summer 2002. As you can see, as you choose more powerful options, you have to put up with more difficulty. Even more powerful (and complicated) options with inscrutable names are available, such as wireless network cards, compact flash modems, and so on. I stick with the top choices because I'm betting that, if you bought this book, you're looking for a simple solution.

Going Wireless with a Palm i705

Palm's wireless model, the i705, is one of the simplest ways of setting up a mobile, wireless connection to the Internet. When you first run the setup program for your i705, an activation program starts up and guides you through the process of getting connected to the Palm.Net wireless service, setting up your e-mail and getting you started. While some of the Palm-powered cell phones give you many of the same benefits, they cost quite a bit more to operate than a Palm i705 when you start surfing the Web frequently. If you need a simple, one-piece solution for mobile e-mail and collecting simple information from the Web while you're on the run, the Palm i705 can help you.

Setting up your i705

Before you begin using your i705, you need to take a few steps to activate your Palm.Net service and connect the unit to the Internet. The process of setting up your i705 is a tiny bit more involved and time-consuming than setting up other Palm devices. However, it's not difficult, and the Palm setup program guides you through everything you need to do. Take the following steps to get ready to set up your i705:

1. **Charge your i705 for about an hour before you run the setup program just to be sure the radio has enough juice to operate.**

   Plug the power cord into the cradle, plug in the AC adaptor and leave the i705 in the cradle until it's charged.

2. **After you've charged the unit, plug the cradle into the USB port on your computer.**

   Make sure your computer is turned on and connected to the Internet when you do this.

3. **Put the i705 setup CD-ROM in your CD-ROM drive and let it run.**

4. **Follow the directions on the screen to set up the Palm Desktop and the Palm.Net service.**

You don't need to know anything special to start Palm.Net service, although you need to remember the username and password you choose when you kick off Palm.Net service. You need to know those things later if you want make changes in your account settings. You'll probably never need to set up Palm.Net service again, so don't worry too much.

Signing up and paying for Palm.Net

When you run the setup program for your i705, have your credit card ready because the first thing the program wants to do is sign you up for the Palm.Net service that makes those wonderful wireless features possible. And why not; that's why you bought a Palm i705, right? Otherwise, you could have saved money and bought a cheaper Palm organizer.

The price of Palm.Net service changes from time to time. As of autumn 2002, you can choose between two types of service:

- ✔ **The Associate Plan:** The low-priced service plan costs $19.99 per month plus a $9.99 setup fee. It lets you check the Internet between 50 and 100 times per month. If you go over your limit, you pay about 20 cents for each screen full of information you get from the Web. That can add up quickly because you pay every time you tap the screen to see more information.

- ✔ **The Executive Unlimited Plan:** If you use the Web a lot from your Palm i705 you may want to consider the unlimited service plan. This plan runs $39.99 per month, plus a $9.99 setup fee, and it lets you check the Web as much as you want. (If you get an annual contract, the price goes down to $34.99 per month.) The other reason to go for an unlimited service plan is that you have to pay to *receive* e-mail on a wireless Palm. Even if you don't send much e-mail, you can end up spending a bundle on the messages you receive.

Controlling the radio

Your Palm i705 contains a radio for connecting to the Internet. It's not a regular radio (like, say, the one in your car); you can't tune it in to Lite FM broadcasts. Your Palm's radio only sends computer information back and forth between your Palm i705 and the Internet. (Nice tune, but you can't dance to it.)

When the radio runs, it wears down your battery charge pretty quickly. When the radio's not running, your Palm i705 goes for a month without a charge, easily. If you run the radio around the clock, you may only get a few days of power from your batteries. One wise precaution is to leave your Palm i705 in its charging cradle each night just to be sure the battery is topped off.

To save battery power, you can turn the radio on and off, or put it on a schedule to avoid draining your batteries overnight when you're sleeping and unlikely to be reading e-mail or checking the Web (unless you have a serious sleep disorder).

To turn your Palm radio on or off, follow these steps:

1. **Hold down the Wireless button for two seconds.**

   The Wireless Preferences screen appears.

2. **Tap the button at the top of the screen corresponding to your preference.**

   Your choices are Always On, Always Off, and Scheduled.

If you turn your radio off, you can't get e-mail or look things up on the Web, but you can use all the other Palm features, such as the Date Book, Address Book, and any other programs installed on your Palm device. If you do decide to send an e-mail or check the Web while the radio's off, a prompt appears asking whether you want to turn the radio on. Just tap Yes to make the radio run long enough to do your work.

Checking signal strength

You can take advantage of your Palm i705's wireless features in many parts of the United States, especially in most big cities and at airports. However, when you're in seclusion deep in the woods, you may be unable to check the head-lines on your Palm i705. But that's what seclusion is for, right? The rest of your Palm i705 will work fine, but you won't be able to check your e-mail until you return to civilization. Also, if you're hiding deep underground in a "secure undisclosed location" or just waiting in a subway station, you won't be able to check the latest stock prices until you emerge.

Your Palm i705 can't retrieve information for you unless you're within range of the Palm.Net signal. The Palm.Net signal is available in some locations but not in others, just like your favorite radio program, so you need to check to be sure.

To check Palm.Net signal strength:

1. **Press the MyPortal button (the second hard button from the right) for two seconds.**

   The Wireless Preferences screen appears.

2. **If the Always Off button at the top of the screen is darkened, tap the Always On button.**

   The radio logs on to Palm.Net and shows you how strong your signal is, as shown in Figure 15-1.

Figure 15-1:
The bars in the Diagnostics application show you how strong the Palm.Net signal is where you are. Five bars indicates a strong signal.

 If the signal is weak or absent at your location, you may do better if you move close to a window. If no signal is in your area, you just have to wait until your area is covered or move closer to civilization.

MyPalm: Your Portal to the Mobile Internet

Getting on the Internet with your Palm i705 is deceptively simple. Press the MyPalm Portal button (the second hard button from the right) to bring up the MyPalm screen, as shown in Figure 15-2. Use your stylus to tap any text on the screen you want to find out more about. For example, if you tap the word News you'll see a screen full of icons for well-known news services such as CNN and USA Today. If you've ever surfed the Web on a regular desktop computer, finding your way around the Palm portal will be second nature. If you ever get lost, just press the MyPalm Portal button to return to the main screen and start again.

Figure 15-2:
The MyPalm Portal is your doorway to wireless information services on your Palm i705.

As you can see in Figure 15-2, the MyPalm Portal screen is organized in four categories, with the most popular choices in each category featured prominently. The best way to find out about them is just to try each one out to see what it has to offer. Here's a quick summary of what you'll find.

Personalizing MyPage

MyPage is a screen on your i705 that you can customize to show the kinds of information you want to see at a glance. You may have run across customizable Web sites like this before; MyPage is like a Web page that you can only view on your Palm i705. If you like to see weather reports and stock prices right away, you can personalize the page to show you those items. If you're more interested in news headlines and your horoscope, you can just see those. If you use the scroll buttons to scroll to the bottom of the page and tap the Personalize This Page button, guess what you get to do? That's right, you get to launch the missiles. Okay, that's a fib — you get to personalize MyPage. (Which is really your page. Why? Don't ask.) You'll have to launch the missiles later.

Updating your Palm with MyPalm Update

Fish gotta swim, birds gotta fly, and software developers gotta software-develop, you know the song. (Stay tuned for my rendition of "Can't Help Loving That Palm of Mine" in my upcoming album, *Songs in the Key of Geek.*)

Keeping up with the latest software for your Palm device can be pretty time-consuming, because new stuff comes out every day. The MyPalm Update page takes some of the detective work out of keeping the software collection on your i705 up to date. To find the MyPalm Update page, press the MyPalm Portal button, tap Personalize, and then tap MyPalm Update to open the MyPalm update screen. Whenever developers release an important new piece of system software for your i705, you'll see it listed on a screen called the MyPalm Update page with a check box next to it. If you tap the check box, a check mark appears in the box and the software automatically gets downloaded and installed the next time you do a HotSync. If you see a piece of software listed in the MyPalm Update page with no accompanying check box, it means you already have that piece of software, so you don't need to worry about it.

Using the Internet

You may be wondering how they crammed the entire Internet into that tiny Palm gadget, no bigger than a pack of cigarillos. It's magic; you don't want to know. Remember how sad you were when you found out there was no Santa Claus? This is worse.

It seems a little silly to label just one part of the MyPalm page Internet since nearly all the information you find there comes from the Internet. But the Internet heading leads you to some of the plain-vanilla tasks that you might associate with using the Internet from a regular desktop computer.

Searching the Web

Great philosophers agree, if a thing isn't on the Internet, it doesn't exist. How many great philosophers say this? Exactly two, including myself and Sir Tom Collins, my philosophical stunt double.

The Google search engine can find nearly anything that exists on the Internet (and therefore exists at all), and you can access Google on your Palm i705 by following these steps:

1. **Press the MyPalm Portal button.**

   The MyPalm page appears.

2. **Tap the word Internet.**

   The Internet page appears.

3. **Tap Search the Web.**

   The Google search page appears.

4. **Tap the line below the words Search the Web.**

   The Insertion Point (a blinking line) appears at the spot you tapped to show what you've selected.

5. **Enter the text you want to search using either Graffiti or your favorite keyboard.**

   The text you enter appears on the line you tapped.

6. **Tap the Go button next to the text you typed.**

   A list of search results appears.

You can tap any of the sites on the list of search results to see a Web page containing your search term. Bear in mind, the page that pops up is unlikely to be designed to be seen on the small, monochrome screen of your Palm i705, so you may have trouble making out what it says.

Web surfing? Web clipping?

Lots of people are excited by the notion of surfing the Web wirelessly from their Palm i705. Unfortunately, that's not exactly what the unit does. When people say "surf the Web," they expect to fire up a program like Netscape and browse to any page, anywhere on the World Wide Web with full text and graphics in beautiful living color. When you enter a URL on the line labeled `Go to a URL`, the Palm i705 does let you view any Web site to a limited degree, but what you see lacks the color, most of the graphic design, and even a lot of the text you'd see if you viewed the same page on a desktop computer. The Palm screen is too small and the wireless connection is too slow to give you the full Web experience. (However, you can expect to see enormous improvements in future Palm models.)

The job your i705 does best is a different thing called *Web clipping,* which is a way of viewing a Web page that is specially formatted to fit on a smaller screen and deal with slower wireless connections. Most of the Web sites you see listed on the MyPalm Portal screen are specially formatted to look good on a Palm screen. You can also install special programs called *PQAs* (Palm Query Applications) that are designed to display particular Web sites on your Palm screen.

Web surfing is to Web clipping what riding the waves at Maui is to dipping your toes in the baby pool. You don't get the full experience of the Internet; you get only selected samples, or *clips.* That's pretty good, though. The Internet is so enormous that some people don't want to see everything — just a few, useful things. That's what Web clipping does: It gives you no more than you need and lets you get your information while you're on the go.

Going to a URL

Web site references are popping up everywhere. You see `www.something.com` on just about every object made: billboards, soda cans, bubblegum wrappers, you name it. If you get a sudden craving to visit `www.freebubblegum.com` while you're standing at the candy counter, you can whip out your Palm i705 and get a peek at that Web site, or any Web site you want to see, provided that you're happy seeing an all-gray version of the upper-left corner of the Web page. Just follow these steps:

1. **Press the MyPalm Portal hard button.**

   The MyPalm page appears.

2. **Tap the word Internet.**

   The Internet page appears.

3. **Tap Go to a URL.**

   The search page appears.

4. **Tap the line below the words Go to a URL.**

   The Insertion Point (a blinking line) appears at the spot you tapped to show what you've selected.

5. **Enter the URL you want to see by using either Graffiti or your favorite keyboard.**

   The text you enter appears on the line you tapped.

6. **Tap the Go button next to the text you typed.**

   The Web site for the URL that you entered appears on the screen.

If you use your Palm i705 to go to a Web site you're accustomed to viewing on a desktop computer, don't be surprised if parts of the site don't work the way you're used to having them work. Animated graphics, for example, don't work on the Palm screen. Also, many Web sites use sophisticated technologies with names such as Java and Flash that just don't work when you load them on a Palm i705 like they do on your desktop computer. On the other hand, you can't use your desktop computer on the cross town bus, so I guess it's an even trade.

Downloading Web clipping applications

Many Web site owners are eager to cater to the influential, forward-thinking, early-adopting kinds of people who carry a Palm i705 (like yourself, naturally). Many of those Webmasters write little programs you can install on your Palm i705 to make their Web sites look attractive and work well on that tiny screen. Those programs are called *Web Clipping Applications,* and you can choose among hundreds for the right one to add to your Palm device. (*Web clipping* is a way of preformatting a Web page before you view it so that it fits on a smaller screen and can deal with slower wireless connections.) You can either download a Web Clipping Application to your desktop computer and install it like any other Palm application (see Chapter 13 for more about installing Palm software), or you can download a Web Clipping Application wirelessly right on your Palm i705 and let it install itself by following these steps:

1. **Press the MyPalm Portal button.**

   The MyPalm page appears.

2. **Tap the word Internet.**

   The Internet page appears.

3. **Tap Download Web Clipping Application.**

   The search page appears.

4. **Tap the line below the words Web Clipping Search.**

   The Insertion Point (a blinking line) appears at the spot you tapped to show what you've selected.

5. **Enter a description of a Web Clipping Application you'd like to find by using either Graffiti or your favorite keyboard.**

   The text you enter appears on the line you tapped. If you're looking for applications related to shopping, for example, enter the word **Shopping**.

6. **Tap the Search button below the text you typed.**

   A list of applications that answer your description appears on the screen.

7. **Tap the word Download next to the name of an application you want to try.**

   The download screen appears, as shown in Figure 15-3.

8. **Tap the Start Download button.**

   The file downloads and the Download Complete dialog box appears.

Figure 15-3:
You can download and install new applications through the MyPalm Portal.

9. **Tap OK.**

After you finish downloading a Web Clipping Application, you see the new program in your list of programs when you tap the Applications button next to the Graffiti area.

Using Palm.Net Wireless E-Mail with Your Palm i705

Oddly, the Palm i705 offers several different tools for exchanging e-mail. Some of those tools are built right into your i705 and get set up automatically, others are built-in but you need to set them up, and others can be downloaded and set up after you've installed them. Whew! Don't despair; I'll show you the simplest solutions first. Later in the chapter I show you where to find more complicated solutions, if you're interested in that sort of thing.

Setting up MultiMail on Palm.Net

The program that your Palm i705 uses to exchange e-mail is called MultiMail Deluxe. When you set up your Palm.Net wireless service, you're automatically assigned an e-mail address on the Palm.Net service, and MultiMail is automatically set up to send and receive message at that e-mail address.

I have good news and bad news about Palm.Net e-mail. The bad news is that your Palm.Net e-mail account has its own e-mail address, usually `yourname@ palm.com`. You've probably given some other e-mail address to everybody you know, so the last thing you want to do is to start handing out a new e-mail address. But don't despair; you can set your Palm i705 to collect e-mail messages from your other e-mail accounts if you wish. I show you how to do that later in the chapter.

The good news is that you can set up MultiMail to notify you when messages arrive at your Palm.Net account, by either beeping, flashing, or vibrating (or all three)! So you can throw out your pager and give your Palm.Net e-mail address to people who urgently need to reach you.

Creating a message

No magic is involved in creating a message for wireless delivery. It's really just another e-mail message. Still, you probably want to know some details, so follow these steps to create a message:

1. **With the MultiMail Deluxe program open, tap New.**

   The New Message screen appears, as shown in Figure 15-4.

2. **If you know your recipient's e-mail address by heart, enter that address by using Graffiti or the on-screen keyboard.**

   If you do this step, skip ahead to Step 9.

3. **If you don't know your recipient's address but you have entered it in your Address Book, you can look it up.**

   If you need to look the address up, continue with Step 4.

Figure 15-4:
Create
a new
message
in the
MultiMail
program.

4. **Tap the word To.**

   The Recipient List screen appears.

5. **Tap Lookup.**

   The To Lookup screen appears, showing the e-mail addresses you entered on your Address List. The screen doesn't show everyone in your Address Book, just those who have e-mail addresses. I like that part.

6. **Tap the name of the person to whom you're sending the message.**

   Your recipient's name is highlighted, as shown in Figure 15-5.

Figure 15-5:
The name of
the recipient
you choose
is high-
lighted to
show you've
selected it.

7. **Tap Add.**

   The address of your recipient appears.

8. **Tap Done.**

   The New Message screen reappears, showing the names of the people to whom you've chosen to send your message.

9. **Tap the line to the right of Subj.**

    A blinking line, named the *insertion point,* appears, and Subj is highlighted.

10. **Enter the subject of your message by using either the on-screen keyboard or Graffiti.**

    The text you enter appears on the Subj line. (Refer to Chapter 2 for more info about entering text.)

11. **Tap the blank area below Subj.**

    The insertion point appears.

12. **Enter the text of your message by using either the on-screen keyboard or Graffiti.**

    The text you enter appears on the screen.

13. **Tap Send.**

    Your message is sent automatically.

If you prefer, you can tap Outbox instead of Send in order to send your message later. You might want to do that if you're out of range of Palm.Net service or in a building that blocks your radio signal. When you want to send your message out, you'll have to tap the Check & Send button on the main MultiMail screen to send the message to your recipient. Don't worry if you need to wait a while to send your message: The message stays in the Outbox until you connect to the network successfully.

Reading a message

The great thing about the Palm.Net e-mail is that it lets you read messages anywhere. Instead of rushing back to the office or lugging a laptop around town, you can just whip out your Palm i705 and see who's trying to reach you.

To read a message:

1. **Press the MultiMail button.**

    The Inbox screen appears showing your list of messages.

2. **Tap the message you want to read.**

    The text of the message you tap appears, as shown in Figure 15-6.

3. **After you finish reading the message, tap Done.**

    Your message closes, and the list of messages reappears. The names of messages you haven't read yet appear in boldface, and the messages you've read appear in a normal typeface.

As long as you leave the radio on, your i705 will automatically collect your messages and alert you when new messages arrive.

Figure 15-6:
The text
of the
message
you want
to read
appears on
the screen.

Replying to a message

If you feel anxious to keep up with your e-mail every second of every day,
you're probably just as anxious to reply to some of those e-mail messages.
Replies are just a simple way of creating a message in direct response to a
message someone else sends you; you can tell the sender what you think of a
message without needing to look up the sender's e-mail address.

To reply to a message:

1. **With the MultiMail Deluxe program open, tap the message you want to
   reply to.**

   The text of the message you tap appears.

2. **Tap Reply.**

   The Reply Options dialog box opens, as shown in Figure 15-7.

Figure 15-7:
Choose
your reply
options,
plain or
deluxe.

3. **Tap Sender.**

   You can choose an additional option: Include Original Text. Including
   some original text is normally a good idea when you reply to a message
   so the recipient knows what you're replying to.

4. **Tap OK.**

   The New Message screen appears. Your recipient's e-mail address
   appears on the To line, and the Subj line shows Re: followed by the

subject of the original message. If you chose in Step 3 to include the original message text in your reply, then that text appears in the body of your new message.

You can change any of this text by deleting and adding text as you normally would.

5. **If you want to add new addresses to the To line of the message, enter the new addresses on that line.**

   You can add an address to a message you're replying to in the same way you do when you create a new message. (See the section, "Creating a message," earlier in this chapter, for details.) Normally, you leave this step alone because the address of the person who sent you the original message is already included on the To line when you tap Reply.

6. **Enter the text you want to add by using either the on-screen keyboard or Graffiti (refer to Chapter 2 for more info about entering text).**

   The text you enter appears with the original message's text.

7. **Tap Send.**

   Your message is sent to your recipient.

You can also tap Outbox instead of Send if you want to wait and send your message later.

Setting up other e-mail accounts

Most e-mail accounts on the Internet use a system called POP3, which stands for Post Office Protocol. The big exception to this rule is AOL, which uses a system totally different than anybody else uses, so what I'm about to say doesn't work for AOL users.

If you have an e-mail account on most normal e-mail services, you can set up your Palm.Net account to collect your messages and forward them to your i705 either daily or hourly. Just log onto `my.palm.com/email` and sign up for external e-mail collection. You'll need to know your e-mail server names and e-mail passwords for the accounts you want to collect on your Palm.Net account in order to get the accounts set up.

Using Other E-Mail

You can send and receive several different kinds of e-mail on your Palm i705, but not always through MultiMail. If you're new to MultiMail, that won't matter much to you. What *will* matter is collecting your messages.

Accessing AOL e-mail

If you have an AOL e-mail account (or several AOL e-mail accounts), you can use the special AOL e-mail program on the Palm i705 and read the same lively messages you read on your regular AOL account. To access the AOL e-mail program, follow these steps:

1. **Press the MyPalm Portal button.**

   The MyPalm page appears.

2. **Tap the word Communicate.**

   The Internet page appears.

3. **Tap the words AOL Mail.**

   The AOL logon screen appears.

4. **Tap the triangle next to the words Screen Name.**

   A drop-down list appears offering choices like Existing Member, Guest, New User, and any screen names you've entered before.

5. **Tap the words Existing Member.**

   The choice you selected appears on the screen.

6. **Tap Sign On.**

   The sign on screen appears, asking for your screen name and password.

7. **Enter your screen name and password on the lines provided by using either Graffiti or your favorite keyboard.**

   The text you enter appears.

8. **Tap Sign On.**

   The AOL mail screen appears.

Unfortunately, you won't hear the little guy say "You've got mail!" but you'll still get your messages. That's a small price to pay for the ability to read your e-mail at the beach.

Retrieving Hotmail, Juno, Yahoo! Mail, and others

Palm also offers a free e-mail program called ThinAir Mail in special, customized versions for people who want to use a Palm i705 to access messages on services such as Hotmail, Juno, and Yahoo! Each version works a little bit differently, so you'll need to go to my.palm.com for details on how to set up the program that works with your particular service.

Using AOL Instant Messaging

AOL Instant Messaging (also known as AIM) is possibly the most popular program on the Internet (after e-mail). More than 150 million people use the AOL Instant Message program every day. Some people love AOL Instant Messaging so much that they're reluctant to even grab a sandwich or take a walk lest they miss that telltale "bing" of AOL Instant Messenger. If you have that kind of boundless AOL enthusiasm, then your Palm i705 can provide that pleasure wherever you go.

Don't feel left out if you're not an AOL member; AOL Instant Messenger is available for free to anyone who signs up. Unfortunately, you can't sign up from your i705; to sign up for AOL Instant Messenger and to download the desktop software, you have to log on to the Web at www.aim.com. After you've created an account on your desktop computer, you can log onto AIM from your i705 by following these steps:

1. **Press the MyPalm Portal button.**

   The MyPalm page appears.

2. **Tap the words Instant Messaging.**

   The AOL Instant Messenger Sign On screen appears.

3. **Tap Setup.**

   The AIM Setup screen appears.

4. **Tap Add.**

   The Add dialog box appears.

5. **Enter your screen name and password on the lines provided by using either Graffiti or your favorite keyboard.**

   The choice you selected appears on the screen.

6. **Tap OK.**

   The name you entered appears in your list of screen names.

7. **Tap the left-pointing arrow at the lower-left corner of the screen.**

   The AOL Instant Messenger Sign On screen reappears.

8. **Tap the triangle next to the words Screen Name.**

   The list of screen names you've set up appears.

9. **Tap the screen name you want to use to log on.**

   The name you select appears on the AOL Sign On screen.

10. **Tap Sign On.**

    The AOL Instant Messenger Main Screen appears.

Can I connect MY phone to MY Palm?

People often ask me, "Can I connect a regular Palm device to a cell phone?" But that's not what they're really asking. They really want to ask, *Can I connect MY cell phone to MY Palm device?* The answer to the first question is yes, but the answer to the real question is *Who knows*? To connect a Palm device to a cell phone and get access to the Internet you need some basics:

✔ The right phone

✔ The right cellular carrier

✔ The right service plan

✔ The right cables or connectors for making the two devices work together.

You can currently choose from among dozens of carriers (such as Sprint, Verizon, Voicestream, and others), scores of service plans, and hundreds of phones, so it's impossible to give directions that speak to every single person's situation. Your best bet is to check with your cellular carrier and see whether a kit is available for using a Palm device on the service with one of their phones. If you are considering shopping for a new cell phone in your effort to make the Palm-to-Internet connection, you may want to take a look at the units that combine a Palm organizer and a phone (just to eliminate some of the guesswork).

True Instant Message (IM) enthusiasts will no doubt be thrilled by the possibilities of being having IM wherever they go. Some of the key benefits include the following:

✔ Nagging your kids by IM

✔ Comparing answers on exams (during the exam)

✔ Sending an IM to someone in the cubicle right next to you, just to hear their computer go "bing!"

I'm sure you'll come up with your own clever ways to take advantage of mobile Instant Messaging.

Combining Palms and Phones

The cell phone is the most popular wireless device on earth. More than 100 million people worldwide carry cell phones, as opposed to around 25 million Palm device owners. Little by little, the Palm computer and the cell phone are merging, which is convenient, because a combined phone/PDA means you have one fewer gadget to fuss with.

As I write this, three companies are offering Palm-powered cell phones. Palm Computing, Inc. doesn't currently offer a hybrid organizer/cell phone, but rumors abound that it'll be releasing its own phone in the very near future.

So far, three major entrants have appeared in the Palm-powered cell phone derby:

- **Kyocera:** Kyocera's phones are available through most of the major cellular phone providers, including Verizon and others. The earlier smart phones were a bit larger than ordinary Palm devices, which made them a bit less popular than they might have been, but the phones included a real, physical numeric keypad for dialing, a real plus for people who make a lot of calls. The company has announced a new model, the Kyocera 7135, that promises the best of all worlds. It has a color screen, a physical keypad, and a Secure Digital expansion port just like other Palm models (see Chapter 18 for more about Palm expansion cards), all in a smaller device than the older phones. The phone also runs on most standard North American cell networks. (Check with your carrier for details.)

- **Samsung:** The i300 from Samsung features a sleek, compact metal case and a bright color screen, but no physical keypad; you have to dial through the touchscreen. Still, size matters when it comes to pocket-sized devices, so Samsung's entry, which is offered most prominently by Sprint, has a leg up on the older Kyocera models in that department. The company is expected to release new models by the end of 2002, so stay tuned.

- **Handspring Treo:** The Treo has attracted lots of attention for its convenient small size and built-in alphabetic keyboard in place of a Graffiti area. Most reviewers have been enthusiastic about Treo's design and features, although current Treo models only run on cellular networks that use the GSM system, which is more popular in Europe than in the United States. To find out more about Treo, take a look at *Treo & Visor For Dummies*, written by yours truly, and published by Wiley Publishing, Inc.

3G: The next generation

Cell phone technology changes as fast as any other technology, so you shouldn't be surprised that a new cell phone system is being installed with a raft of bells and whistles. The new system is called 3G (for Third Generation) and it promises to add super-speedy Internet connections to your cell phone. By the time you read this, Sprint will have introduced its version of this zippy new system, called Sprint PCS Vision, along with the new Handspring Treo 300 to take advantage of the system. Verizon has also announced a new high-speed data/cell phone network, and other carriers are following suit. I have every reason to believe that some kind of Palm-powered phone will come down the pike soon enough to take advantage of all the new services that these speedy new networks can provide.

Chapter 16

Professional Palm Software

*T*hat tiny little Palm device can take on thousands of different personalities when you add any of the myriad software titles that developers are constantly cooking up. If I were to describe every existing Palm software title in this volume, you'd need a wheelbarrow to carry the book around. Thus, the programs I discuss in this chapter are among the best known and are loved by Palm aficionados.

Access Dining Guides

Since the dawn of humanity, the eternal question remains: "What'll we have for dinner?" Whether you're hungry for moo shoo, manicotti, or macaroni, a Palm dining guide can help you find a restaurant to suit your taste.

Vindigo

Vindigo, possibly the most popular program for the Palm platform, is an electronic guide to most of America's major cities. If you live in or visit any of America's dozen most populous cities, just tell Vindigo exactly where you are in the city — and you get a quick, comprehensive guide to everything nearby — restaurants, movies, shops, banks, and art exhibits, or anything you want in the way of dining, entertainment, or recreation. To locate Vindigo, go to www.palmpilotfordummies.com/vindigo.

TealMeal

What do you want for dinner? Pizza, Chinese, or burgers (again)? TealMeal can help you pick a restaurant that has what you want. You can either enter a list of your own favorite restaurants in TealMeal or download TealMeal databases for cities around the world, from Milwaukee to Kuala Lumpur. Discover more about TealMeal at www.palmpilotfordummies.com/tealmeal.

Bill for Your Time

TimeReporter for TimeSlips is a tool for people who earn a living through hourly billings. Record the time you spend on all your various clients and projects on the job by using TimeReporter and automatically synchronize the data you enter with TimeSlips, the desktop time-tracking application that's so popular with lawyers, consultants, and other professionals. You can find out more at www.palmpilotfordummies.com/timereporter.

Browse the Internet

The Internet seems to be everywhere these days, so you might as well have it on your Palm device, too. Most Web-browsing programs for the Palm device are much less speedy and sophisticated than the ones you use on your desktop, but many people find it mighty convenient to have Web information on a Palm device that's right in their pocket.

AvantGo

Many Palm owners wouldn't be caught dead without AvantGo, a Web-page reader designed especially for the Palm platform. I guess it's a stretch to call AvantGo a browser, because it really captures copies of your favorite Web pages and formats them for viewing on your Palm device. One drawback to using AvantGo is that it increases the time it takes to HotSync your Palm device, a fact that many people find frustrating. But if you need to take information from the Web and carry it around on your Palm device, AvantGo is a popular tool for the job. You can find out more at www.palmpilotfordummies.com/avantgo.

Blazer

The people at Handspring who make the Visor and Treo offer their own Web browser called Blazer, specially designed to deliver the best possible Web-browsing experience on that tiny little screen, as shown in Figure 16-1. The program is included free with the Treo, as well as with certain Visor accessories. If you didn't get a free copy because you bought a different kind of Palm device, you can find out how to buy the program online at www.palmpilotfordummies.com/blazer.

Figure 16-1: Blazer puts big-time Web browsing on that little Palm screen.

Create Outlines

You can find several outliner programs for Palm devices. BrainForest is one of the best known of the outliner programs. It allows you to organize your thoughts into "trees" with "branches" and "leaves" you can move, copy, sort, and delete. You can investigate BrainForest at www.palmpilotfordummies.com/brainforest.

Dictate by Phone

Copytalk lets you enter data into your Palm device with a simple phone call. The system is actually a typing service you can call — actual (live!) human typists transcribe the appointments, addresses, e-mail messages, and other items you dictate. They then forward your items to you via the Internet; the Copytalk software pops your dictated items directly into the right place on your Palm device. Monthly fees for the service start at $9.95 per month or $49.95 per year and go up depending on how many items you dictate each month. It's the next best thing to having a personal assistant. You can check Copytalk out at www.palmpilotfordummies.com/copytalk.

Gather Addresses

Most business involves a lot of selling; any successful entrepreneur is constantly hunting for new prospects. Address Grabber from ProdEx Technologies snaps up names and addresses you find on the Internet and pops 'em into your Palm Desktop, Microsoft Outlook, or nearly any other name-and-address program on your computer. Why waste time typing addresses when you could be dialing for dollars? Check out Address Grabber at www.palmpilotfordummies.com/addressgrabber.

Get Tech Support

Remedy Help Desk, from Peregrine Remedy Corporation, is part of an elaborate system you can use to track and manage computer problems in a large organization. If you've ever worked as a computer-help-desk person, you know how much trivial information you need to organize and keep current. You also need to know how many times technicians visit a certain computer and how many things are done to that machine. With Remedy Help Desk, field technicians can enter information about problems and solutions while in the field and then update the big company database by performing a simple HotSync. For more about Remedy Help Desk, see www.palmpilotfordummies.com/remedy.

Keep Your Finances in Order

It was only a matter of time before someone said, "Gee, I'd sure like to have a copy of Quicken on my Palm." The nice people from LandWare worked with the people who make Quicken to produce Pocket Quicken, a convenient way to keep your most important financial data on a Palm organizer. The program synchronizes with Quicken to help you keep track of your current balances and lets you make entries to Quicken from your Palm device while you're roaming around. For more information, go to www.palmpilotfordummies.com/pocketquicken.

Manage Real Estate Sales

Those on the upper tiers of the real-estate business know that Top Producer is the software of choice among successful realtors. The program has a desktop portion and a Palm portion (called Top Producer for Palm Organizers), so you need to use both if you want to keep track of clients, listings, sales calls, and all the other details that move you closer to closing. You can find out all about Top Producer from the developer's Web site at `www.palmpilot fordummies.com/topproducer`.

Manage Your Portfolio

How do you make a million dollars in the stock market? Start with 10 million. If your money is tied up in stocks (and if there's any left), you want detailed information about what's happening on Wall Street. Years ago, you needed an expensive stock ticker to get the latest from the exchanges. Now you can use a Palm device for a complete set of stock management tools like Handango's Finance Suite no matter where you are. Becoming a Palm investment mogul isn't all that expensive; check out the package at `www.palmpilotfordummies.com/handangofinance`.

Play Games

You can choose from games such as Atum, Bejeweled, Blackjack, Hangman, Solitaire, Zap!, and many others. Call it a personal problem, but I just can't handle having games on my Palm device. I've been forced to delete several of the suspects mentioned here because I just can't stop playing 'em. I'm especially fond of Atum and Blackjack. If you surf the Web a bit, you're sure to find plenty of Palm games to keep you occupied at `www.palmpilotfordummies.com/games`.

Proof and Edit Text

Some people just can't stop themselves from changing what other people wrote. (Hey, somebody's got to do it, right?) When you need to find just the right word, TrueTerm can find it for you in a variety of languages. The program is available in several versions:

- ✔ An English-only dictionary
- ✔ A thesaurus
- ✔ A program that provides a rough-and-ready translation from English to another language

TrueTerm runs best on a Palm device that has at least 8MB of space. (TrueTerm takes up well over 1MB of space, so it may be too big to fit on a 2MB unit such as a Palm M105 after you add other stuff.) You can find out more about TrueTerm at `www.palmpilotfordummies.com/trueterm`.

Read Documents

If you spend any time at all reading documents on the Web, you've probably come across items in the popular Adobe Acrobat format, also known as PDF. Adobe Acrobat Reader is the preferred electronic publishing program for lots of businesses and government organizations. Acrobat's claim to fame is that it displays a document almost exactly the same way on many different kinds of computers, including PCs, Macs, and even Palm devices. You can find out more about Adobe Acrobat Reader for Palm OS at www.palmpilotfor dummies.com/acrobat.

You can also download a free guide to getting the most from Palm eBooks. Go to www.palmpilotfordummies.com/ebooks.

Record Your Automobile Expenses

You can enter the cost of gas, oil, repairs, and mileage into a handy program called Time Expense Automobile Keeper (TEAK) so that you know the overall cost of operating your vehicle. The program simplifies the process of tracking your time, expenses, and automobile mileage on your Palm organizer as well as on your PC. With the click of a button, you can easily generate comprehensive time, expense, and mileage reports. With the click of a mouse, you can find out more at www.palmpilotfordummies.com/teak.

Remove Duplicates

Once in a blue moon, the HotSync process messes up and creates two of everything on your Palm device. UnDupe automatically converts your double vision back to normal. You can get a clearer picture of what UnDupe does at www.palmpilotfordummies.com/undupe.

Research

The Palm organizer is a gift for this writer; I always get my best ideas when I'm farthest from a computer. The most useful program I've ever run across for use as a writer is Info Select, which is shown in Figure 16-2, from MicroLogic (www.palmpilotfordummies.com/infoselect). Info Select is an amazing, triple-jointed information manager that keeps all the scraps and tidbits of information you gather, putting them in a huge outline that you can search, arrange, and print nearly any way you want. The program runs under

Windows and includes a Palm version that you can install to your Palm device so you can synchronize information between the Palm device and your desktop. The best thing about Info Select is that you can find information with it on the desktop almost instantly.

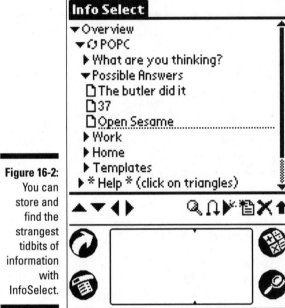

Figure 16-2:
You can store and find the strangest tidbits of information with InfoSelect.

Store Passwords

You probably have so many passwords and secret ID numbers to keep track of that you can't remember half of them. Of course, you don't want to write down your secret passwords where the bad guys could find them and do nasty things, so what do you do? Use a program like Cloak to store your passwords by using a safely encrypted storage system, keeping secret numbers safe from prying eyes. To learn the secrets of Cloak, see www.palmpilot fordummies.com/cloak.

Stay Fit

I won't mention any names, but many people need help in the diet and exercise departments. Diet & Exercise Assistant from Keyoe, Inc. (www.palmpilot fordummies.com/diet) is one of the most popular Palm programs for munch-management.

Research shows that nothing shocks you into good behavior faster than recalling just how badly you've eaten in the recent past. Diet & Exercise Assistant helps you track your food intake and set suitable diet goals for your age, sex, height, and weight. You can download a free trial copy of the program, which runs for five days. If you haven't given up on your diet by then, you can order the full-featured version. I plan to start using Diet & Exercise Assistant . . . tomorrow.

Study

Who says memorization is boring and old-fashioned? Okay, maybe it's old-fashioned, but you can make memorization fun by using one of the flash card programs available for your Palm device. One of the most versatile programs, SuperMemory, lets you create lists of text on your desktop and convert them into a system that you can use to drill students in collections of facts. You can sneak a peek at SuperMemory by going to `www.palmpilotfordummies.com/supermemory`.

Synchronize

The folks who invented the original PalmPilot were smart enough to make it work with the programs you already have on your Windows PC. You may already have a *PIM* (personal information manager) that you're attached to (or stuck with) for good reasons. As Palm devices have caught on, more and more companies make PIMs and offer ways to link their products to Palm devices. Other companies make their fortunes by creating ways to connect your Palm device to programs from companies that prefer not to support Palm devices (yes, Microsoft is one of those — how did you know?).

The Palm Desktop program that comes with your Palm device talks directly to your Palm device every time you hit the HotSync button. (For more info about HotSyncing, see Chapter 13.) Because the Palm device was made to talk to the Palm Desktop, you don't need another program to act as a go-between. If you're already using a different program for your PIM, such as Microsoft Outlook or ACT!, you need a program to translate and move information between your Windows PC and your Palm device. Several programs, called *conduits* or *synchronizing tools,* can do the job for Windows users.

You can choose between several well-known conduit programs for Microsoft Windows. Although these programs all do a similar job, each offers a slightly different set of features at a different price:

✔ **PocketMirror Standard, from Chapura:** This is the least expensive synchronization program. In fact, you get a copy of the program free when you purchase any Palm device. PocketMirror can synchronize your Palm device only with Microsoft Outlook and offers relatively few of the more advanced features that competitors offer, but for the many people who don't *use* the more advanced features, PocketMirror is a perfectly good choice. To find out how to soup up PocketMirror, see www.palmpilot fordummies.com/pocketmirror.

For more information about Microsoft Outlook, check out *Microsoft Outlook 2002 For Windows For Dummies,* written by yours truly and published by Wiley Publishing, Inc.

✔ **PocketMirror Professional, from Chapura:** This is the next step up from the free program that comes with your Palm device. It does everything the free version does, and it also lets you synchronize Outlook subfolders and Public folders if you use Outlook in a large enterprise with Microsoft Exchange.

✔ **Desktop To Go, from DataViz, Inc.:** You can buy this program to synchronize a Palm device with Microsoft Outlook and Schedule+. The program enables you to do a couple of fancy things with Outlook when you synchronize (tricks you can't do with PocketMirror), such as tell Outlook to send information from your Outlook custom fields to certain fields on your Palm device. Because almost nobody uses more than one type of PIM, Desktop To Go does a fine job of synchronizing your Palm device. You can also use Desktop To Go to synchronize a limited date range in the Date Book so that you spend less time waiting for your Palm device to finish synchronizing. For example, if you have 100 appointments in your schedule, spread out over the next year, a HotSync takes longer than if you have only a few appointments scheduled in the next week. You may want to tell the conduit to synchronize only the appointments for the next week to speed up the HotSync process. You can find more information at www.palmpilotfordummies.com/desktoptogo.

✔ **Intellisync, from PumaTech:** The most powerful and best-known conduit available for the Palm device, Intellisync enables your Palm device to trade information with just about every major personal information manager out there, including Goldmine, ACT, and Lotus Organizer. If you're an Outlook user, Intellisync also lets you synchronize your Palm device to any Outlook folders you choose, and it retains the categories you assign to your items in Outlook when those items turn up on your Palm device. Using Intellisync is overkill if you use Outlook in only the simplest way, but if you're an Outlook power user or use organizers other than Outlook, Intellisync is indispensable. Further intelligence on Intellisync can be gleaned at www.palmpilotfordummies.com/ intellisync.

You can also find Intellisync products for synchronizing handheld computers with Web sites, laptop computers with desktop computers, and heaven knows what else. (If the company made a product to synchronize your VCR with your popcorn popper, I wouldn't be surprised.)

Before you rush out and buy a special program to synchronize your Palm device with your PIM, check with the people who make your PIM to see whether you can get a free conduit for the program you use. For example, the people who make ACT! offer a special program to link their product with Palm devices. In fact, recent versions of ACT! 4.0 include a Palm link right on the CD.

The three most popular PIMs have books devoted to them. I wrote a book about Microsoft Outlook, cleverly titled *Microsoft Outlook 2000 For Windows For Dummies,* which, as you might guess, I highly recommend. For ACT! users, Jeffrey J. Mayer has written a great book just for you: *ACT! 4 For Windows For Dummies.* Lotus Organizer, which remains popular after years as one of the top PIMs, is covered in *Lotus SmartSuite Millennium Edition For Dummies,* by Michael Meadhra and Jan Weingarten. (All of these books are published by Wiley Publishing, Inc.)

Take an Opinion Poll

Nothing is more crucial to marketers than focus groups and public-opinion polls. You have to know what your customers are thinking long before they whip out those credit cards. Stay one step ahead of the competition with a program called SurveyMate (see Figure 16-3) from www.palmpilotfordummies.com/surveymate. This program lets you enter a list of questions and record the answers people give you, whether those answers are true/false, yes/no, or multiple-choice.

Figure 16-3:
What's your opinion? Find out with SurveyMate.

Use a Launcher

You don't need to switch between the Palm Computing applications to enter your appointments and to-dos if you have Actioneer. You can enter plain-English statements like *Call Bob tomorrow at 2 p.m.* into Actioneer and let the program create the appointment or to-do as necessary. Actioneer also offers a similar program for Microsoft Outlook users. You can take action to find out more at www.palmpilotfordummies.com/actioneer.

Use a Word Processor

WriteSmart Pro consists of three small programs you can use to enter text on your Palm organizer more quickly and accurately:

- ✔ **Jot** is a plain-language Graffiti replacement.
- ✔ **QuickNotes** helps create and organize drawings and diagrams.
- ✔ **WordComplete** is a program that intelligently guesses what word you're entering and fills out the word to save you time.

Find out more at www.palmpilotfordummies.com/writesmart.

Utilize Databases

The term database sounds spooky and Big-Brotherish, but databases are usually fairly harmless and often pretty useful. The card catalog at your library is a database, and so is your list of Christmas card recipients. You'll probably run across dozens of databases you'd like to carry around on a Palm device, so it's good to know that you can choose from several good Palm database programs.

HanDBase Plus Edition

I use HanDBase more than any other Palm database program because it's both powerful and easy to use. With HanDBase you can easily create databases right on your Palm device without using a desktop program at all, as shown in Figure 16-4. The manufacturer also offers a good set of easy-to-use desktop tools. You can find out more about HanDBase at www.palmpilotfor dummies.com/handbase.

JFile

JFile is the granddaddy of database programs for Palm devices. It's not as snazzy or powerful as some of the more recent database programs like HanDBase or MobileDB, but because it's the oldest Palm database program, it can run a huge range of prepackaged databases. You can find ready-made JFile databases covering everything from drink recipes to chemical elements.

Figure 16-4:
You can
create your
own data-
bases on
your Palm
device with
HanDBase.

JPack

The people at Land-J who developed JFile have wrapped up a collection of their most popular programs in a suite called JPack. In addition to JFile, the collection that you'll find at www.palmpilotfordummies.com/jpack includes the following:

- ✔ **JShopper:** This program is a shopping list organizer. You can arrange your list by store at as many as ten different stores. It also helps you keep up with coupons.

- ✔ **JTutor:** This flash card program is great for memorizing information and drilling to improve your recall.

- ✔ **Jookerie:** This game was derived from the classic dictionary game in which people make up definitions of words to try to fool their opponents.

- ✔ **JStones:** Described as "an addictive board game," JStones demands that you earn points by placing markers, or "stones," on a playing board according to an elaborate set of rules.

MobileDB

MobileDB is another fine database program for the Palm whose claim to fame is its ability to connect to FileMaker Pro, which is an extremely popular database program for desktop computers that runs on both Windows machines and Macs. On your Palm device, MobileDB can print, beam, and even clone items. (Sorry, it can only clone database items; you can't use MobileDB to clone yourself, at least not in this version.) Find out more about MobileDB at `www.palmpilotfordummies.com/mobiledb`.

View Images

You can display photographs on your Palm device with the help of a program such as AcidImage from Red-Mercury. Several programs can display photos on your Palm device, including Roxio PhotoSuite Mobile Edition (which is included on many Palm models), FireViewer, and SplashPhoto, but AcidImage specializes in displaying photos in the popular JPG format without making you convert them to a Palm-specific format first. That makes it possible to take photos directly from your digital camera on a Multimedia card and view them directly on your Palm device. Although showing photos on your Palm device may seem awfully geeky, you may have your reasons for wanting to see pictures on your Palm device. I know of a Palm-toting couple who keep their wedding pictures on their matching Palm devices. Isn't that romantic? (You can find out more about AcidImage at `www.palmpilotfordummies.com/acidimage`.)

Work with Office Suites

Your Palm device isn't quite ready to replace your laptop, but programs like Documents To Go, which I discuss at length in Chapter 10, and Quickoffice bring that possibility one step closer. Quickoffice is fairly similar to Documents to Go, but it has a slightly different set of strengths. The product consists of three programs: Quicksheet, Quickword, and Quickchart. This trio performs many of the jobs for which most people use a desktop word processor or spreadsheet program. The files you create with Quickoffice can be synchronized with Microsoft Office documents on your desktop so that you can keep and update critical information while you're on the run. Quicksheet, the spreadsheet program, was the first program in the Quickoffice collection, and the suite's greatest strength is its capability to deal with numbers. For details about Quickoffice, see `www.palmpilotfordummies.com/quickoffice`.

And Plenty More

This list is not exhaustive (although perhaps exhausting). If you want to hunt for more software for your Palm device, check out `www.palmpilotfordummies.com/software`.

Chapter 17

Special Delivery: Using Palm Mail

Although e-mail is convenient, the business of sitting in front of a computer to read and write e-mail isn't so convenient. Your Palm device includes a rather basic e-mail program that enables you to carry a little bucket of messages wherever you go. You can read messages and compose replies while you're sitting by the Seine or riding the subway. I have to admit that the program has its limits, but I often find using my Palm device a handy way to deal with my e-mail.

Don't let the convenience of Palm e-mail lull you into carelessness. Driving while reading e-mail on your Palm device is a pretty risky business, so please pull over first. I don't want anyone to get arrested for DWE (Driving While E-mailing).

Making Sense of the Palm Postal System

The Palm e-mail program doesn't exchange messages like a desktop e-mail package does. The e-mail program acts as an accessory to the e-mail program on your desktop. When you perform a HotSync, the e-mail program copies the messages in your desktop's Inbox and stores those copies on your Palm device. You can read or reply to those messages or compose new messages on your Palm device when you're away from your desktop computer. When you get back to your desktop computer, you have to perform another HotSync to move your outgoing messages to your desktop e-mail program, which does the work of actually delivering the messages. See Chapter 14 for more about the HotSync program.

The Palm i705 features a mail program called MultiMail Deluxe. It works much like the Palm e-mail program, except that it sends messages directly from your Palm i705 to the recipient wirelessly without connecting to any other computer. This chapter is about the original Palm e-mail program, which is not that clever. (You can read more about the Palm i705 in Chapter 15.)

The Palm e-mail program can't send messages directly to their recipients without a desktop e-mail program to do the heavy lifting. Palm Mail does not work well independently. (You probably know people like that at work.) That's not what it's designed to do.

You can overcome this limitation by taking a few extra steps. If you want to send e-mail directly from your Palm device, you need something that connects it to the Internet, such as the PalmModem, which I discuss in Chapter 11. You also need to buy one of the independent e-mail programs for your Palm device that I mention at the end of this chapter.

In the following sections, I focus on showing you how to use what comes out of the box with your Palm device.

Working with Your Messages

You can use the built-in Palm e-mail program only if you have a desktop mail program with which to synchronize it. You can do many of the same tasks with Palm Mail that you can with your desktop e-mail program, such as read and write messages, reply to messages, and forward messages. However, some popular e-mail features, such as attaching files or reading attached files, aren't available in Palm Mail. You may be willing to trade those features for the ability to read your e-mail on a bicycle built for two (preferably on the back seat), but the choice is up to you.

To access your Palm e-mail program, tap the Applications soft button to the left of the Graffiti area and then choose Mail. The Inbox screen opens.

Creating a message

Creating a new e-mail message is much like writing a regular paper letter. All you need is an address and a message. Actually, all you need is an address; but sending a message as well is a sign of good manners.

Follow these steps to create a new message:

1. **With the mail program open, tap New.**

   The New Message screen appears. If you know your recipient's e-mail address by heart, enter that address by using Graffiti, the on-screen keyboard, or an external keyboard like the Palm Portable keyboard. If you do any of these things, skip ahead to Step 7.

   If you don't know your recipient's address, you can look it up in the Address Book. Continue with Step 2 if you're in this particular boat.

2. **Tap the word To.**

   The To screen appears.

3. **Tap Lookup.**

   The To Lookup screen appears, as shown in Figure 17-1, showing the e-mail addresses you've entered. It doesn't show everyone in the Address Book, just those who have e-mail addresses. Convenient, eh?

4. **Tap the name of the person to whom you're sending your message.**

   The name you tap is highlighted to show you selected it.

Figure 17-1:
If you don't know your recipient's e-mail address, you can pick a name from the Address Book on the To Lookup screen.

5. Tap Add.

The e-mail address of the person you selected appears on the To screen. You can repeat Steps 3 through 5 for each person to whom you want to send copies of the message.

6. Tap Done.

The New Message screen reappears, showing the names of the people to whom you've chosen to send your message.

7. If you want to send copies of your message to additional people, tap the line to the right of CC.

CC is highlighted to show you have selected it. If you know your recipient's e-mail address, just write it by using Graffiti or the on-screen keyboard. If you don't know the e-mail address and want to check your Address Book, repeat Step 2 (tap CC rather than To) through Step 6 for each CC addressee you want to add.

8. Tap the line to the right of Subj.

A blinking line (the *insertion point*) appears, and Subj is highlighted, as shown in Figure 17-2.

Figure 17-2:
On the New Message screen, enter the subject of your message as you would enter any other text.

```
┌─────────────────────────────────┐
│ New Message                     │
│   To: fredda.dedark@night.com   │
│   CC: obearly@snoozer.com       │
│  Subj: ........................ │
│  Body: ........................ │
│       ......................... │
│       ......................... │
│       ......................... │
│       ......................... │
│       ......................... │
│       ......................... │
│       ......................... │
│  (Send) (Cancel) (Details...)  ↑│
└─────────────────────────────────┘
```

If you tap Subj itself, the Subject screen appears. Opening the Subject screen is an extra step you don't really need to take because you can enter your subject on the New Message screen. If you prefer to use the Subject screen, tap Done when you finish entering your text and continue to Step 10.

9. **Enter the subject of your message by using either the on-screen keyboard or Graffiti (see Chapter 2 for more info about entering text).**

   The text you enter appears on the Subject line.

10. **Tap to the right of Body.**

    The insertion point appears, and Body is highlighted.

    If you tap Body itself, the Body screen appears. Just as with the Subject line, you don't really have to take this extra step. If you prefer using this screen to enter your message, just tap Done when you finish and continue to Step 12.

11. **Enter the text of your message by using either the on-screen keyboard or Graffiti or an external keyboard.**

    The text you enter appears on the screen.

12. **Tap Send.**

    Your message closes and moves to the Outbox.

Even though you've tapped Send, your message isn't on its way to your recipient. Tapping Send simply moves your message to the Outbox. The next time you HotSync your Palm device, everything in the Outbox moves to your desktop e-mail program, which then sends your message.

Reading a message

You already know how busy people at work can look when they're really reading jokes someone sent by e-mail. Now you can pull the same trick with your Palm organizer if you use Palm Mail. As long as you don't laugh out loud, people don't know how much fun you're having and leave you alone. They also leave you alone if you laugh a bit too much, so the trick works either way.

To read your messages:

1. **With the mail program open, tap the pull-down list in the upper-right corner of the Mail screen to see the list of available folders.**

   The list includes Inbox, Outbox, Deleted, Filed, and Draft. You can expect to find new messages in the Inbox.

2. **Tap the name of the folder you want to view.**

   The folder you tap appears on the screen, showing a list of messages.

3. **Tap the message you want to read.**

   The text of the message you tap appears.

4. **After you finish reading the message, tap Done.**

   Your message closes, and the list of messages reappears. A check mark appears next to the message you just read.

If you want to cycle through your messages but don't want to return to the message list, just use the two left- and right-pointing triangles at the bottom of each message screen. Tapping one of those triangles enables you to see the next message or the preceding message. Although that feature is useful, for some reason I think of the next message as being *below* the current message, rather than to the right. Anyway, that's what those triangles do, in case you are wondering.

While you're reading a message, you may also notice a pair of icons in the upper-right corner of the message screen. One looks like a tiny message containing a great deal of text, and the other looks like a tiny message with only a little bit of text. If you tap the icon that looks like it holds a great deal of text, you reveal all the message *headers*. These include the information that comes before the body of the message, such as who sends the message, who receives it, what its subject is, and the date the message was sent. The other icon shows only the name of the person who sent the message and the subject of the message. You can tap either icon at any time to see as much or little header information as you want. I prefer to see less header information.

Replying to a message

The simplest way to address a message to somebody is to reply to a message he sent you. Here's what to do:

1. **With the mail program open, tap the message that you want to reply to.**

   The text of the message you tap appears.

2. **Tap Reply.**

   The Reply Options dialog box opens, as shown in Figure 17-3.

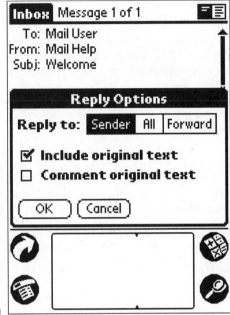

Figure 17-3:
Reply only to
the person
who sent
the message
or to every-
one it was
sent to.

3. **Tap either Sender or All.**

   If you choose Sender, your reply goes only to the person (or persons) listed on the To line of the message. If you choose All, your reply goes to the person (or persons) on the CC line, also. To see what happens when you tap Forward, see the following section, "Forwarding a message."

   You have two additional options: Include Original Text and Comment Original Text. If you check the first option, the text of the message you're replying to is included with the message you're sending. Checking the second box puts a caret symbol (>) in front of every line of the original text so the person getting your reply can quickly see which text she wrote and which text you added. You can check the first box, neither box, or both boxes; if you just check the second box, though, nothing happens. You can't add comment marks to the original text unless you include the original text. Normally, I leave both boxes checked.

4. **Tap OK.**

   The New Message screen appears. Your recipient's e-mail address appears on the To line, and the Subject line shows Re: followed by the subject of the original message. If you chose in Step 3 to include the original message text in your reply, that text appears in the body of your new message.

   You can change any of this text by deleting and adding text as you normally would.

5. **If you want to add new addresses to the To or CC line of the message, enter the new addresses on the line you want.**

   You can add an address to a message you're replying to in the same way you do when you create a new message. See the section "Creating a message," earlier in this chapter, for details.

6. **If you want to add text to your message, tap to the right of Body.**

   The insertion point appears. If you chose to include the original message's text, your Palm device conveniently leaves you a blank line to start writing your reply text.

   If you tap the word *Body* itself, the Body screen appears with the subject of your message at the top. If you enter your text on the Body screen rather than on the New Message screen, just tap Done when you finish entering your text and continue to Step 8.

7. **Enter the text you want to add by using either the on-screen keyboard or Graffiti (see Chapter 2 for more info about entering text).**

   The text you enter appears with the original message's text.

8. **Tap Send.**

   Your message closes and waits in the Outbox for delivery.

Forwarding a message

Forwarding a message is just like replying to a message (see the preceding section), except that rather than send a message back to the person who sent you the original message, you send a message to a third person.

To forward a message:

1. **With the mail program open, tap the message that you want to forward.**

   The text of the message you tap appears.

2. **Tap Reply.**

   The Reply Options dialog box opens.

3. **Tap Forward.**

   When you forward a message, the text of a message that you received from one person is sent to another person.

4. **Tap OK.**

   The New Message screen appears, containing the text of the message you're forwarding. On the Subject line, you see Fwd:, followed by the subject of the original message.

5. **On the To line, enter the e-mail address of the person to whom you're forwarding the message.**

   You address a message you're forwarding in the same way that you create a new message. See the section "Creating a message," earlier in this chapter, for the lowdown.

6. **If you want to add text to your message, tap to the right of Body.**

   The insertion point appears. If you tap the word *Body* itself, a new screen appears for the body text, with the subject of the message at the top. You can enter text on either this screen or the New Message screen — your choice. If you choose to enter text on the Body screen, just tap Done when you're finished and continue to Step 8.

7. **Enter the text you want to add by using either the on-screen keyboard or Graffiti (see Chapter 2 for more info about entering text).**

   The text you enter appears with the message text.

8. **Tap Send.**

   Your message closes and waits in the Outbox for delivery.

People seem to enjoy forwarding jokes by e-mail. I guess forwarding a joke to 25 people is faster than standing around the water cooler and waiting for them to show up so you can repeat the joke to each of them, one by one. Also, using your Palm device to forward jokes by e-mail makes you look like you're working (except to those who know better).

Deleting a message

Your Palm device seems to have plenty of space until you start loading it with e-mail. You'd be surprised how easily you can collect enough e-mail to fill a couple of megabytes of memory. Fortunately, deleting a message is just as easy. Here's how:

1. **With the mail program open, tap the message you want to delete.**

   The text of the message you tap appears.

2. **Tap Delete.**

   Your message disappears. If you have the Confirm Deleted Message option checked in the Preferences dialog box (tap the Menu soft button, and then choose Options⇨Preferences), the Delete Message dialog box opens, as shown in Figure 17-4. Just tap Yes to get rid of that pesky message.

Figure 17-4:
Tap Yes to
delete a
message.

Presto! Your message has magically disappeared — sort of. Actually, when you choose to delete messages, they move to the Deleted folder and wait for you to clear them all out by running the Purge function that I describe in the next section.

If you change your mind after deleting a message, you can undelete a message from the Deleted Items folder. Open the Deleted Items folder by tapping the list of folder names in the upper-right corner of the Mail screen, and then choose Deleted. When the list of deleted messages appears, tap the message you want to undelete to open it, and then tap the Undelete button at the bottom of the message screen. When you tap Undelete, the message returns to the Inbox.

When you HotSync, your Palm device's Inbox is forced to match the Inbox on your desktop e-mail program. Therefore, if you delete a message from your desktop e-mail program, the next HotSync removes that message from your Palm device's Inbox. Deleting messages from your desktop before you HotSync may be easier for you. Most desktop e-mail programs enable you to delete batches of messages at one time, which is faster and easier than deleting messages one by one on your Palm device. See Chapter 14 for more about the HotSync program.

If you want to take a message out of the Inbox but leave it on your Palm device, you can move the message to the Filed folder. Just tap the Menu soft button and then choose Message➪File. That way, when all the messages in your Inbox are replaced by a new set during the next HotSync, the ones you sent to the Filed folder stay put. To see the contents of your Filed folder, tap the folder list in the upper-right corner of the Inbox screen and then tap Filed.

Purging deleted messages

Deleting a message doesn't eliminate that message from your collection. A deleted message moves to the Deleted folder until you purge your deleted items, like this:

1. **With the mail program open, tap the Menu soft button at the bottom-left corner of the Palm screen.**

   The menu bar appears.

2. **Choose Purge➪Deleted.**

   The Purge Deleted Message dialog box opens, as shown in Figure 17-5.

Figure 17-5: This dialog box warns you about wiping out your deleted messages.

3. Tap Yes.

The Purge Deleted Message dialog box closes, and your messages are gone forever.

The Deleted folder exists to save you if you accidentally delete an item and then change your mind and want to undelete it. But the best way to save space on your Palm device is to purge deleted messages frequently.

One big difference between deleting e-mail messages and deleting other items on your Palm device is that no archive for deleted messages exists on the Palm Desktop. Your desktop e-mail program serves as the archive, so make sure you really want those messages to disappear forever before you delete them. See Chapter 12 for more about archiving items.

Saving drafts

If you tap Cancel while composing a new message, the Save Draft dialog box asks whether you want to save a draft of the message. If you tap Yes, your incomplete message moves to the Drafts folder, where you can return to it later. Isn't that thoughtful?

Tapping No deletes your incomplete message forever, and Cancel simply returns you to the message itself.

Sending a blind copy

Sending blind copies of your messages is a sneaky way to inform someone about your communications with a third person without that third person knowing. For example, if you need more cooperation from someone in another department of your company, you can send that person an e-mail asking for the help you need and at the same time send a blind copy to the person who supervises both of you. The person you're addressing the message to doesn't know that you've clued in the boss.

Blind copies, or *BCCs,* are so sneaky that the line for them is hidden unless you know how to find and use it. That said, here's the secret:

1. With the mail program open, tap New.

The New Message screen appears.

2. Tap Details.

The Message Details dialog box opens.

3. Tap the check box labeled BCC.

A check appears in the box, as shown in Figure 17-6.

New Message

To: ....
CC: ....

Message Details ℹ

Priority: ▼ Normal

BCC: ☑

Signature: ☐

Confirm Read: ☐

Confirm Delivery: ☐

(OK) (Cancel)

Figure 17-6:
To send a
secret blind
copy of a
message,
find the
secret
check box.

4. **Tap OK.**

   The Message Details dialog box closes, and the BCC line appears on the New Message screen.

5. **Tap BCC on the New Message screen.**

   The BCC screen appears. If you know the e-mail address of your BCC addressee by heart, enter the address by using Graffiti, the on-screen keyboard, or an external keyboard. Tap Done when you're finished, and continue creating your message. If you need to look up the address of the BCC addressee, continue to Step 6.

6. **Tap Lookup.**

   The BCC Lookup screen appears, showing all the names and e-mail addresses in the Address Book. Not everyone in the Address Book shows up on this list — only the ones with e-mail addresses.

7. **Tap the name of the person to whom you want to send a blind copy.**

   The name you tap is highlighted to show you have selected it.

8. **Tap Add.**

   The name you chose appears on the BCC screen.

9. **Tap Done.**

   The name you chose appears on the BCC line of your message.

10. **Continue creating your message.**

Well, now the secret is out. Don't forget; you saw it here first.

Sorting messages

Most of the time, I like to read messages in the order in which I receive them. However, sometimes I want to see all the messages from a certain person lined up in a row or read messages about a certain subject all at once. You can sort your messages in three different ways, depending on what you need.

To change the sort order of your messages:

1. **With the mail program open, tap Show.**

   The Show Options dialog box opens.

2. **Tap the triangle next to Sort By.**

   A list of ways to sort your messages appears, including Date, Sender, and Subject, as shown in Figure 17-7.

Figure 17-7:
In the Show Options dialog box, you can sort messages by category.

3. **Tap your choice.**

    The sort type appears next to Sort By.

4. **If you want to display the date you received each message, tap the check box next to Show Date.**

5. **Tap OK.**

    Your messages appear sorted the way you chose.

This sort order remains in effect until you choose a different sort order.

Customizing Your Palm E-Mail

After you develop a serious Palm e-mail habit, you need to know some techniques for managing the messages you get, customizing the messages you send, and speeding up the process of synchronizing your messages with your desktop. You may never use these tricks, but I want you to know they're available.

Setting HotSync options

After you accumulate a healthy number of items on your Palm device, the HotSync process may slow down quite a bit. At first, a HotSync takes only a few seconds, but after a couple of months, a HotSync may take several minutes, which is a big deal for people as busy as you and me. To speed up your HotSync time, you may want to limit e-mail activity on your Palm device to sending messages or receiving unread messages. You can ignore the HotSync options if you want, with no ill effect. See Chapter 13 for more about the HotSync process.

To set HotSync e-mail options:

1. **With the mail program open, tap the Menu soft button at the bottom-left corner of the Palm screen.**

    The menu bar appears.

2. **Choose Options⇨HotSync Options.**

    The HotSync Options screen appears, as shown in Figure 17-8.

3. **Tap the triangle next to Settings For.**

A list appears that enables you to choose either Local HotSync or Remote HotSync. Typically you need to connect a modem to your Palm device to perform a Remote HotSync. You may want to make different things happen when you perform a Remote (or Modem) HotSync than when you do a local HotSync. Modem HotSyncs are slower than local HotSyncs, so if you download only unread messages, for example, you save time and money when you do a long-distance modem HotSync. On the other hand, you may want to get all your messages when you do a local HotSync, so you need to be able to create different settings for the two types of HotSyncs. If you never attach your Palm device to a modem, you don't need to think about modem HotSync options.

4. **Tap either Local HotSync or Remote HotSync.**

Your choice appears next to Settings For. You're not limited to setting only local or only remote HotSync options; you just have to set the options for each type of HotSync one at a time.

5. **Tap one of the boxes below Settings For.**

A definition for each setting appears in the space. Here's the skinny on each setting:

- **All:** All messages in your desktop Inbox are copied to your Palm device, and all outgoing messages are transferred to your desktop when you HotSync.

- **Send Only:** Only outgoing messages are transferred to your Palm device when you HotSync. Incoming messages stay on your desktop computer.

- **Filter:** You can tell your Palm device to accept certain kinds of messages and reject others. For example, you can set up a filter to accept only messages marked as high priority. I discuss message filtering in greater detail in the following section, "Filtering messages."

- **Unread:** Your Palm device accepts only those messages you haven't read yet. The ones you've read stay on your desktop.

6. **Tap OK.**

   The HotSync Options screen disappears, and your message list reappears.

Filtering messages

Filtering is a fairly sophisticated HotSync option. It enables you to set up rules to limit the messages the system copies to your Palm device, based on the priority of the message, the name of the person whose address appears in the To or From line, or the text on the Subject line.

I know people who get hundreds of e-mail messages every day. If performing a HotSync copied all their messages to their Palm devices, they would have room to do only e-mail. Filtering is a good idea for those who get more e-mail than they want on their desktop e-mail but who still want to take some messages on their Palm device.

Here's how to filter your messages:

1. **With the mail program open, tap the Menu soft button at the bottom-left corner of the Palm screen.**

   The menu bar appears.

2. **Choose Options⇨HotSync Options.**

   The HotSync Options screen appears.

3. **Choose either Local or Modem HotSync.**

4. **Tap Filter.**

   Options for filtering messages appear, as shown in Figure 17-9.

5. **If you want to copy only high-priority messages to your Palm device, tap the check box next to Retrieve All High Priority.**

6. **If you want to create a rule for selecting a type of message to retrieve, tap the triangle at the left edge of the screen.**

   A list appears with two choices: Ignore Messages Containing and Retrieve Only Messages Containing.

Figure 17-9:
You filter the
junk from
your water,
so why not
filter the
junk from
your e-mail?

7. **Choose the type of rule you want to create.**

8. **If you want to ignore or receive messages according to the address of the person they're sent to, enter that e-mail address on the To line.**

   "Wait a minute," you say. "I'm the recipient of my own e-mail, so if I choose to ignore my own e-mail address, I won't get any messages, right?" Technically, yes. Although filtering messages addressed to yourself may seem silly, you may discover reasons to exclude certain messages. First, you may get e-mail addressed to a mailing list. People on mailing lists often get dozens of messages every day, and you may not want to clutter up your Palm device with that kind of stuff. Besides, you can still look at the excluded messages on your desktop computer.

   Another reason is that your desktop e-mail program may collect messages from two e-mail addresses. If you have one address for business and another for personal messages yet receive both in the same desktop program, you can filter out one or the other type of message by putting that e-mail address on the To line.

9. **To ignore or receive messages from a particular sender, enter that sender's address on the From line.**

   You can enter multiple addresses on this line; just separate them with a comma.

10. **To ignore or receive messages in which the subject line contains a certain word or phrase, enter that text on the Subj line.**

11. **Tap OK.**

The HotSync Options screen disappears, and your message list reappears.

Remember that only the items in the Inbox of your desktop program are copied to your Palm device. If you're used to the more elaborate rules and filters in your desktop e-mail program, you can have your desktop computer do all the filtering for you before you HotSync your Palm device. Most people I know are perfectly happy without ever using any kind of e-mail rule or filter, so if you ignore filtering, you're probably just as well off.

Using signatures

Lots of people like to personalize their e-mail with a standard bunch of text at the end of each message. Most popular e-mail programs enable you to set up a signature, so why not use signatures on the messages you create with your Palm device?

Why not, indeed, when the process is this simple:

1. **With the mail program open, tap the Menu soft button at the bottom-left corner of the Palm screen.**

The menu bar appears.

2. **Choose Options⇨Preferences.**

The Preferences screen appears, as shown in Figure 17-10.

Figure 17-10: Individualize your e-mail with a flashy signature.

3. **Enter your signature text by using the on-screen keyboard or Graffiti (see Chapter 2 for more info about entering text).**

   The text you enter appears on the Preferences screen.

4. **Tap OK.**

   The Preferences screen disappears, and your message list reappears. Your signature is automatically added to all your outgoing messages from now on.

One little detail about signatures: You can't see them yourself when you create your messages. Palm Mail adds the signature when you send a message.

Setting truncating options

One of the limitations of using a tiny gadget like a Palm device for reading e-mail is the small amount of space. You may not care much about megabytes or RAM until you run out of it. That's why the Palm e-mail program automatically *truncates* (chops off) messages at a certain length. Although you can determine the length, you're still limited to 8,000 characters. Because your desktop computer stores the full text of your messages, you can always look in your desktop e-mail program to see what's missing.

Here's how to set the length at which messages are truncated:

1. **With the mail program open, tap the Menu soft button at the bottom-left corner of the Palm screen.**

   The menu bar appears.

2. **Choose Options⇨HotSync Options.**

   The HotSync Options screen appears.

3. **Tap Truncate.**

   The Truncate Options dialog box opens, as shown in Figure 17-11.

4. **Tap the maximum message length you want.**

   The choice you tap is highlighted to show that you selected it.

5. **Tap OK.**

   The Truncate Options dialog box closes, and the HotSync Options screen appears.

6. **Tap OK.**

   The HotSync Options screen disappears, and your message list reappears.

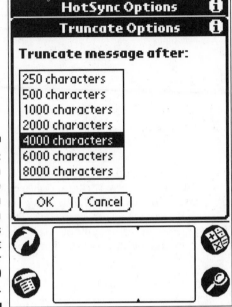

Figure 17-11:
You can
include
anything you
want in a
message, as
long as it
has fewer
than 8,000
characters.

In addition to long e-mail messages, your Palm mail program chops off attachments. If someone sends you a file — such as a word-processing document or a spreadsheet — that's attached to a message, you don't see the extra file on your Palm device. Although you can still see the file on your desktop computer, the Palm device just doesn't have space for the extra file. Instead, it tells you a file is attached.

Other E-Mail Programs

For a few dollars more, you can get a richer, more capable mail program for your Palm device. You still probably don't want to send and receive all your e-mail through your Palm device because the screen is so tiny, but if you need more than the built-in Palm mail program offers, you do have choices. Here are some of my favorites.

MultiMail Professional

Power e-mail users can have it all (well, most of it, anyway) with MultiMail from Actual Software in their Palms. A free copy of MultiMail comes preinstalled on every Palm i705 for sending wireless email. You can send and receive messages as big as 256K in size, which is mighty, mighty big on a Palm device. You can also attach documents you've created in other programs to your e-mails, in much the same way you may have done on desktop e-mail programs. MultiMail can connect to a variety of desktop e-mail programs on both Windows computers and Macs. You can get more information at `www.palmpilotfordummies.com/multimail`.

One-Touch Mail

I like a program that's rich and easy, like me. (All right, so I'm not rich.) One-Touch Mail from JP Systems includes lots of convenient features, like canned responses you can call up with one or two taps, such as "Call me" or "Need more info." You can also create your own responses, such as "Fuggedaboutit!" or "Get lost, ya low-life spammer!" (For non–New Yorkers, polite custom responses are also acceptable.) The Palm-powered Handspring Treo cell phone includes One-Touch Mail as its wireless e-mail program. The program also lets you e-mail entries from your Palm Address Book, Date Book, To Do List, or Memo Pad. You can find more info at `www.palmpilotfordummies.com/onetouchmail`.

riteMail

A very slick little Palm e-mail program called riteMail turned up recently from a clever group of former Russian rocket scientists. (Seriously! Actual Sputnik-heads!) The program lets you hand write messages on your Palm screen or draw pictures or diagrams and send out your scribblings via e-mail. riteMail is especially impressive on a color Palm device, such as the m130 or m515, because it's a full-color program with a set of surprisingly sophisticated drawing tools. I've always felt that exchanging synchronized e-mail from your Palm device took a little more effort than it was worth, but riteMail makes Palm email worth the trouble. You can find out more at `www.palmpilotfordummies.com/ritemail`.

AOL Mail

In my personal opinion, AOL e-mail is just awful. The world's largest online service could easily afford to give its members normal e-mail like all those free mail sites out there. But it doesn't. You're better off getting e-mail some-where else, anywhere else. (Oh, please, don't get me started on AOL.) Plenty of Web sites offer free e-mail, and you can find two of the more popular free e-mail services at `www.hotmail.com` and `www.mail.com`.

Anyway, if you must stay with AOL for your e-mail and get your AOL e-mail on your Palm device, AOL Mail does that job very nicely. At least the program is free, but then it should be. You can find the program on the Web at `www.aol.com/anywhere` (as in get your e-mail anywhere except AOL).

Chapter 18

Brain-Building with Palm Expansion Cards

*Y*ou may have noticed a little opening on the side of your Palm device that looks like the coin slot on a pay phone. You don't need to put a quarter in there; they haven't started selling coin-operated Palm organizers just yet. (But I think the world may be ready for that Palm-Powered Piggy Bank!) That little slot is called the *expansion card slot*. Instead of slipping change in the slot, you slide a postage-stamp-sized card that can add functions that weren't built in at the factory or expand the brainpower of your Palm device. I wish I had a slot like that on the side of my head.

As I write this book, the first expansion cards for Palm devices have been on the market for about a year, and so far only a handful of cards have been introduced. The people at Palm tell us that big things will be available on those small cards in the foreseeable future, but the forecast as to what will be available when is pretty cloudy.

Right now, there are a few distinct kinds of expansion cards:

- ✔ **Expansion modules:** You can use expansion modules to add room to your Palm device so that you can add more stuff.

- ✔ **Software modules:** These add programs and games to your Palm device.

- ✔ **eBooks and other reference materials:** Digital information is portable information.

- ✔ **Interface cards:** These make it possible to connect your Palm device to other kinds of devices.

✔ **Gadgets:** It's possible to connect various gadgets to your Palm device that have a function of their own, although only a few devices fitting that description are currently available. For example, it's rumored that a teeny-weeny camera that plugs into your Palm Expansion slot will soon be available, and a company called Margi offers a gizmo called Presenter To Go that allows you to make PowerPoint presentations right from your Palm device.

I still haven't seen expansion cards that do the things I really want done — say, cook dinner, do the dishes, and drive me home. I guess those gizmos are still in the future.

Storage Cards

The most common task for a Palm expansion card is to make more room on your Palm device for programs and other kinds of information. Many of the expansion cards that are sold as things like eBooks and game cards are really just plain old expansion cards that are modified to offer an easy way to store and install those programs.

Palm Memory Expansion Card

If you're like a cowboy and yearn for more wide-open space on your Palm organizer, saddle up and lasso yourself an expansion card or three. Palm Computing, Inc., sells these little doggies in 16MB and 32MB sizes, and other manufacturers offer SD memory cards as large as 512MB, enough to store several thousand pictures of your horse along with the names of all your cattle. Yippee-ti-yi-yo!

Palm Backup Card

Every time you put the Palm device in the cradle and push the HotSync button, a second copy of all your information is stored on your desktop computer. Techies call this a *backup copy*. I recommend doing a HotSync at least once a week to safeguard your data. But at times, you can't be near your computer but want to keep your data safe anyway. That's where the Palm Backup Card comes in. It's a specially designed Expansion Card that stores up to 16MB of data. Just plug in the Backup Card, let the built-in software run, and tap the screen to start your backup and your data is safe. Also, some programmers like to write programs on a Palm device and use the Backup Card as an easy way to recover from the crashes that normally happen when you're testing new Palm programs. That's what these programmers tell me, anyway. They probably just enjoy crashing their Palms for the fun of it. Boys will be boys.

Games and Entertainment

Ever since the first astronaut played Pong on his flight computer ("Oops! Houston, we have a problem!"), people have been enjoying computer games. Besides, what's the point of getting yourself a slick gadget like a Palm organizer if you don't have a little fun, right? You'll find plenty of entertaining choices for your Palm device; here are a few:

PalmPak Games Card

With enough games to keep you distracted for hours in any airport waiting room, subway station, or dull staff meeting, the PalmPak Games card includes some of the most popular games for the Palm Platform. Some of the better-known titles include Blackjack, Solitaire, chess, checkers, backgammon, and slot machines as well as high-tech titles such as Zap 2016, SimCity, and Bubblet.

Handmark Scrabble Card

What self-respecting Scrabble fiends wouldn't want a pocket-sized version of their favorite word game on their Palm organizers? This edition even includes a 10,000-word electronic Scrabble dictionary, to prevent cheating. Cheaters will have to settle for the regular board version of Scrabble.

Pocket Express Entertainment Pack

Games! More games! The Pocket Express Entertainment Pack includes classic games such as Tetris, Pocket Chess, Pocket Dice, and Lode Runner. It also includes the kind of Palm Blackjack game that I've personally used to lose thousands and thousands of imaginary dollars. Fortunately, I made it up by earning all the imaginary dollars I get for writing this book.

eBooks and Reference

In 1999 the experts were saying that within a few years eBooks would be the next big thing. They told us that before we knew it, eBooks would be selling like hotcakes. Well, now it's a few years later and eBooks are selling like cold hotcakes. The much-ballyhooed eBook revolution just ain't happening, folks. Sorry.

There's no denying that reading a traditional paper book is a pleasure, but reading an eBook is a job. If reading certain books is a part of your job, your Palm organizer may be a good place to read them. An electronic version of an important reference book can be a very valuable thing to have on your Palm organizer; maps are useful, too. The current crop of eBook cards for the Palm includes several different genres, some of which are enormously useful, others are . . . well, pleasure reading, if that's your pleasure.

You can download a free guide to getting the most from Palm eBooks. Go to www.palmpilotfordummies.com/ebooks.

PalmPak eBook Series: Personal Finance

Some people are rich, some are poor. Rich is better, from what I've heard. The books in this collection will show you how to get rich by managing your money wisely. The collection would cost $100 if purchased separately, but it's only $39.99 if you buy the whole group, so buying the collection makes you about 60 bucks richer already! (Or are you $39.99 poorer? I'm not sure; maybe that's why I'm not rich.)

PalmPak eBook Series: Mystery

This collection of mysteries by Michael Connelly includes six exciting page-turners with no pages! How does that work? It's a mystery! You can read these books while you ride the commuter train to work, but try not to scream at the scary parts when the train goes through a dark tunnel, okay?

PalmPak eBook Series: Sci-Fi

What could be geekier than reading science fiction books on an electronic organizer? Hardly anything, except perhaps wearing a pocket protector with your "I Love Linux" T-shirt. If you do read this trilogy by Peter Hamilton on your Palm organizer, you'd do well to avoid mentioning that fact on a first date.

PalmPak Dictionary/Thesaurus Card

If you carry the Palm Dictionary, you could describe it by using a word like practical or useful, functional, constructive, valuable, effective, or hundreds of other words that mean pretty much the same doggone thing. For $39.95, that's a bargain, a deal, and a good buy, don't you think?

PalmPak Travel Card: Rand-McNally Road Atlas

Most guys love gadgets and hate asking for directions. If you have a Palm device containing a road atlas, you can have it both ways! When you're driving somewhere and get lost, er, I mean when you end up on the "scenic route," you can spend hours finding your location on your Palm organizer rather that wasting precious minutes asking someone for directions. Sounds good to me! Now if I can only find a Palm gizmo that can pick up my socks and do the laundry!

PalmPak Travel Card

You can get three geographically distinct PalmPak Travel Cards (US Cities, European Cities, and Asia-Pacific Cities) to help you get around cities in different parts of the world. Each card contains information on how to get around in the major cities in each region, with guides to shopping, dining, hotels, nightlife, and transportation. The European version of the card also includes programs for dealing with time-zone changes, currency conversion, and SmallTalk, a translation program.

PalmPak Language Translator Card

Everyone understands the universal language of pointing at stuff. The problem is, in many cultures it's impolite to point, and in all cultures there are certain things you don't want to point at. The PalmPak Language Translator card simplifies everything by letting you point at your Palm organizer. That's always polite and much more informative.

Connections

Most Palm users only connect their organizer to a desktop computer (if they even do that). But there are lots of clever developers out there who are figuring out ways to connect your Palm device to all sorts of things in all sorts of ingenious ways. Right now your choice of things to connect through your Palm expansion slot is pretty small, but you can count on seeing more and more choices as time goes on.

Palm Bluetooth Card

Bluetooth is a technology that was designed to let tiny devices like Palm computers connect wirelessly to other tiny devices such as cellphones, portable printers, and even laptop computers. But Bluetooth developers don't plan to think small forever. Toshiba has announced a Bluetooth-enabled refrigerator and microwave oven, in case your Palm organizer gets hungry and wants to raid the fridge.

You can be the first kid on your block with Bluetooth if you buy the Palm Bluetooth Card. However, the people at Palm Computing, Inc,. have been saying that future Palm devices will have Bluetooth built right in, which would make a Bluetooth Card unnecessary. So unless you're a very early adopter and you have a burning desire to make your M515 mate with a microwave oven that you don't have yet, you might wait a bit until all the pieces are in place.

WiFi Cards

The most popular way to connect devices wirelessly at the moment is a technology called WiFi, also known affectionately as 802.11b (by geeks who feel sentimental about these things). As I write this there are no WiFi cards that go in your Palm device's SD slot, but several companies are rumored to be planning products that will probably be available by the time you read this. A WiFi card would let you connect your Palm device to your laptop, your office network, and even to the Internet in many situations. Bluetooth and WiFi do the same job, except that WiFi connects at a higher speed and over a greater distance but drains your batteries a lot faster. At the moment, you'll find a much wider array of products that connect via WiFi, so when a WiFi card becomes available for your Palm device, it'll probably more useful more quickly than a Bluetooth Card.

Presenter-to-Go

Are you ready to deliver a PowerPoint slide show from your Palm device? You can do just that with Presenter-to-Go. You can leave your laptop at home and connect the Presenter-to-Go module to a monitor or LCD projector to show your PowerPoint slides in beautiful living color. I've given presentations using Presenter-to-Go, and my audiences are always impressed with the sharpness and clarity of the slides that I get from a little bitty Palm organizer (www.palmpilotfordummies.com/presentertogo).

Part VI
The Part of Tens

The 5th Wave   By Rich Tennant

"Well, here's what happened—I forgot
to put it on my 'To Do' list."

In this part . . .

Sometimes the good stuff comes in tens — in this part of the book, for example. Here I tell you where you can go on the Internet to solve problems you may have with your Palm device (and to read the latest Palm gossip). I also tell you about the coolest Palm accessories on the market.

Chapter 19

Ten Nifty Palm Accessories

As citizens of a consumer-based society, we all have an important respon-sibility: *to buy stuff!* Thank heavens you bought this book. Don't stop there, though; buy another copy, and then check out the list in this chapter to see which Palm device gewgaws you simply can't live without. Remember that our economy depends on you!

Palm/Stowaway Folding Keyboard

Right now the hottest accessory for handheld computing is the fold-up Palm Portable Keyboard, also known as the Stowaway keyboard for the Handspring Visor and other brands of Palm devices. An astonishingly well-crafted gadget, the Palm/Stowaway keyboard looks like something straight out of a James Bond movie. But you want a keyboard that not only makes you look cool but also helps you be more creative and productive. A Palm/Stowaway combina-tion can improve your productivity because you can get things done anytime, anywhere. You can be more creative, too, if you're like me and always get your best ideas when you're nowhere near a computer. You can buy the keyboard from the retailer who sold you your Palm device for about $99. If you use a Handspring Visor, you can buy the Targus Stowaway keyboard, which is

absolutely identical to the Palm Portable Keyboard except that it only con-
nects to a Visor. You get more info about the Stowaway online at `www.palmpilotfordummies.com/stowaway`.

Palm MiniKeyboard

If you're all thumbs when it comes to typing, you might be happy with the
Palm Mini Keyboard. It's a tiny keyboard that clips to the bottom of your Palm
device and allows you to enter text on your Palm device by typing with two
thumbs. Thumb-typing seems a little awkward at first, but many people
become pretty zippy thumb-typists in short order, and they never need to learn
Graffiti. Find out more at `www.palmpilotfordummies.com/minikeyboard`.

Canon BJC-85 Printer

Canon makes several portable, battery-powered printers with an *IR* (infrared)
port that makes them compatible with your Palm device. If you use printing
software on your Palm device (such as PalmPrint or IrPrint), you can print
memos, appointments, or any number of things that you've created on your
Palm organizer on normal ink-jet paper. My favorite printer model is the tiny
Canon BJC-85, which is smaller than a carton of cigarettes (and much better
for your health). You can also connect the Canon BJC-85 to your regular computer with a cable and use it just like any other printer. Sometimes you just
need to commit something to paper, so the Canon portable printers fill the
bill quite nicely. For more info, see `www.palmpilotfordummies.com/canon`.

NavMan GPS

You've seen those luxury cars that use satellites to keep track of where
you're traveling so you never get lost. The NavMan GPS system does the
same thing for you, and you don't even need to attach it to a car — just
attach it to a Palm device. Besides, your Palm organizer is much cheaper
than a Cadillac and far easier to put in your pocket. NavMan GPS keeps track
of your speed, direction, and heading. It also tracks your location and displays all that information on a customized map. And remember, guys, when
you use one of these gadgets, you're not actually asking for directions, so it's
okay. For more info, see `www.palmpilotfordummies.com/navmangps`.

Seiko InkLink

Some people just don't like writing on the Palm screen; to them, nothing beats good old ink on paper. The Seiko InkLink offers the best of both worlds: Just put the special InkLink clip onto a plain old paper writing pad, then when you write on the pad with a special smart pen, InkLink beams everything you write straight to your Palm device or laptop computer. You can buy InkLink from many of the stores that sell Palm organizers or check out www.palmpilotfordummies.com/inklink.

Extra Styluses

You can find scads of new and improved styluses (or is that *styli?*) for your Palm device. The same folks who make fancy and expensive writing pens make many of these styluses. If you want a stylus that displays your taste, class, and distinction, check out the better office-supply stores. I happen to like the snazzy combination stylus-pen that the Cross Pen people make, which works wonderfully and makes a splendid gift. (I only mention that so when the holidays come, you'll know what to send me. Thank you very much!) If you want a plain old stylus that fits in the little stylus well on your Palm organizer, you can get a three-pack of plastic styluses for about five bucks. Check with the merchant who sold you your Palm device.

Palm Travel/Recharger Kit

If you own a Palm device with rechargeable batteries, such as a Palm m515 or m705, one of the portable recharging kits now on the market is essential if you take overnight trips. Yes, keeping your Palm device fully charged by putting it in its cradle each night is possible, but Murphy's Law says you'll run out of juice when you're farthest from home and the stores are all closed. You can get the Palm Travel Kit from most stores that sell Palm devices, or find out more at www.palmpilotfordummies.com/travelcharge.

Card Scanner

A company called Corex Technologies makes a number of products for entering business-card data into your Palm device. My current favorite is a special scanner that's perfectly sized for business-card scanning called CardScan 600c (www.palmpilotfordummies.com/cardscan) and is sold as part of a bundle called CardScan Executive. If you travel regularly to attend trade shows or conferences and need to get business card info entered into your Palm device and desktop contact manager in a hurry, the CardScan system can help. The scanner doesn't attach directly to your Palm organizer; you attach the scanner to the desktop or laptop computer you use as the host for your Palm device. Scan your collection of business cards into the host computer first. When all the cards are entered into the host computer, put your Palm computer in its cradle and do a HotSync.

Extra Cradles

If you use your Palm device at work and at home, you may want to synchronize with both computers every day. That's why Palm sells extra cradles. You can find out more at www.palmpilotfordummies.com/cradle.

Cases

Scores of people — from the very classy Coach leather works to inmates at the Funny Farm — seem to be turning out wallets that can store and protect your Palm device. Personally, I use the Co-Pilot, from E&B Cases, because it has room for cash and a few cards, but it's still small enough to keep in my front pocket. You can check out E&B at www.ebcases.com. Another popular case manufacturer is RhinoSkin, at www.rhinoskin.com. The best-known RhinoSkin product is a titanium Palm-device case that looks like it was torn off a tank and could probably survive being shot from a cannon. I prefer a softer, gentler Palm-device case.

Chapter 20

Ten Internet Resources for Palm Computing

*T*ime flies at warp speed in the technology business! Every few weeks, a smashing new program for the Palm platform turns up from some emerging software genius. Every so often, some genius releases a whole new Palm device. How can you possibly keep up? Your best bet for staying abreast of developments is to turn to the Internet. You can find thousands of sources of information on the Internet; this chapter is a list of my favorites.

PalmPilotForDummies.com

Keeping a book about Palm devices up-to-date is nearly impossible. But I can easily post news and developments about the things you'll want to know and keep you fully informed. I also post all the Web links in this book to www.palmpilotfordummies.com, to save you from having to type all those goofy Web addresses over and over. Just go to www.palmpilotfordummies.com and click the links you want to see.

The PalmPilot Web ring is a great place to start. If I were to give you a list of all the Web sites devoted to Palm devices, the list would number in the hundreds, and it would be out of date by the time you read it. A great place to begin your Internet search for Palm Web sites is the PalmPilot Web ring, which you can access at www.palmpilotfordummies.com/web_ring.htm. The PalmPilot Web ring is a chain of hundreds of Web sites that advise Palm users on how to get the most from their handheld computer. If you explore the Web ring long enough, you'll encounter all the other sites I mention in this chapter.

Palm

If you want good information, you might as well go right to the horse's mouth, which in this case is www.palm.com. You can find out about the latest products and accessories for your Palm device and even buy stuff. The Handspring Web site is also a good place to look for tech support.

InSync Online

The people at Palm Inc. run an Internet mailing list called InSync Online, which sends regular messages describing tips, tricks, and special offers for Palm users. You can sign up at the InSync Web site (www.insync-palm.com).

The Palm Computing Newsgroups

```
comp.sys.palmtops.pilot
alt.comp.sys.palmpilot
```

Gee, what funny looking Web-site addresses. Well, that's because they aren't Web addresses; they're the addresses for two Palm computing newsgroups. The Internet has thousands of online discussion forums called *newsgroups,* in which people post and reply to questions, opinions, and announcements on nearly every conceivable topic. You can read any newsgroup through a news-reading program, such as Microsoft Outlook Express, or by pointing your browser at www.dejanews.com and searching for the word Palm.

PalmPower Magazine

PalmPower Magazine can be found at www.palmpower.com (I read it daily). Every morning, PalmPower lists up to half a dozen stories that may be of interest to Palm users around the Web. Also, the editors of the site prepare monthly features about technology and reviews of new Palm accessories. If you want to follow what goes on in the Palm universe on a daily basis, PalmPower is an important resource.

Smaller.com

Good things come in small packages, right? So it figures that better things come in smaller packages. And really super-duper, great things come in itsy-bitsy, teeny-weeny. . . . Anyway, Smaller.com (www.smaller.com) is devoted to the latest news about itty-bitty computers such as the Palm handheld. Smaller.com discusses Palm organizers as well as the palmtop computers made by HP, Casio, and others. Smaller, Inc., a firm that sells some of the accessories I mention elsewhere in this book, runs this site.

VisorCentral

A useful Web site and news archive, VisorCentral (www.visorcentral.com) includes reviews of products and software carefully organized into categories. I like to check this site daily for the latest rumors, gossip, and dish about the latest developments from Handspring, Inc. This site isn't run by the Handspring company itself, but its creators often seem to have a good inside scoop on what's going on.

pdaMD.com

Even if you're not a doctor (and you don't even play one on TV) you can learn a lot from pdaMD.com (www.pdamd.com). This site is for physicians who use Palm organizers. The medical profession is picking up Palm devices pretty quickly to deliver better medical care faster with fewer errors. You'll get a view of how a Palm organizer can literally be a lifesaver.

MemoWare

Some people say that electronic books, or e-books, will be the next big thing. If you want try the next big thing in a nice small way, go to www.memoware.com and download an e-book to see how you like it. MemoWare offers more than 10,000 e-books formatted for Palm handhelds. That should keep you busy for a while.

Part VII
Appendixes

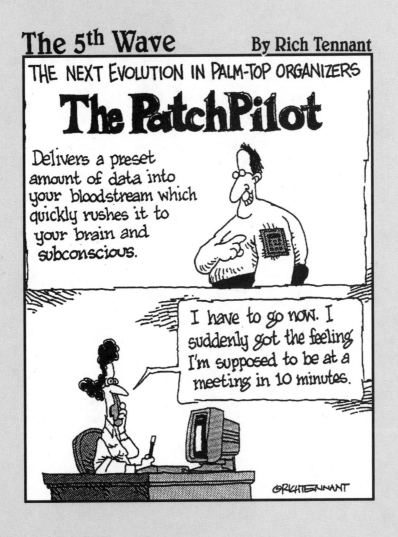

In this part . . .

In your body, an appendix is a thingamajig you don't
even know you have until it gives you trouble. If your
doctor takes it out, you won't even miss it. The appendixes in this book are practically the opposite — they're
added bonuses that you may not notice till you need
'em, but you'll be glad to have 'em — especially if you're
buying a new Palm device or planning to use Palm devices
in a large organization.

Appendix A

Enterprise Applications: Palm Software for Big Business

. . . .

*I*t won't kill you if you don't know about Palm enterprise applications, but it might kill you if your doctor doesn't. Thousands of doctors and other hospital personnel now pack a Palm organizer when they go to examine patients in order to have up-to-the-minute patient data at the ready and to minimize the kinds of hospital errors that cause thousands of deaths every year.

But the Palm device that your favorite surgeon uses at work doesn't work miracles all by itself. It's typically attached to an elaborate system of hardware and software that the people at Palm Computing, Inc. refer to as a Palm *enterprise application*. The kinds of applications used in hospitals include programs such as ePocrates, a prescription drug manager or PatientKeeper, a program for automating hospital patient records.

There's no exact definition of what makes a given product an enterprise application. You can generally assume that truly big-time enterprise applications are usually not available for purchase by individuals, because they often cost thousands of dollars to buy and install, and they tend to require specially trained technicians to make them run. To get an enterprise application for yourself, you have to hire a company called a *value-added reseller* or a consulting firm to acquire and install the product for you.

What Is a Client/Server System?

Because there's no official rule about what constitutes an enterprise application, I draw the line between enterprise applications and other applications at the point where the programs require what techies call *client/server architecture*. A *client/server system* is an arrangement in which most of the information you're dealing with isn't physically located on the machine you're actually using; it's typically sitting on a more powerful computer, called a *server*, usually in another location. Sometimes a server is a huge computer or a collection of computers that takes up a whole room, other

Pain-reducing programs

"Prompt pain relief" is the promise you get from dozens of home remedies you see advertised on TV. However, the process of getting new pain-relieving medicines to the market is anything but prompt. Drug companies spend many years and millions of dollars testing medications before those drugs become available for general use. A company called PHT Corp has created a series of Palm Enterprise applications that streamline the process of collecting data from people participating in clinical trials. (Please don't call them guinea pigs — at least not to their faces.)

PHT Corp's program, called LogPad, is a good example of how a Palm Enterprise application can make a sophisticated task seem simple. In the past, participants in drug trials had to enter information on paper and send the information in to researchers. People often made mistakes or forgot to make entries, which made trials take longer and cost much more. Now each participant receives a Palm device with a copy of the LogPad program preinstalled and a modem for transmitting information back to the researchers. Whenever it's time for the participant to enter some information, the Palm device can be set to beep; then the person enters the required information and goes on with the day. Meanwhile, the LogPad program sends the data entered by the participant to a powerful server that stores and processes the information for researchers — who can size up the data *as it's collected,* rather than having to wait weeks or months for all the data to be sent in and entered. This allows scientists to see whether their research is working out or perhaps to decide to modify (or even cancel) the experiment if it's really going awry. When the test is over, researchers end up with better data more quickly, participants end up doing less work, and you and I end up with better medicines sooner.

times it's just an ordinary-looking machine, very similar in appearance to a desktop computer you might use at home. The *client* computer (the one you're actually looking at) in a client/server system, could be another desktop computer, a laptop, a Palm device, or even a cell phone, but it's usually a less powerful machine than the server holding the data. If the client machine is a Palm device, you can bet that one reason for using an enterprise application is to make the power of a big computer available in a handy portable form to a mobile professional, such as a doctor on rounds or a warehouse manager who has to find items that might be scattered around a large area.

If you follow the handheld-computing business closely, you may have heard a lot of hype about enterprise applications being slung about by PR and Marketing people. To the people at Palm Computing, there's no doubt that enterprise applications (that is, the prospect of selling *lots* of Palm devices to big business) are important to their hopes of making a profit in the future. I hope they succeed; Palm has to make profits so Palm can make Palms.

Enterprise Applications and Ordinary People

For the average Joe or Jane, an enterprise application looks and acts just like any other software program that you might add to your Palm device; there's no noticeable difference in daily use between an enterprise application and any other Palm program. Now that nearly half of all Palm devices are issued by companies to their workers, there's a chance that you're using an enterprise application and you don't even know it.

Can you put up an enterprise application on your own? Probably not. Unless you're a pretty well-trained technician and have tens of thousands of dollars to throw around, you'd be better off leaving that work to the professionals.

Familiar-Looking Enterprise Applications

You may run across enterprise applications that look strikingly similar to Palm programs you've used as an individual. It's not uncommon for companies that sell popular Palm applications to build bigger versions of those programs for the enterprise market. The difference between a regular version and an enterprise version of a program is that the *enterprise editions* are built to serve hundreds (even thousands) of people at once — and to do so over large corporate computer networks running sophisticated programs that you and I wouldn't want to mess with.

A good example of this is Intellisync Enterprise Edition from Pumatech.

If you use a synchronization program like Intellisync, you may be familiar with configuration screens that point the data on the desktop to the right place on your Palm device. However, Intellisync Enterprise Edition does a lot more than the personal version. The program allows a company administrator to manage the way information is synchronized to all Palm devices in the company, rather than leaving each individual to fuss with all those confusing details. Another benefit of Intellisync Enterprise Edition is that it can manage information being sent to a variety of different kinds of mobile devices, from Palm devices to cell phones to Pocket PCs and others. The program can also automate software updates to all the mobile devices in a company so that software upgrades to everyone's devices can occur without the end-user having to deal with it.

Enterprise Applications Straight from the Source

If you want, you can enterprise-enable your vast fleet of Palm devices (or Palm-enable your vast enterprise, however you prefer to say it) by getting a solution right from the people who make your Palm organizer. One simple choice is to go with the Palm Enterprise Software suite for the Palm i705. The latest Palm device is already equipped with wireless connections that the Palm people manage for you; you don't need to hire another geek to keep another network running. When you send your mobile workforce into the field with Palm i705s in their pocket, you can keep them connected to the latest, most accurate information on your company network all day, every day, without keeping your workers chained to a desk.

The Promise of Palm Enterprise Applications

Businesses have only scratched the surface of what they can accomplish with a well-considered deployment of Palms and the appropriate enterprise applications. As Palm OS 5-powered devices become more widely available with faster processors and richer collections of features, you can bet that a handheld computer will be as familiar to every working person as a cubicle and a paycheck.

Appendix B

Which Palm Device Is Which?

*T*he list of Palm devices changes constantly, but you can bet that you can always find at least one model to suit your needs. All Palm organizers run Palm-compatible software, synchronize with a desktop computer, and fit in your pocket.

Table B-1 covers the devices made and sold by Palm Computing, Inc., but that's not the end of your choices. Handspring offers a series of Palm-powered devices that might suit you, as I detail in Table B-2. Sony's Palm-powered lineup (described in Table B-3) offers bright, clear screens, Memory Stick expansion to increase your capacity, and a jog dial for easy access to files and programs. You can also find excellent Palm-powered devices made by companies such as Kyocera, Samsung, Acer, HandEra, and others.

Table B-1		The Palm Product Line	
Model	*Memory*	*Features*	*Battery*
m105	8MB	Budget model with basic organizer features. Monochrome screen.	AAA
m125	8MB	Lowest-priced Palm model with SD expansion port. Monochrome screen.	AAA
m130	8MB	Lowest-priced model with color screen. Includes SD expansion port.	Rechargeable
m500	8MB	Slim, metallic case, monochrome screen, SD expansion port.	Rechargeable
m515	16MB	Slim, metallic case, color screen, SD expansion port.	Rechargeable
i705	8MB	Wireless connection to Internet, with e-mail and AOL Instant Messenger. Monochrome screen and SD expansion port.	Rechargeable

Table B-2		Handspring Products	
Model	*Memory*	*Features*	*Battery*
Visor Neo	8MB	This economical Visor comes in assorted colors and can certainly do the work you need to do.	AAA
Visor Platinium	8MB	A faster Visor for people who crunch lots of numbers or who run unusually sophisticated programs.	AAA
Treo 90	16MB	Color version of the organizer.	Rechargeable
Treo 180	16MB	Combines an organizer, cell phone, and pager. Monochrome.	Rechargeable
Treo 270	16MB	Combines an organizer, cell phone, and pager. Color screen.	Rechargeable

Table B-3		Sony Products	
Model	*Memory*	*Features*	*Battery*
Clie PEG-SL10	8MB	Economy model. High-resolution monochrome screen.	Rechargeable
Clie PEG-S360	16MB	Monochrome screen, more memory than PEG-SL10.	Rechargeable
Clie PEG-T615C	16MB	Brilliant color screen.	Rechargeable
Clie PEG-T665C	16MB	Same screen as Clie PEG-T615C, plus built-in MP3 player for listening to music.	Rechargeable
Clie PEG-NR70	16MB	Bigger, brighter color screen, MP3 player, built in keyboard.	Rechargeable
Clie PEG-NR70V	16MB	Same features as Clie PEG-NR70, plus built-in camera.	Rechargeable

Index

● *T* ●

Notes

Notes

Notes

FOR DUMMIES®

A world of resources to help you grow

HOME, GARDEN & HOBBIES

0-7645-5295-3

0-7645-5130-2

0-7645-5106-X

Also available:

Auto Repair For Dummies
(0-7645-5089-6)

Chess For Dummies
(0-7645-5003-9)

Home Maintenance For Dummies
(0-7645-5215-5)

Organizing For Dummies
(0-7645-5300-3)

Piano For Dummies
(0-7645-5105-1)

Poker For Dummies
(0-7645-5232-5)

Quilting For Dummies
(0-7645-5118-3)

Rock Guitar For Dummies
(0-7645-5356-9)

Roses For Dummies
(0-7645-5202-3)

Sewing For Dummies
(0-7645-5137-X)

FOOD & WINE

0-7645-5250-3

0-7645-5390-9

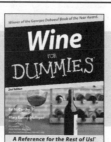

0-7645-5114-0

Also available:

Bartending For Dummies
(0-7645-5051-9)

Chinese Cooking For Dummies
(0-7645-5247-3)

Christmas Cooking For Dummies
(0-7645-5407-7)

Diabetes Cookbook For Dummies
(0-7645-5230-9)

Grilling For Dummies
(0-7645-5076-4)

Low-Fat Cooking For Dummies
(0-7645-5035-7)

Slow Cookers For Dummies
(0-7645-5240-6)

TRAVEL

0-7645-5453-0

0-7645-5438-7

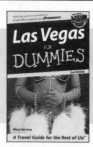

0-7645-5448-4

Also available:

America's National Parks For Dummies
(0-7645-6204-5)

Caribbean For Dummies
(0-7645-5445-X)

Cruise Vacations For Dummies 2003
(0-7645-5459-X)

Europe For Dummies
(0-7645-5456-5)

Ireland For Dummies
(0-7645-6199-5)

France For Dummies
(0-7645-6292-4)

London For Dummies
(0-7645-5416-6)

Mexico's Beach Resorts For Dummies
(0-7645-6262-2)

Paris For Dummies
(0-7645-5494-8)

RV Vacations For Dummies
(0-7645-5443-3)

Walt Disney World & Orlando For Dummies
(0-7645-5444-1)

Available wherever books are sold. Go to www.dummies.com or call 1-877-762-2974 to order direct.

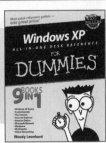

FOR DUMMIES®

Helping you expand your horizons and realize your potential

INTERNET

0-7645-0894-6

0-7645-1659-0

0-7645-1642-6

Also available:

America Online 7.0 For Dummies
(0-7645-1624-8)

Genealogy Online For Dummies
(0-7645-0807-5)

The Internet All-in-One Desk Reference For Dummies
(0-7645-1659-0)

Internet Explorer 6 For Dummies
(0-7645-1344-3)

The Internet For Dummies Quick Reference
(0-7645-1645-0)

Internet Privacy For Dummies
(0-7645-0846-6)

Researching Online For Dummies
(0-7645-0546-7)

Starting an Online Business For Dummies
(0-7645-1655-8)

DIGITAL MEDIA

0-7645-1664-7

0-7645-1675-2

0-7645-0806-7

Also available:

CD and DVD Recording For Dummies
(0-7645-1627-2)

Digital Photography All-in-One Desk Reference For Dummies
(0-7645-1800-3)

Digital Photography For Dummies Quick Reference
(0-7645-0750-8)

Home Recording for Musicians For Dummies
(0-7645-1634-5)

MP3 For Dummies
(0-7645-0858-X)

Paint Shop Pro "X" For Dummies
(0-7645-2440-2)

Photo Retouching & Restoration For Dummies
(0-7645-1662-0)

Scanners For Dummies
(0-7645-0783-4)

GRAPHICS

0-7645-0817-2

0-7645-1651-5

0-7645-0895-4

Also available:

Adobe Acrobat 5 PDF For Dummies
(0-7645-1652-3)

Fireworks 4 For Dummies
(0-7645-0804-0)

Illustrator 10 For Dummies
(0-7645-3636-2)

QuarkXPress 5 For Dummies
(0-7645-0643-9)

Visio 2000 For Dummies
(0-7645-0635-8)

Available wherever books are sold. Go to www.dummies.com or call 1-877-762-2974 to order direct.

FOR DUMMIES®

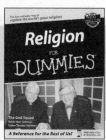
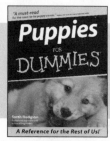